The Methodology of Macroeconomic Thought

In loving memory of my father, Rev. William Grant Anderson,
who taught by example the importance of, and pleasure to be derived from,
reasoned argument (where reason is necessarily bound up with belief) while
respecting the beliefs of others.

The Methodology of Macroeconomic Thought

A Conceptual Analysis of Schools of Thought in Economics

Sheila C. Dow
University of Stirling

Edward Elgar
Cheltenham, UK • Northampton, MA, USA

Published by
Edward Elgar Publishing Limited
8 Lansdown Place
Cheltenham
Glos GL50 2HU
UK

Edward Elgar Publishing, Inc.
6 Market Street
Northampton
Massachusetts 01060
USA

Reprinted 1998

British Library Cataloguing in Publication Data
Dow, Sheila C.
    The methodology of macroeconomic thought: a conceptual
    analysis of schools of thought in economics
    1. Macroeconomics
    I. Title
    339.3

Library of Congress Cataloguing in Publication Data
Dow, Sheila C.
    The methodology of macroeconomic thought: a conceptual analysis
of schools of thought in economics / Sheila C. Dow. — [2nd ed.]
    Rev. ed. of: Macroeconomic thought. 1985.
    Includes bibliographical references and indexes.
    1. Macroeconomics. I. Dow, Sheila C. Macroeconomic thought.
II. Title
HB172.5.D69 1996
339—dc20   96–922
                                                              CIP

ISBN 1 85278 980 8 (cased)

Printed and bound in Great Britain by
MPG Books Ltd, Bodmin, Cornwall

Contents

Preface to the Second Edition

Much has happened in the ten years since I wrote *Macroeconomic Thought: A Methodological Approach*, of which this is a substantially-revised second edition. Many of the changes are intended simply as improvements on the first edition. The change in title for example simply reflects the shift in emphasis in this edition more towards methodology.

But the purpose of putting together a second edition is to restate the argument in the first edition in the context of developments since the publication of the first. The understanding of methodology and its role in economics has changed significantly over the last ten years. There is now a much greater willingness among economists in general, and methodologists in particular, to contemplate a range of schools of thought with different methodological foundations. But this willingness has often gone too far. By reacting against the previous situation in which methodology's role was to establish rules for best practice, many went to the other extreme of attempting to avoid judgement altogether. The description of different schools of thought was seen as sufficient in itself, whereas I had approached description as a necessary first step towards more constructive debate. Some commentators misinterpreted *Macroeconomic Thought* as advocating a retreat from an active role for methodology, when in fact it was intended as preparing the way for reasoned argument, based on a mutual understanding of the methodological foundations of different approaches to economics.

The point of *Macroeconomic Thought* was thus not that, in economics or in methodology, anything goes. I had set out to describe and analyse the methodology and content of four schools of thought in their own terms. This was intended to contrast with the common practice of appraising one school of thought, unconsciously, using the criteria specific to another school of thought. What I was arguing for, and continue to argue for, is methodological awareness among practising economists as a basis for constructive debate. Now there is a limit to how far any individual can analyse schools of thought in the schools' own terms, since each of us has our own approach, to methodology as well as to economics. Having tried to 'get inside the heads' of economists in four different schools of thought simultaneously, I can attest that it is not a sustainable activity.

Preface to the Second Edition

Much has happened in the ten years since I wrote *Macroeconomic Thought: A Methodological Approach*, of which this is a substantially-revised second edition. Many of the changes are intended simply as improvements on the first edition. The change in title for example simply reflects the shift in emphasis in this edition more towards methodology.

But the purpose of putting together a second edition is to restate the argument in the first edition in the context of developments since the publication of the first. The understanding of methodology and its role in economics has changed significantly over the last ten years. There is now a much greater willingness among economists in general, and methodologists in particular, to contemplate a range of schools of thought with different methodological foundations. But this willingness has often gone too far. By reacting against the previous situation, in which methodology's role was to establish rules for best practice, many went to the other extreme of attempting to avoid judgement altogether. The description of different schools of thought was seen as sufficient in itself, whereas I had approached description as a necessary first step towards more constructive debate. Some commentators misinterpreted *Macroeconomic Thought* as advocating a retreat from an active role for methodology, when in fact it was intended as preparing the way for reasoned argument, based on a mutual understanding of the methodological foundations of different approaches to economics.

The point of *Macroeconomic Thought* was thus not that, in economics or in methodology, anything goes. I had set out to describe and analyse the methodology and content of four schools of thought *in their own terms*. This was intended to contrast with the common practice of appraising one school of thought, *unconsciously* using the criteria specific to another school of thought. What I was arguing for, and continue to argue for, is methodological awareness among practising economists as a basis for constructive debate. Now there is a limit to how far any individual can analyse schools of thought in the schools' own terms, since each of us has our own approach, to methodology as well as to economics. Having tried to 'get inside the heads' of economists in four different schools of thought simultaneously, I can attest that it is not a sustainable activity.

But, insofar as knowledge advances by argument between different approaches, it is unlikely to advance if there is no awareness of the implications of difference in approach; therein lies the basis for acrimonious argument-at-cross-purposes with which we are all too familiar in economics, and in macroeconomics in particular. There is no point in castigating a New Classical economist for assuming that markets clear, or a Post Keynesian for assuming that money matters, for example, without understanding the methodological imperatives which drive those assumptions.

In particular, my approach was non-dualistic, that there is a range of methodologies, each with its own set of appraisal criteria. We can discuss the relative merits of each in its own terms, and in our own terms, but there is no universal set of appraisal criteria by which to decide on the best methodology for all, and thereby the best economic theories. This incommensurability is the key feature of Kuhn's approach which influenced the argument. (Kuhn continues, in my view, to be misunderstood; but, in order to deflect unnecessary argument, it is perhaps helpful to point out that it is only his incommensurability concept which is crucial for the approach adopted here.) But some interpreted my approach dualistically: either there are universal appraisal criteria or there are none. Since I set out the arguments against the first, I must be supporting the second. It was important therefore, in this edition, to try to make it more clear that tolerance and understanding are required among methodologists as well as among economists, but that neither precludes reasoned argument between those with different perspectives. It is through such reasoned argument that knowledge progresses.

Methodological awareness has increased immeasurably in the last ten years; this has taken the form of a greater willingness among many economists to accept the legitimacy of different schools of thought, and has fuelled an explosion of interest in the field of methodology. That field itself has also been changing radically. But it has changed in a way which makes it important still for the arguments I put forward in the first edition to be reiterated. Most methodologists now are engaged primarily in description, rather than the traditional practice of prescription. This has been very constructive, spawning a wide range of useful accounts of different methodologies and discouraging intolerance. But the understanding of the pitfalls of prescription has become so well entrenched that there has been a dualistic switch to arguing for the removal of judgement from methodology altogether. There is still a need for awareness of differences in mode of thought, among methodologists as much as among economists; methodologists, just like economists, need to be aware that their approaches are coloured by their own modes of thought, which others may not share.

Because of the importance of mode of thought for methodology and theory, a whole chapter (Chapter 2) is now devoted to this topic. While in the first edition I focussed on two modes of thought, the traditional Cartesian/Euclidean mode of thought and the Babylonian mode of thought, I refer in this edition to a third, which is 'not-Cartesian/Euclidean thought'. It was this dualistic, rejectionist, reaction against Cartesian/Euclidean thought which led to the attempt to remove any element of judgement from methodology. Babylonian thought is different; it represents a move beyond dualism. Further, I have become increasingly convinced of the importance of thinking in terms of knowledge, of the methodologist, the economist, and individuals and groups in the economy. This view owes much to Brian Loasby. In particular it is helpful to focus on the distinction between information and knowledge (or, similarly, between 'knowing that' and 'knowing how'). Cartesian/Euclidean thought concentrates on the known and knowable, i.e. information, while its dual, not-Cartesian/Euclidean thought, concentrates on the unknowable. Babylonian thought transcends this dual by setting up a system for generating knowledge, where knowability is a matter of degree.

The discussion of methodology as such is now the subject matter of Chapter 3, with new sections added to address the major developments in methodology which have occurred in the last ten years, notably the development of the anti-methodology position based on not-Cartesian/Euclidean thought. The implications of differences in mode of thought and methodology are again illustrated by considering four schools of thought in macroeconomics. It was not strictly necessary to update these chapters, since their purpose was more one of illustration than of providing a comprehensive account of the schools of thought. However, the detail on schools of thought has been updated to capture some recent developments, particularly in mainstream macroeconomics. These developments are important in themselves, but also show interesting parallels with recent developments in methodology; both sets of developments in turn reflect similar developments in the general intellectual climate of the last ten years, which have been conducive to fragmentation. The conclusion has also been revised, taking account of recent developments in methodology and theory, and looking forward to where these developments might lead.

There has been a range of recent publications explicitly designed to set out a range of schools of thought, at least two of them focusing explicitly on macroeconomics (see for example Phelps, 1990, Mair and Miller, 1991 and Snowdon, Vane and Wynarczyk, 1994). Each of these volumes is a most welcome addition to the literature, each approaching an account of schools of thought in its own way. This volume is complementary to them in a variety of respects. First, the emphasis here on mode of thought goes further in trying to identify the source of differences between schools of thought as well as potential and actual commonalities. Second, this emphasis led naturally to an account of differences between schools of thought at the conceptual level, with particular theories considered as illustrations; other volumes focus much more directly on theories. The emphasis here on the four selected concepts (micro-foundations, equilibrium, expectations and money) is designed to be applicable to a range of actual and potential theoretical developments within each field. Finally, unlike other accounts, mainstream economics is treated here as one school of thought, on a par with neo-Austrian economics, Post Keynesian economics and Marxian economics. This demarcation is retained in the second edition in spite of persistent and undeniable differences within mainstream economics and the disproportionate scale of support it still attracts within the discipline. This demarcation follows logically from the judgement that mainstream economics is united by a common mode of thought and a common conceptualization. This choice of demarcation itself thus serves to illustrate that distinctive conclusions emerge when the analysis starts at the level of mode of thought and proceeds at the conceptual level.

I am most grateful to Edward Elgar for encouraging me to undertake this project, and for his patience in waiting for the outcome. As ever, the thoughts expressed here owe much to many fruitful discussions over the years, with many people but especially with my husband Alistair, for which I am most grateful. Particular thanks are due to Vicky Chick, Bill Gerrard and Tony Lawson who commented on some of the new material in this edition, and to John Hillard for having the stamina and heart to cast an editorial eye over the full manuscript and to compile the indices. The project was taken over its first hurdle by Carlos Rodriguez Fuentes, who converted the manuscript of the first edition into wordperfect by scanning. Lorraine Annand helped it along its way with some additional typing. The final hurdle of preparing the manuscript for publishing was cleared for me by Lynne O'Rourke. I am most grateful for all of their help.

Preface to the First Edition

The increasing disarray in macroeconomics has encouraged a search for roots. On the one hand, the result has been a growing concern with methodology and, on the other, a greater willingness to classify different strands of thought and trace their origins. The guiding principle of this book is that these two approaches are best pursued together.

Methodology has long been regarded as a specialist topic in economics. As such it has often pursued questions not directly related to the pressing theoretical questions of the day. More important, it has often been couched in a specialist language which has effectively excluded specialists in other fields. At the same time, macroeconomic theory has splintered into separate strands, each requiring specialist knowledge, and making difficult any attempt to analyse the whole.

This study represents an attempt to bridge the gap between methodology and macroeconomic theory. Methodology is thus viewed with a wider perspective than is customary, encompassing mode of thought and world-view as well as technical procedures. Within this methodological perspective, macroeconomics is considered primarily, not in terms of 'issues', like crowding-out, but in terms of concepts, like equilibrium. Once it is seen how differently these concepts are used within different schools of thought, different positions on theory and policy issues follow on quite naturally.

The book is designed as a text, suitable for intermediate and advanced students in macroeconomics, and in methodology. It presumes some familiarity with macroeconomic theory. But, as far as possible each piece of theory to which reference is made is expressed in terms of first principles. Indeed, the methodological approach to macroeconomics requires that most discussion be conducted in terms of first principles. The methodological content and the range of schools of thought covered are likely to be unfamiliar to many macroeconomic students. But it is hoped that the descriptions provided here, within a cohesive format, will not only increase understanding but also help to put into an overall perspective the issues involved. Similarly, for methodology students, it is hoped that the integration of methodology with theory will aid understanding by adding perspective to specialist methodological theory. The overview approach, designed to provide perspective, is of necessity limited in the extent to which particular topics can be pursued. There, is, however no shortage of specialist material; references are provided throughout to guide the reader to the relevant sources for pursuing particular topics.

The study was also written with academic colleagues in mind. Indeed, it is the result of my own attempts to make some sense of the debates within macroeconomics, attempts which led me to methodology as the appropriate level for starting enquiries. The study is thus offered as a contribution to the growing literature produced by others engaged in a similar search.

A great debt is owed to all those with whom I have discussed ideas in methodology and macroeconomics. The first debt is owed to the late Sidney Weintraub, who provided me with the invaluable opportunity of communicating my initial ideas to others through the pages of the *Journal of Post Keynesian Economics*; he provided encouragement and advice at a crucial, early stage in the development of many of the ideas which now appear in this study. Since then I have benefited greatly from numerous discussions, both formal and informal, with numerous individuals and groups. It has been invaluable to have discussions with specialists in the many particular fields covered here; however, I accept full responsibility for any misrepresentations of others' ideas. I am grateful to those who have provided comments on individual chapters, including Andrea Boitani, Lawrence Boland, Victoria Chick, Peter Dooley, Geoffrey Harcourt, Arjo Klamer, Jan Kregel, Brian Loasby, Carlo Panico and John Pheby. I am particularly grateful to Dieter Helm who provided detailed comments on the entire manuscript, and to Peter Earl who did likewise, as well as engaging in many discussions throughout the production of the first draft. The greatest debt, however, is owed to my husband, Alistair. Not only did he provide detailed comments on chapters, encouragement and emotional support, but also he influenced strongly my early interest in methodology and the subsequent emergence of ideas. Finally, I would like to express my gratitude to Mrs Ann Cowie who has, with her typing and organisational skills, nursed the manuscript through its various stages with patience, cheerfulness and efficiency, to Mrs Shirley Hewitt for preparing the index, and to Sue Corbett of Basil Blackwell who provided encouragement throughout.

1 Introduction

It is the popular view of economists that we are incapable of agreeing amongst ourselves. This is particularly evident in the area of macroeconomic policy where theoretical debates are aired in the popular media. The general public appear to be mystified that economists cannot get together and agree on a 'correct' economic policy stance for the government.

Among many economists also there is a deep-seated and genuine wish that all economists might agree on a range of general principles and argue only about the details. Hence Friedman's attempt to pour oil on waters he had troubled with his monetarism: 'We are all Keynesians now' (qualified, however, in Friedman, 1968a), echoed later by Laidler's (1981) statement: 'We are all monetarists now'. More recently, Bleaney (1991, p.145) has asserted:

> One of the characteristics – perhaps in retrospect it will be viewed as the chief characteristic – of theoretical economics over the past decade has been the cooling of controversy and a gradual re-establishment of some form of consensus in the profession for the first time since the mid-1960s.

Yet serious disagreements appear to persist. This phenomenon is open to a variety of explanations. First, Johnson (1971) suggested that economists presenting new theories differentiate their product unduly from prevailing theory in order to attract adherents and to increase the importance of their theories. Apparent disagreements are thus grossly exaggerated, masking the underlying consensus. Second, others such as Wiles (1979-80) identify disagreements as arising from ideological differences. Synthesis would be possible once ideology was eradicated from analysis. Third, it has been argued by Myrdal (1953), that it is in the nature of economics that there will be disagreements; while these may have ideological elements, ideology cannot be eradicated from theory. If this is the case, denial of the existence of valid disagreements should be regarded with some suspicion.

Were it possible to conduct completely objective empirical tests of the range of available theories, it would be possible to promote a synthesis around the most empirically successful theories. But, while facts themselves may be

1

distinguished from values, their organization for the purposes of theory testing is itself theory-laden. Further, if the evidence contradicts the predictions of a theory, it is impossible to identify precisely which element of the theory is being contradicted, from basic premises to the form of data used. A failure of prediction is thus not sufficient to justify rejecting the theory which generated the predictions. At best, there can emerge a collection of different theories, each of which is confirmed in some sense by the evidence. Appraisal of these theories then must rely on the relative merits of the particular form and content of abstraction adopted by each. Since there is little strictly factual basis for choosing between these abstractions, the choice must have other origins. These origins can be understood in terms of vision of the economic process, world view or, in Myrdal's terms, ideology. It is significant that the term 'ideology' has dropped out of common parlance in economics, reflecting the continuing view that it is something to be eradicated. In terms of dictionary definition, the term can still accurately be applied to economics. But, to avoid the baggage that now goes along with the term, the alternatives of 'vision' and 'world view' will be employed (see Dow, 1990b; Snowdon *et al.*, 1994).

Because of an absence of conclusive empirical grounds for theory appraisal, therefore, we will pursue the third approach, identified with Myrdal, that fundamental theoretical differences can persist which cannot be isolated from difference of vision. In focusing particularly on macroeconomics, we will attempt to identify broad categories of theory, or schools of thought, in macroeconomics, between which there are fundamental theoretical differences. As a corollary, the search for synthesis is much more likely to meet with success within these broad categories than between them. This framework can then contribute to a better understanding of debates in macroeconomics, by categorizing them according to whether or not they reflect fundamental differences as to choice of theoretical abstraction.

The demarcation criterion to be used here to identify fundamental differences is a methodological one. A school of thought will be defined by its common methodology. The method of a school of thought refers to its technical procedures, i.e. to its modelling techniques, its choice of categories, and its preferred testing procedures. But these in turn derive from an underlying conceptualization of reality and preferred mode of reasoning. We use the term 'methodology' to encompass both the methods actually employed within a school of thought and the underlying world view, or vision, which generated them.

Within any school of thought there will be diversity of technical procedure, but we group them together because the common world view allows constructive debate about the relative merits of these procedures. Similarly, some technical procedures may be employed by more than one school of thought, but the persisting differences of underlying world view dog any discussions in terms of these common procedures. The IS-LM framework within macroeconomics, for example, has frequently been used in textbooks to compare different theories (as was its initial purpose, when designed by Hicks). The monetarist-Keynesian controversy was expressed in terms of this framework as if it were a controversy over the slope of the LM curve. Yet empirical estimation of the relationship between money holdings, the interest rate and the income level has not resolved the differences between those monetarists and Keynesians who approach the issue instead on the basis of different world views. For them, the slope of the LM curve only captures one element of the different theoretical structures which they put forward. And indeed, within those theoretical structures, the IS-LM framework, to the extent that it is employed, takes on different meanings which condition how they may be tested against empirical observation. Thus, for example, it is significant whether the curves themselves are regarded as inherently stable or not, and whether observations are interpreted as positions of intersection on the curves, or not necessarily on either of the curves.

By attempting to identify broad groupings of theory according to underlying world view, or methodology, therefore, we hope to focus on those areas where debate is most constructive. Where debates stem from fundamental methodological differences, it is only at this level that any resolution is feasible. Debates at other levels are of course also constructive, in the sense that they promote exchange of ideas as well as the impetus to improve the quality of technical procedures, including testing procedures. But ultimately, debates require some basis for theory appraisal. Since each school of thought derives its criteria for appraisal from its methodology, any constructive discussion involving appraisal must include an awareness of methodological differences. Within each school of thought, the criteria for appraisal are held in common, so that both active debate and promotion of synthesis are much more feasible without explicit reference to methodology.

The view that there is already a synthesis in macroeconomics implies that there is agreement on a common set of criteria for appraisal. The view that synthesis, although not yet reached, is nevertheless possible implies that such agreement is possible. Indeed, traditionally, the theory of methodology has been designed to establish general criteria for theory appraisal. Not only could theories be ranked according to their empirical success, according to this approach, but testing procedures themselves could be ranked according to how closely they met the established criteria for appraisal. On the basis of this approach to methodology, therefore, it is possible for economists to reject schools of thought on the grounds that their methodology is unsatisfactory. Synthesis is envisaged as emerging in favour of a body of theory which 'best' satisfies the 'best' criteria for appraisal.

The focus here is on methodology as a basis for description first, and only then as a basis for critical analysis. The aim is to establish that there are some basic methodological differences which divide bodies of theory, and that these differences include differences as to theory appraisal. In the absence of a value-free set of criteria for appraisal comprehensive enough to override those criteria internal to each school, there can be no assurance that these methodological differences can be resolved.

While it is the aim primarily to describe, rather than to sit in judgement, it is inherent in this approach that any economist (if consistent) employs a particular methodology and, as we shall see, an underlying mode of thought. In pursuing the aim of this study, therefore, I must employ a particular methodology, even when describing others. Indeed the aim itself reflects a particular methodological position. It is a problem to which there is no solution, given the absence of absolute appraisal criteria, for methodology or theory. But the methodological perspective goes some way to minimizing the problem of lack of objectivity. By identifying the world view underlying a school of thought, there is a better chance of 'getting inside the head' of a representative member of that school; without that recognition, the imposition of one's own world view would be much greater, and the more insidious for not being acknowledged.

The arguments to be developed here, therefore, reflect the view that the absence of objective appraisal criteria does not preclude rational discussion of alternative theories, or schools of thought in general. An anchor is provided by the objective existence of a reality which theories are intended to explain or predict. Theories are the outcome of the interaction of external reality with the theorist's understanding of it. We will thus occupy a methodological middle ground between the extremes of presuming that objective knowledge is attainable on the one hand, and a nihilistic interpretation of relativism on the other. Within this middle ground, different schools of thought may be discussed together, but may be compared only with great caution. The primary purpose of attempting such a joint discussion here is to demonstrate the distinctiveness of schools of thought in the hope that practitioners of each will themselves exercise great caution in judging each other, and to focus serious debate on the relative merits of their respective methodological positions.

In categorizing schools of thought, we are imposing a simplification on an extremely complex structure. Such simplification is subject to the pitfalls of any theory, that abstraction requires some departure from reality. But in any sphere of existence, including that of formal theory, some categorization is necessary to impose some order on our observations of the world. The psychological appeal of such categorization by 'but one single quality, that is common to a great variety of otherwise different objects' (Smith, 1795, p.65), was a theme of Adam Smith's *History of Astronomy*. Inevitably, differences within each category may at times override the one quality held in common. Shackle (1972, p.52) warns of the dangers, as well as attractions, of what he calls 'codes'.

The categories selected here are very broad, each encompassing a variety of methods. Four schools of thought are discussed which can be distinguished by their broad methodological positions; differences within each position are discussed, but the emphasis is on the differences between the four as a sufficient demonstration that there is no basis at present for a complete synthesis in macroeconomics. Further it is methodology and theory which are being categorized, not economists as such. Many economists do belong clearly to one of the four schools, but many do not. Indeed, we will tend to focus on particular individuals whose work exemplifies one or other school of thought, and especially on those who are 'methodologically aware', i.e. those who make explicit their methodological positions.

But it is often the most notable economists who evade a unique categorization. Perhaps the classic example is Hicks, whose work has consistently sparked off new research programmes in a range of fields. Indeed, his contributions could be described as resulting from a creative admixture of ideas from different schools of thought. His work is an advertisement for the benefits of communication across schools of thought. Further, the fact that Hicks could be identified with different schools of thought at different times if anything reinforces the value of these categories. In order to understand Hicks' work, we must understand the general character of the schools of thought to which he has at different times veered, and their underlying methodology. In the case of many other economists, whose espousal of different methodologies and whose debates with users of other methodologies have often been conducted without any methodological awareness, only a specification of these methodologies allows us to eliminate the ensuing confusion.

The four schools of thought to be explored are classified as: mainstream, Neo-Austrian, Post Keynesian and Marxian. The first group in particular is very broad. It is defined here to include both Walrasian and non-Walrasian general equilibrium theory and disequilibrium theory; both New Classical and New Keynesian theory. The most significant common factor uniting this collection of theory is the use of some kind of general equilibrium framework. (This is the common factor identified by Weintraub, 1985; Hausman, 1992, argued for equilibrium, rather than general equilibrium, as the defining characteristic of mainstream economics, but he was referring exclusively to microeconomics). Another common factor is the view of methodological exclusivity: that mainstream economics is coterminous with economics. To readers within the mainstream school, classifying mainstream economics as a 'school of thought' may thus seem rather odd; within mainstream economics then schools of thought are generally understood to refer to differences within mainstream economics (as in Phelps, 1990).

Another way of understanding mainstream economics is in the negative sense of non-political economy (see Dow, 1990b). The other three schools of thought are examples of political economy, chosen for their distinctive methodologies, which stem from their different visions of the economic process. The coverage of schools of thought is not intended to be complete. One school of thought in particular which has been attracting increasing support is the institutionalist ('old institutionalist', or 'evolutionary') approach. The coverage here has not been extended to take account of this because the overlap, particularly with Post Keynesian economics, prevents the kind of sharp delineation which is possible with the four schools originally selected; sharpness of delineation is still regarded as central to my purpose of illustrating the significance of any methodological differences. (This purpose arose from the – in many cases unwarranted –*presumption* on the part of many, of methodological commonality.)

Much discussion will be devoted to the methodological differences within each school of thought. They are indeed important. But the existing *corpus* of mainstream literature, both on theory and methodology, is devoted almost exclusively to these differences within mainstream thought. The purpose of this study rather is to demonstrate the even greater methodological differences which exist between mainstream macroeconomics and the other three schools under consideration. The differences within each school of thought will thus be discussed only insofar as they may threaten the coherence of that school, or its relationship with other schools of thought. If there is to be some understanding among diverse schools of thought there must be some understanding of their differences.

Before discussing the methodology of macroeconomics as such, it is necessary to devote some thought to methodology in general. It is also necessary to trace back historically the development of widely accepted modes of thought which govern methodological enquiry as much as enquiry within scientific disciplines; these modes of thought have been ingrained for so many centuries that a special effort is required for us to recognize them. Chapter 2 is devoted to elucidating differences in mode of thought and their implications. Further, economic methodology has always developed in the shadow of the methodology of the physical sciences; so in Chapter 3 we trace the development of ideas in the methodology of the physical sciences first, and then explore their adaptation to the social sciences.

Traditional methodology is demonstrated to have arisen from a dominant Western mode of thought which requires theories to conform to a system of reasoning unified by a set of axioms. Recent developments in methodology on the other hand are influenced more by alternative modes of thought which allow for greater diversity of approach in addressing particular problems. These developments provide the initial justification for considering macroeconomic thought in terms of schools of thought. While Kuhn's approach as such has met with some problems in application to economics, it nevertheless contains the elements required to serve the purpose here of giving an account of different bodies of theory without an objective basis for appraisal. It is the incommensurability of schools of thought which requires that we pay attention to their methodological foundations.

Chapter 4 then explores the background to the four selected schools of thought in macroeconomics. By considering the economic, political, historical and theoretical context in which each set of ideas emerged, it is possible to build up a picture of the concepts, theories and basic principles of reasoning which make up each school of thought, as well as an understanding of why particular technical procedures were employed by each.

In the next group of chapters, particular features of each methodology are picked out to allow a focus for comparing the methodologies under consideration. Thus, in Chapters 5 to 8, we discuss the main features of how each school of thought deals with the concepts of micro-foundations, equilibrium, expectations and money, respectively. These concepts are central to any macroeconomic methodology. The account of the use of these concepts by each school of thought is not intended to be exhaustive; it will be selective of those main features which differentiate one school from another.

Once a particular methodology is adopted, a particular range of theories becomes admissible. Similarly, taking this a stage further, this set of theories admits of a particular range of policy proposals. Chapter 9 is devoted to exploring the policy proposals of each school of thought in three broad areas, but deals first with the approach of each school to deriving policy prescriptions from theory. Particular attention is then paid to the prescriptions generated for inflation/unemployment policy, techniques of money supply control, and international policy. It is not uncommon for members of different schools of thought to come up with similar policy proposals, e.g. a recommendation to control the rate of growth of the money supply. But, because each makes the recommendation on the basis of a different view of the economy, there may be disagreement not only about the policy package of which it is a part but also the techniques employed to implement it. It is the occasional apparent agreement on policy which makes continued theoretical arguments seem rather vexing. An understanding of the reasons for these arguments, however, could allow more effective communication between economists and policy makers.

2 Modes of Thought in Economics

2.1 Introduction

Science tells us what we can know, but what we can know is little, and if we forget how much we cannot know we become insensitive to many things of great importance... Uncertainty, in the presence of vivid hopes and fears, is painful, but must be endured if we wish to live without the support of comforting fairytales. It is not good either to forget the questions that philosophy asks, or to persuade ourselves that we have found indubitable answers to them. To teach how to live without certainty, and yet without being paralysed by hesitation, is perhaps the chief thing that philosophy, in our age, can still do for those who study it. (Russell, 1946, p.14)

The formulation of theories in economics, as much as theories within philosophy, represents an attempt to deal with the fact that we can never attain a state of complete knowledge about the past, and even less about the future. Methodology is concerned with the way in which theories are formulated, the way in which knowledge is generated under conditions of uncertainty. It is thus concerned with theory formulation at a variety of levels. As individuals we must formulate theories (however subconsciously) about the environment in which we live in order to function at all, in order not to be 'paralysed with hesitation' (see Kelly, 1963). Economists in turn form theories about individual behaviour, and the consequences in aggregate of that behaviour. Methodologists variously form theories about how economists form their theories, establish prescriptions for how theory ought to be formed, and establish criteria for appraising and comparing theories. At each level there is an attempt to direct thought and investigation along lines which will generate as much knowledge as possible.

Methodology can be approached from a variety of standpoints, depending on the particular path chosen for generating knowledge. Here we will adopt simultaneously two conventional definitions of methodology, allowing it to span several levels: the study of 'the technical procedures of a discipline' as well as the 'investigation of the concepts, theories, and basic principles of a subject' (Blaug, 1980, p.xi). In other words, we will consider methodology as spanning the study of theory formulation at the technical level of model building and at

9

the level of the underlying, and often implicit, world view of the theorist. Indeed it is to be shown that the range of levels of thought involved are interdependent, that a particular world view is generally associated with a particular technical approach to a subject.

Implicit in *any* methodology (whether or not this is the stated intention) are criteria for theory appraisal, i.e. for prescription. We shall, as far as possible, limit our enquiry to description of the content of different methodologies which correspond to different bodies of theory. Thus, rather than treating methodology as something which transcends all theory content, providing universal appraisal criteria, we will use it primarily as a means of classifying bodies of theory.

In order to understand the issues addressed by methodologists, we have to go back one stage further to the very basic level of how people think, or believe they ought to think according to their implicit appraisal criteria. In this chapter we focus on two of the strands of thought which seem to have most influenced methodologists as well as practitioners within disciplines like economics. Traditional methodology, or philosophy of science, has been more influenced by one of those modes of thought as the ideal for scientists. Following a brief introduction to the two modes of thought, we explore their differences in terms of the difference between open and closed systems, between atomism and organicism and between dualism and a move beyond dualism. We then consider the significance of mode of thought for questions of uncertainty, and probability and expectations. Finally, we address the question of communications between scientists of differing mode of thought.

Some readers may find it quite challenging to address questions of mode of thought; this is inevitable in that we naturally approach these questions using the mode of thought to which we are accustomed. Some background reading which may be helpful is Pirsig (1974); he provides a narrative approach to expressing ideas about modes of thought. (I'm told its also good background reading on motorbikes.)

2.2　Two Modes of Thought

By mode of thought is meant the way in which arguments (or theories) are constructed and presented, how we attempt to convince others of the validity or truth of our arguments. It is concerned as much with the rhetoric used as means of communication as with the logical structure of the argument. It is a broader concept than 'methodology', and indeed influences our judgement as to what constitutes an acceptable methodological position.

At the general level of an argument on any subject, it may seem at first that there are simply good arguments and bad arguments. But a particular mode of thought is instilled in us from an early age, at least as being what we should aspire to. Education teaches us how to reason and how to organize our observations of the world. Unless we are already conscious of a conflict, say between the mode of thought which we prefer and another which we are being encouraged to adopt, it takes some effort to recognize our own mode of thought objectively and accept that there may be alternatives. Indeed some modes of thought more than others limit the ability to admit the possibility of alternatives. Once it is admitted that there are alternatives, however, it must be accepted that what constitutes a good argument within one mode of thought may be a bad argument within another. At this stage we are not considering questions of the truth or falsity of arguments, or their correspondence with reality. We are concerned with the initial stage at which arguments are judged as to whether they are worthy of consideration at all.

Within the complex history of Western thought, we can identify in general terms at least two strands, or patterns, of thought which underlie the traditional and more recent approaches to methodology respectively, and which have echoes too throughout economic theory. These modes of thought encapsulate quite different ways of constructing arguments and of appraising theories. They are not opposites, nor are they all-encompassing; other patterns may also be identified. The purpose of focusing attention on only two modes of thought is to demonstrate the importance of awareness of mode of thought, as well as the other levels in the hierarchy (methodology, theory, policy prescription), if we are to understand debates in economics and use them constructively. Debates in macroeconomics have frequently stemmed from a lack of recognition that different participants were employing different modes of thought, or that there was a divergence between the mode of thought professed and the one used in practice.

The first, which we call the Cartesian/Euclidean mode of thought, is named, not by coincidence, after two mathematicians, the third-century BC Greek, Euclid, and the seventeenth-century Frenchman, Descartes. Both were path-breaking mathematicians who, through their geometric method, had a profound influence both on philosophy and on scientific method. The method involves establishing basic axioms, which are either true by definition or 'self evident', and using deductive logic to derive theorems, which are not self-evident. It is, however, only in mathematics that it is possible to establish incontestable axioms, because mathematics alone is a definitional system which can be pursued totally independently of observations of reality. The axiomatic method is aesthetically appealing because it allows a complete logical system to be constructed. Within this mode of thought, mathematics is thus regarded as the apex of scientific purity.

We will employ the term 'Cartesian/Euclidean' very broadly, to include all scientific thought influenced by the ideal of closed systems of axiomatic logic. The term is sometimes used strictly to refer to Descartes' or Euclid's mathematical method. But it is retained here for much broader application on the grounds that this mathematical method has been retained as an ideal (not always explicitly) within traditional methodology. The fact that most discussion within traditional methodology has ranged around issues peculiar to applied science does not detract from the position adopted here, that these issues have been couched in terms of how to formulate a closed axiomatic system, however the axioms are arrived at, to apply to observable phenomena in general.

For applied sciences, the difficulty of identifying self-evident axioms is a perpetual problem, since they must have some anchor in observed reality. In economics, for example, the axioms of consumer rationality allow a wide range of theorems to be derived by deductive logic, but they cannot be regarded as self-evident as a universal representation of human behaviour (Earl, 1983, pp.112–15). In the physical sciences, methodological developments have often been counterposed to the Cartesian method, in the sense that axioms were to be derived from empirical investigation, with all its attendant problems. But as long as the axiomatic systems approach is retained, we apply the term Cartesian/Euclidean. (See Losee, 1972, chapter 8, for example, discussing Newton's method in relation to Descartes.)

The second mode of thought has not represented an ideal within Western philosophy of science, and as such its origins, development and characteristics are less clearly established. Rather than using a linear system of logical deduction from basic axioms, this mode of thought starts from the view that it is impossible in general to establish watertight axioms and points to the way in which axiomatic error is compounded by each link in the deductive chain of logic. The alternative approach is to employ several strands of argument which have different starting points and which, in a successful theory, reinforce each other; any argument, therefore, does not stand or fall on the acceptability of any one set of axioms. Knowledge is generated by practical applications of theories as examples, using a variety of methods.

Various traditions can be identified as having something in common with the mode of thought described here (pragmatism and structuralism, for example). Its historical origins have been described variously as Babylonian (see Feynman, 1965, for the original usage, and also Wimsatt, 1981, and Stohs, 1983) as well as Stoic and Roman (Macfie, 1955). The Babylonian tradition can refer both to the non-axiomatic style of mathematical reasoning (see Feynman, 1965) as well as to the rabbinical tradition represented by the Babylonian Talmud. More generally, this style of reasoning is found typically in theological and legal argument. This mode of thought characterizes the philosophy of Keynes, whose influence on economics will be explored in chapter four. Keynes (1972c, p.364) himself used the term 'Babylonian' to refer in admiration to the scientific method Newton actually employed (as opposed to the positivist, mechanistic method conventionally ascribed to him). We will therefore use the term 'Babylonian' deliberately as a relatively unused term which does not pick up baggage from past debates. In fact, the dominance of the Cartesian/Euclidean style of reasoning has tended to colour the formulation and presentation of alternative modes of thought, particularly in perpetuating dualism. Babylonian thought is presented here not as 'not-Cartesian/Euclidean thought' (which would constitute a dual; see section 2.5 below) but rather as something different. This distinction is important. Thought in the last ten years has increasingly been influenced by a dualistic rejection of Cartesian/Euclidean thought; unlike Babylonian thought, this involves the rejection of any notion of system at all.

While the examples which spring to mind of Cartesian/Euclidean thought tend to be mathematical, the examples of Babylonian thought tend to be more 'applied'. For example, if one were debating the relative merits of cutbacks in financial provision for the university system, a whole range of reasoned arguments would generally be presented, referring to the benefits to society of higher education, comparisons with other countries, historical analysis of the role of the university sector, and so on. Indeed this is the way in which arguments are commonly conducted verbally, even by those whose papers written for academic journals take on a distinctly Cartesian/Euclidean air (McCloskey, 1983). Argument in the Babylonian style is thus conditioned by the problem at hand, employs a range of methods suited to the problem, and these methods cannot be combined into one formal deductive argument without drastically changing their nature.

While Cartesian/Euclidean thought is characterized by atomism and dualism, Babylonian thought is characterized by organicism and a move beyond dualism (Dow, 1990a). These characteristics follow in turn from the Cartesian/Euclidean practice of thinking in terms of closed systems and the Babylonian practice of thinking in terms of open systems. We now look at these characteristics in more detail to draw out the significance of the two modes of thought.

2.3   Closed and Open Systems of Thought

A closed system is one whose bounds are known and whose constituent variables and relations are known, or at least knowable. Closed systems are the province of classical logic, where the truth value of premises can be established and deductive logic applied, in order to arrive at demonstrable conclusions. Reality may be understood as a closed system, in the sense that there is a natural order which can be captured in laws of nature, or in terms of divine preordination. But, even if there is no presumption of reality as a closed system, the choice may be made of concentrating scientific knowledge on closed theoretical systems. This requires that reality can be segmented into parts which are closed, even if the whole is open. Thus, for each closed system, it must be presumed that unknown elements are stochastic, i.e. conform to a known frequency distribution. Thus, for example, for economics to be developed as a closed system, a deterministic account of economic behaviour must either be presumed to account for all behaviour, or else be separable from other elements of behaviour (Drakopoulos, 1991). The determinacy of relations within a closed system lends itself to formalism; classical mechanics and general equilibrium theory are excellent examples of closed theoretical systems.

An open system is one where not all the constituent variables and structural relationships are known or knowable, and thus the boundaries of the system are not known or knowable. This is the province of fuzzy mathematics, with indeterminate boundaries of sets (Dubois and Prade, 1980). It is also the province of non-classical logic, where logical relations are applied to uncertain knowledge; this logic is variously known as ordinary logic or human logic, as exemplified by Keynes's (1973a) probability theory. If reality is understood as an open system, then scope is allowed for free will, for creativity and for indeterminate evolution of behaviour and institutions. An open system, understood as the dual of a closed system, has often been interpreted, as in the New Physics, as a lack of system, and thus as posing severe limitations on scientific knowledge (Capra, 1975). It is this mode of thought, exemplified by postmodernism (see section 3.5), which lies behind a notable anti-methodology position which developed in the 1980s.

But an open system can also be understood to entail order as well as chaos, as, for example, in Prigogine and Stengers's (1984) theory of self-organizing systems in chemistry. Thus, as in Babylonian thought, an open system can be segmented into subsystems which can be approximated to closed systems for partial analysis, but which are always open organically to influences from other parts of the overall system. While there is no inevitability of order, there are understood to be underlying forces which can maintain, or restore, order in an indeterminate way. The Babylonian approach offers the foundations for reasoned argument in the face of uncertainty. It allows for, and uses, regularities rather than laws, as a starting-point for knowledge with a view to action. It allows for segmentation along disciplinary lines, but requires the openness of each discipline to other disciplines because of the organic interconnectedness of their subject-matter.

2.4   Atomism and Organicism

Atomism, or reductionism, follows from the axiomatic structure of Cartesian/ Euclidean thought. Because the entire logical structure in Cartesian/Euclidean thought depends on the basic axioms, it is important to make them as widely acceptable as possible, i.e. as close as possible an approximation to being 'self-evident'. As a result, propositions are broken down into their smallest components, such that one set of axioms can be identified from which all propositions can be derived by means of deduction. The term 'atomism' contains a clear reference to physics, at the stage when atoms were the smallest physical units to be identified. If all could agree on the nature of atoms, then the nature of molecules established by applying a logical chain of reasoning to the nature of atoms is likely also to attract agreement. Within economics, reductionism requires that basic axioms refer to the smallest unit of enquiry, i.e. the individual (although the application of psychology or microbiology might justify even further reduction to the determinants of human behaviour).

The Babylonian approach rather is characterized by organicism. This may stem from the view that the subject-matter of science is itself organic; or it may stem from the view that the subject-matter is ultimately unknowable in any complete sense, so that the most appropriate knowledge system for understanding it is organic. An organic system involves interdependencies which preclude the selection of one set of axioms as universally causal; it also involves interdependencies which are complex and evolutionary, and thus not amenable to formalization with respect to separable elements within a single system of reasoning. In practice, the organic system must be segmented in some way in order for knowledge to progress; it is then legitimate to have separate disciplines, separate fields within disciplines, and separate chains of reasoning within each field. But the underlying presumption is of the openness of each, and the need for the scientist to be aware of other lines of reasoning on related issues.

Typical of the Cartesian/Euclidean approach is the importance given to identifying the origins of the universe. Physicists and 'creationist' theologians who are concerned with identifying these origins are using reductionist, Cartesian/Euclidean thinking, presuming that all useful (physical or theological) results can be derived from the axioms which define the origins of the universe. Others who employ a more Babylonian style of thinking regard the limitations on knowledge as being so great that agreement on the origins of the universe would not be sufficient to allow conclusions to be drawn about contemporary events by means of deductive reasoning. The chain of logic would be so long, requiring so many ancillary assumptions, that any error would be seriously compounded by the time theorems emerged.

Rather, within Babylonian thought, it is regarded as preferable to start with contemporary problems, choosing starting points for reasoning which are best suited to these problems. The evolution of the universe and God's role in it are regarded as so complex that it is inconceivable that human minds could capture it in a complete system of deductive logic. Each line of enquiry then is limited; and there is no necessity for each to have the same starting point. This does not mean that Babylonian thought disregards logic. Rather, logic is applied within partial systems. Two lines of argument may have conflicting assumptions or conclusions. But the conflict is not a logical one if it simply reflects different choices as to which part of the system is chosen for enquiry. In Simon's (1955) terms, rationality for the scientist, as for the entrepreneur, is bounded. In Babylonian thought, there is more than one way of dealing with this limitation, reflected in different ways in which problems can be broken down and decomposed. Knowledge can thus be generated by decomposing systems, or, equivalently, by analysis. Any chosen decomposition, or analysis, is not universally applicable; it 'depends upon a limited range of environments and is likely to fail in critical instances' (Loasby, 1983, p.405). The scientist should thus be prepared to alter the decomposition (change her analysis) in different circumstances.

Since the ability to agree on any one set of axioms is doubted within the Babylonian approach, there is no particular incentive to make the axioms as narrow as possible. Indeed, since Babylonian arguments or theories can draw on a range of facets of a system, depending on which is singled out for particular attention (physical, economic, political, or whatever) it is more useful to focus on the nature of the system as a whole. Rather than being reductionist or atomistic, this approach is 'holistic'. A Cartesian/Euclidean system of thought is bound together by the set of axioms from which all theorems are derived. Babylonian thought is holistic in the sense that the binding factor of theories is a general perception of how the system as a whole works. Different schools of thought will reflect different choices as to which facets of the system to concentrate on, derived from different perceptions as to how the system works, no one body of theory purporting to present a complete, closed system. Thus some economists might see the whole in terms of market relationships, and study some particular aspect of markets, while others see the whole in terms of power relationships and consider different aspects of the economy in that light.

As a corollary, no axiom is basic to the Babylonian system, and some theorems may be axioms in other parts of the system. If the same theorem crops up as a result of applying logic to axioms derived from different parts of the system, then the acceptability of that theorem is increased because it is not dependent on the validity of any one set of axioms. A parallel argument was used by Keynes (1973a) about conclusions to be drawn from statistical inference where observations reflect an absence of *ceteris paribus*. If a conjunction of events persists in spite of a changing economic structure, this increases the probability of a causal relationship (Dow and Dow, 1985).

2.5   Dualism

Perhaps the most important feature of Cartesian/Euclidean thought, and one which permeates all aspects of analysis, is dualism. Dualism is the propensity to classify concepts, statements and events according to duals, as belonging to only one of two all-encompassing, mutually-exclusive categories with fixed meanings: true or false, logical or illogical, positive or normative, fact or opinion, and so on. Reliance on duals has a strong tradition in the rather different debate within Greek philosophy (to which Euclid subscribed) as to whether mind/soul could be separated from matter, or the mental/spiritual from the material. Indeed virtue was associated with cultivating the mind/soul at the expense of matter. Since truth and logic were the products of the pure application of the mind/soul, their pursuit was thus also virtuous.

The principle of the excluded middle is encapsulated in the dualistic notion of all-encompassing, mutually-exclusive categories. Yet this has been challenged in a variety of ways. For example, in Hegelian dialectics, there is a notion of opposites in the thesis and antithesis, but this opposition coalesces to form a third category, the synthesis. And the opposition is not dualistic, in that the thesis and antithesis derive their meaning from each other. The thesis and antithesis are polarizations, each of which may have their own legitimacy. We shall see evidence in Chapter 3 of a dialectical process in the evolution of ideas in the philosophy of science, whereby a polarization has emerged between traditional philosophy of science (modernism) and the anti-methodology position of postmodernism. Yet postmodernism is often presented as evolving out of modernism. Babylonian thought transcends this polarization; it represents the synthesis.

Another challenge comes from intuitionist logic which addresses the difficulty in practice of identifying categories. For example, in number theory, we can specify a dual in principle as follows: n is either the greatest prime number for which $(n - 2)$ is also a prime, or it is not. But if we cannot in practice identify the greatest prime for which $(n - 2)$ is also a prime, we need another category for 'n is undefined' (Heyting, 1971, p.2). Ziman (1979, p.2) has suggested three rather than two categories: 'true', 'false' and 'undecided' for the practical application of dualistic theoretical systems but, as we shall see in Chapter 3, it is not at all straightforward to decide whether an empirical proposition is true, false or undecided. Quantum physics concluded that all observations are in the 'undecided' or 'uncertain' category, in contrast to the dualism of classical mechanics. But rather than staying with the dual of certain/uncertain, quantum mechanics moved beyond dualism by developing theory to deal with uncertainty of different kinds and different degrees (Capra, 1975, Chapter 4).

A theoretical structure based on a Babylonian mode of thought discourages the use of strict, universal duals. Rather than limiting analysis to one side of the dual of truth/falsity, logical/illogical, and so on, the Babylonian approach starts from the presumption that any chain of reasoning has shortcomings when applied to an existing reality. The Cartesian/Euclidean approach concentrates on the elimination of error; a system of thought is limited to one which eliminates error. The Babylonian approach designs a system of thought in such a way as to deal with error, where error is not logical error, but the result of the uncertainty with which most knowledge is held. Such an approach involves 'hedging', in order to reduce dependence on a particular line of enquiry, just as firms hedge with respect to production processes and product lines (Kay, 1982). The result is less aesthetically appealing because the system cannot be closed. But while Euclid regarded usefulness as irrelevant to mathematics, the Babylonians, Romans and Stoics governed their enquiries by how conclusions, or theorems, could be applied: usefulness here means the ability to deal with a wide range of practical problems, in spite of the difficulties in establishing axioms. The particular collection of intertwining chains of reasoning which are employed will differ depending on the problem at hand and the prior view taken of the underlying causal forces. While the Cartesian/Euclidean mode of thought is universal in terms of its structure, the Babylonian mode of thought is universal only in the sense of its adaptability in the face of different problems.

2.6   Uncertainty, Probability and Expectations

These two modes of thought determine the view taken of scientific knowledge, and also, in the case of the social sciences, of the knowlege held by the objects of study. Thus knowledge, in Cartesian/Euclidean terms, is represented by information: facts about separable entities (which have fixed meanings) which are known, or not known, but knowable in principle. Uncertainty then refers to something quantifiable by means of frequency distributions. There is no room in theory for unknowability; the concept only has relevance for disciplinary boundaries. Thus behaviour which is irrational in relation to known information, according to the orthodox economic sense of rationality (and so, to the economist, unknowable), is the province of the psychiatrist, not the economist.

The rationale for the Babylonian mode of thought is that reality is too complex to yield much certain knowledge. While Cartesian/Euclidean thought represents the choice of focusing exclusively on certain (at least in principle) knowledge, Babylonian thought represents the choice of building up rational grounds for belief in propositions, even if most of the underlying knowledge is held with uncertainty. This indeed is how Keynes (1973a) understands how knowledge is in general built up as a basis for action; most propositions are believed to be known, subject to uncertainty of various degrees which are unquantifiable. As Keynes (1973c, p.2) put it: 'As soon as one is dealing with the influence of expectations and of transitory experience, one is, in the nature of things, outside the realm of the formally exact.'

Keynes (1973a) developed his theory of probability in a more general sense than quantifiable probability based on frequency distributions. In his sense of the term, '[a] degree of probability is not composed of some homogeneous material, and is not apparently divisible into parts of like character with one another' (Keynes, 1973a, p.32). He saw the scope for probability in the statistical sense as being limited to systems which were approximately atomistic, where there was 'limited independent variety'. But he saw reality (particularly the economic system) as organic, precluding the general application of the probability calculus (Keynes, 1973a, p.262 and 1973c, p.286; see also Carabelli, 1988, 1995).

> [T]here might be quite different laws for wholes of different degrees of complexity, and laws of connection between complexes which could not be stated in terms of laws connecting individual parts. In this case natural law would be organic and not, as it is generally supposed, atomic. (Keynes, 1973a, p.277)

Just as quantum physics evolved to address uncertainty, Keynes's theory of probability provides the basis for a similarly non-dualistic treatment of the concept. Thus Keynes argued that the confidence held in the understanding of the (unquantified) probability attached to a proposition would be greater the more weight attached to the probability. Weight increases the more relevant evidence is available. But this is fundamentally different from the notion of an increase in sample-size for a frequency distribution calculation. First, more evidence may either increase or reduce relative probability. Second, if the evidence reveals wider realms of ignorance than were previously anticipated, the increased evidence might actually reduce the confidence held in the probability judgement (Runde, 1990). Within a Cartesian/Euclidean argument, more information reduces uncertainty, but within an open system of thought, more information can increase uncertainty. Third, there is the prior judgement as to whether to recognize new evidence, and whether to recognize its relevance to the probability judgement. Conventions play a large part in the formation of judgements under uncertainty; these conventions also play a part in how much uncertainty is recognized (Dow, 1995). These conventions are important because, without them, choice of theory or, more generally, action, would, in the absence of certain knowledge, be unfounded. Cartesian/Euclidean thought can be understood as the convention that all knowledge be treated as certain, or at least certainty-equivalent (i.e. in principle knowable with certainty).

2.7   Communications Between Modes of Thought

Scientific activity governed by different modes of thought can and does coexist. What then is the relation between them? Chick (1995) identifies four possible reactions of scientists using one theory to those scientists using another theory. These reactions can be seen to be governed by modes of thought, over which the scientists may also differ. The first is the reaction most clearly stemming from a Cartesian/Euclidean mode of thought: *rejection*. This reaction employs the dualism inherent in the Cartesian/Euclidean mode of thought. If one theory establishes truth, a contrary (or even just a different) theory can only be false. If one is scientific, then the other is unscientific. If one is good, the other is bad. From this perspective, the concept of schools of thought itself is difficult to accept because the choice in favour of one closed theoretical system precludes the choice of any other system of thought (or any lack of system). The reaction to another school of thought is one of rejection. We shall see that even those schools of thought which most clearly adopt non-dualistic reasoning still retain elements of Cartesian/Euclidean thought to the extent that some take the stance of rejecting Cartesian/Euclidean thought.

The second reaction, which is typical of Babylonian thought but is also consistent with Cartesian/Euclidean thought, is one of *containment*. As Chick (1995) argues, this reaction has been typical of the physical sciences in recent years, with physics containing both Newtonian mechanics and the theory of relativity, for example. Closed-system theorizing can be contained within an open theoretical system for application to those subsystems which conform reasonably closely to closed systems, or for partial application, as in partial equilibrium analysis. Keynes for example specified the conditions for applying quantifiable probabilities, econometrics and mathematics; the closed-system theorizing that these entail is feasible, although its application is limited, and the onus is on the economist to justify the application (Dow, forthcoming, b). While neo-classical economists (as we shall see in section 4.6), reformulated Keynes's economics to contain it within the neo-classical system, some Post Keynesians now see the mainstream theoretical system as contained within the broader Post Keynesian system but only applicable under special circumstances (Gerrard, 1989).

The third reaction is to accept both, even if apparently conflicting, approaches as respresenting a *paradox*. What is meant by paradox of course depends on mode of thought. In Cartesian/Euclidean terms, a paradox involves a logical contradiction which is unacceptable within an axiomatic deductive framework; paradox is thus unavailable as a solution within Cartesian/Euclidean thought. Within a Babylonian approach, paradox and ambiguity may well arise between two lines of reasoning. Beyond dualism, inconsistency too may be perfectly acceptable. As Whitehead (1938, p.75) noted with respect to open-system modes of thought: 'By means of process the universe escapes from the limitations of the finite. Process is the immanence of the infinite in the finite; whereby all bounds are burst, and all inconsistencies dissolved.' But here the paradoxes and inconsistencies are only acceptable within certain bounds. Thus, for example, one chain of reasoning could select a variable as endogenous which is exogenous in another chain of reasoning. In general a paradox as between a closed subsystem and an open system is acceptable only given the logic of open systems; a paradox between an open system of thought and a closed system of thought as the foundation for theorizing in general would not be acceptable within a Babylonian approach. The notion of paradox has however been embraced by postmodernism. The argument will be developed in the next chapter that postmodernism involves a mode of thought which is the dual of the Cartesian/Euclidean mode of thought,

Babylonian thought being rather something other than Cartesian/Euclidean thought. Paradox is then acceptable as a general principle in not-Cartesian/ Euclidean thought, although in practice the dominant reaction to modernist (or Cartesian/Euclidean) thought is one of rejection.

The final reaction posited by Chick is one of *synthesis*, or *transcendence*, as the resolution of paradox. Synthesis entails transcendence of a thesis-and-antithesis paradox. The term 'synthesis' is being used here in a quite different way from the way it has in the past been used in economics. Most notably, the neo-classical synthesis was more an exercise in containment than a true synthesis in the sense of transcendence. Prigogine and Stengers (1984) see the emergence of synthesis in chemistry with their argument that the instability generated by the internal structure of systems is what governs change and evolution; instability is not the threat to order (as generated by some external life-force) feared from a Cartesian/Euclidean perspective – it is not paradoxical. Instability is what in fact provides the solution. Chick argues that economics is a long way away from addressing, far less achieving, such integration. The ingredients are there, however, in the paradox between the passive, equilibrating behaviour of mainstream economics and the originative behaviour and accumulation motive variously present in non-mainstream schools of thought. The need for a resolution of this paradox should become more apparent if mainstream macroeconomics continues its switch of attention further towards issues of economic growth (see section 4.9). The impetus for the motion which generates growth can be found in the type of originative behaviour which prevents equilibrium being established in the short run.

2.8   Conclusion

These observations of necessity (because of their brevity) have been selective in focusing on two broad strands within Western thought, and noting a third, which is the dual of Cartesian/Euclidean thought. But, as we turn in the next chapter to discuss the philosophy of science, we shall see how influential these modes of thought have been. First we look at the traditional philosophy of science, which has generally formulated its ideals according to Cartesian/Euclidean principles. It has continued to run up against the difficulties posed by uncertain knowledge. Then we look at more recent developments in the philosophy of science, some of which are grounded in the dual of Cartesian/Euclidean thought (in the form of an anti-methodology position) and some of which are grounded more in what we have called the Babylonian tradition.

3 Methodological Issues in Economics

3.1 Introduction

In this chapter we explore the influences on economic methodology, bearing in mind the modes of thought underlying these influences. First we consider traditional philosophy of science which aimed to set out rules for good science according to Cartesian/Euclidean principles. Then we consider the new philosophy of science which emerged in the 1960s, which conformed more to Babylonian principles. All of these developments in the philosophy of science referred initially to the physical sciences. So in section 3.4 we discuss the application of philosophy of science to economics. Finally, we consider developments in philosophy of science which have emerged predominantly within social science in the 1980s and 1990s.

The purpose of this chapter is to distill the breadth and complexity of methodological issues into those central issues which have ultimately influenced the development of thought in economics. The cost of covering such a large literature in one chapter is related to its benefits: a great deal of detail must be sacrificed. This is necessary if we are to develop a view of the whole in such a way as to grasp the connection between mode of thought, methodology, theory and policy. It is hoped that an understanding of some of the main issues will encourage the reader to pursue further areas of interest within the field. Surveys of the literature may be found in Hausman (1989, and 1992, Appendix), Gerrard (1990 and 1995), Backhouse (1994, Introduction) and Dow (forthcoming, d). Textbook accounts of methodology can be found in Blaug (1980), Caldwell (1982), Glass and Johnson (1989), Gordon (1991), Pheby (1988) and Redman (1991).

3.2 Traditional Methodological Issues

Methodology has traditionally been concerned with defining good scientific practice, and thus specifying a dividing line between science and non-science (note the dual). The Cartesian/Euclidean pattern of theorems logically derivable from a unifying set of axioms was taken as the basic requirement, whether the starting point of enquiry was observation or axioms. But in applying that framework in any area other than mathematics, the fundamental question was how to connect that chain of reasoning to reality. How were the basic axioms to be chosen? How were the axioms and theorems to be assessed as representations of reality?

The history of methodology in this mode of thought can be seen primarily as a debate about the relative merits of deduction and induction (another dual). We have already met deduction as the classic method of logic in the Cartesian/ Euclidean tradition. It involves applying logic to some general law, or axiom, possibly in conjunction with some initial conditions, to derive particular theorems. It is the type of logic employed in arriving at predictions. Induction starts at the other end of the chain; particular conjunctions of events are observed to occur and, if these conjunctions are taken to be causally connected (and expressed as theorems), logic is applied to work backward towards the axioms. Thus, for example, if the velocity of circulation of money is observed to fall over a long period during which income is rising, an economist using the general equilibrium system, working back to the axioms of rational individual behaviour, could conclude that money is a luxury good. Induction can also provide a means of dealing with the difficulty in some sciences of establishing basic axioms as the first stage in analysis. In economics, observation of consistent negative relationships between demand and price, for example, can be used to justify the axioms of consumer rationality (whether or not any claim is being made as to the empirical validity of axioms themselves, other than their ability to explain observed conjunctions of events). Inductive logic is best suited to explanation, rather than prediction; the initial step is to hypothesize that conjunction of events involves causality.

Each method is subject to serious limitations. The problem of deduction derives from its dependence on the validity of the general laws or axioms from which the theorem is deduced. Validity of the deductive logic itself does not immunize the argument from the need for demonstrating its empirical validity. The problem of induction is that conjunction of events may not in fact reflect causality, so that different sets of observations could suggest different conjunctions.

Deductive logic applied to a simple monetarist model could predict that, given the assumptions of that model, and certain initial conditions being satisfied, a ten per cent increase in the money supply this year will lead to ten per cent inflation in, say, eighteen months' time. But not all economists accept the assumptions of the monetarist model, or agree that the initial conditions are met, so there will be no agreement on the value of the prediction. And if the prediction proves to be incorrect, the 'axioms' of the monetarist model are so complex that it is generally impossible to identify which is the faulty axiom. This problem is inevitable with any applied discipline whose theorems refer to real rather than conceptual events. The organization of observations by which the validity of theorems is assessed is a product of the theoretical structure which generated the theorems (see Duhem, 1906; Quine, 1953). Thus, even if axioms are to be immune from assessment in the light of observation, there is no conclusive method by which theorems can be shown empirically to be true. They can at best be shown to be confirmed by a particular set of observations.

Induction in turn is subject to a drawback arising also from the limitations to objective observation. Suppose inflation does correspond consistently to the rate of change in the money supply. Induction could suggest that something like the monetarist theory holds, but it does not prove that the monetarist theory is in some sense true. The conjunction of rates of inflation with similar rates of growth in the money supply could be explained by reasons totally unconnected with the monetarist model. The classic example of the problem of induction is to generalize from the observation of several white swans that all swans are white, although there are in fact black swans. Most uses of induction, however, require that a causal mechanism be imputed which would allow explanation of a conjunction of events (rather than simply a classification system).

Within the Cartesian/Euclidean mode of thought, in applied fields, induction and deduction are often combined to deal with the limitations of each. Observations are made with a particular system of deductive logic in mind. The observed conjunction of events is then explained in terms of that system, adapting it if necessary by means of induction. The adapted deductive system may then be employed to make predictions. Philosophers of science, on the other hand, have demonstrated a greater tendency to think in terms of duals. Given the acknowledged limitations of both induction and deduction, they have tended to opt for one or the other as the ideal for which scientists should strive. The inevitable problems resulting from such reliance on one would eventually justify a reversal in favour of the other.

The initial preference, arising from the Greeks, was for pure deduction. Plato maintained that the only true knowledge was available through the mind, not through the senses:

> there is nothing worthy to be called 'knowledge' to be derived from the senses, and...
> the only real knowledge has to do with concepts. In [Plato's] view, '2 + 2 = 4' is
> genuine knowledge, but such a statement as 'snow is white' is so full of ambiguity
> and uncertainty that it cannot find a place in the philosopher's compass of thoughts.
> (Russell, 1946, p.163)

This preference for deduction persisted through the Middle Ages, reinforced by a theological preference for deduction from axioms which took the form of statements of faith. Scientific discoveries in the sixteenth century appeared to challenge some of the articles of faith, and provided the impetus for further questioning of the traditional scientific method of deduction. In particular, the argument that the world is round rather than flat, based on empirical evidence, raised new questions about the relation between theory and observation. Descartes' response in taking up this philosophical challenge was to question all axioms. He concluded (in accordance with Plato) that his senses were too imperfect a basis on which to rely; the only certain knowledge was his knowledge of his own thought: 'I think therefore I am'. From this position, Descartes reinforced the dualism between conceptual knowledge, and observation using the senses, between mind and matter.

In Britain, however, there was the opposite response led, among others, by the eighteenth-century philosopher–economist Hume. Hume also emphasized the subjectivity of perception but, rather than concluding that only the mind and not the senses be consulted, he maintained that the only potential source of true knowledge was the observation of matter. Given the logical inability of induction to allow general laws of cause and effect to be derived from limited observations, however, Hume was extremely sceptical of any rational basis for general laws. But he influenced the emergence of empiricism, the use of observation and experiment as a basis for science. It must be noted that empiricism remained within the Cartesian/Euclidean framework. It simply changed the basis on which axioms were established; what was self-evident in an applied science generally required more explicit reference to the real world than did mathematics.

While empiricism and the inductive method were dominant in British philosophy of science until late in the nineteenth century, the deductive method was reinforced on the continent by the work of the eighteenth-century German philosopher, Kant. He divided knowledge into the dual of *a priori* knowledge and *a posteriori* knowledge. *A priori* knowledge is innate or self-evident knowledge, which is brought to the surface of the mind by observation; it is the source of the axioms, or general laws, of theory. This knowledge includes not only ideas such as that '2 + 2 = 4', but also causal relations; causation is the concept by which we organize our observations. *A posteriori* knowledge refers to empirical facts of which we can have no innate knowledge, e.g. that the rate of unemployment was at a particular level in a particular year. Such facts may constitute the predictions of theories, i.e. the theorems by which theories are tested. This approach provides justification for the deductive method as applied to axioms based on *a priori* knowledge (albeit elicited by empirical observation).

For the physical sciences, the necessity for ostensive observation to elicit *a priori* knowledge in effect meant that induction from experimental information was still required. However we shall see that in the social sciences such as economics, the difficulty of collecting data by experiment was one of the factors which led to a continued emphasis on deduction. Within economics, debates between the inductivists and the deductivists could be extreme, where participants insisted that a choice be made between induction and deduction. A notable case was the methodological debate in the 1870s and 1880s between the Austrian subjectivists led by Menger (1883), who favoured deduction from subjectively-derived axioms, and the German historical school, led by Roscher and Schmoller who favoured induction (Schumpeter, 1954, pp.814–15 and section 4.3 below).

From Kant also came the notion that statements could be classified according to the dual of analytic statements and synthetic statements. The former are those whose truth or falsity depends on pure logic, and the definition of terms, such as 'all white swans are swans' or the Quantity Theory equation, $MV = PT$; all other statements are synthetic and their truth or falsity depends on their consistency with observed facts. It was thus concluded that meaningful statements must either be analytic, or be synthetic and capable of checking against facts, i.e. of being verified. This specification of what is and is not meaningful is what generally became known by the term 'logical positivism'. It is the logical consequence of the Cartesian/Euclidean mode of thought when applied beyond the field of pure mathematics (Quine, 1953).

This 'verifiability principle' provided a criterion for identifying science (as opposed to non-science), as generating meaningful statements. These statements were generated by means of the hypothetico-deductive method: hypotheses were constructed on the basis of observations, from which theorems could be derived and tested against further observations. At a general level, this view of science was taken as an attack on any metaphysical, or normative, content in knowledge. It also threw up the symmetry thesis, that induction (from observations to hypotheses) is symmetrical to deduction (from hypotheses to testable theorems), where both are employed within the same axiomatic system. In practice, however, that symmetry seemed to be violated. Newton's theory of gravity, for example, provided an excellent basis for prediction of the outcome of falling bodies. But Newton's law of gravitation is a purely mathematical law; it does not yield a plausible explanation in the form of a mechanism of gravitation. In contrast, Darwin's theory of evolution provides an explanation of the survival of some species at the expense of others in terms of a mechanism: those species not suited to their environment die out. The theory does not allow prediction of which species will survive in the future. In principle, if we knew more about gravity and about natural selection, we could perhaps explain and predict with both theories. But we construct theories precisely because we do not know everything.

But, more important for the philosophy of science, logical positivism also highlighted the role of theory testing. If verification were the criterion for continuing to accept theories, absence of verification should suggest theory rejection. But, as Duhem (1906) (and, later, Quine, 1953) pointed out, it is not at all straightforward to know what to reject (see, further, Harding, 1976). Rather than theories being of the simple form 'if A then B', they are generally complex compendia of a range of axioms and initial conditions. In the simple monetarist example given earlier, a ten per cent rise in the money supply was predicted to be followed by a ten per cent rate of inflation eighteen months later. If in fact inflation turned out to be twelve per cent, does that justify rejecting the entire monetarist model? It could be that the monetarist model is correct, but that the initial conditions of the hypothesis were not met; or that the money supply definition chosen was not the correct one; or that the hypothesis of expectations formation is flawed; or that portfolio preferences cannot be represented by twice-differentiable functions; and so on. This problem implied that only the simplest theorems were capable of verification, and thus meaningful by the logical positivist criterion. Duhem thus advocated relative simplicity as a means of choosing between theories; otherwise a retreat into deductivism might be implied.

The capacity to test theories was further thrown into doubt by the inescapable logical problem of induction; verification did not guarantee necessary causation. If the theory is of the form 'if A then B', and B is found to be true, then A need not be true; in fact C might be true instead where 'if C then B' is the case. The rescue of logical positivism was attempted in this respect by one of its critics, Popper, who in many ways spearheaded the subsequent developments in methodology with which we deal in the next section. Whereas the prevailing, conventionalist approach was to adopt conventions for inferring propositions from induction in as satisfactory a way as possible given the problem of induction, Popper sought to provide an alternative solution which avoided the problem of induction. (See Boland, 1982, for a critical discussion of conventionalism.) Popper (1934) argued that the only watertight empirical test did not involve verification, but involved falsification. As long as observations are taken as true statements, the only real knowledge we have is that certain theories are not true; that if 'if A then B' is implied by deductive logic, and B is found not to be true, then A cannot be true either. (If at the same time B has been shown to follow from C, then C also is shown to be false.)

Falsifiability constitutes Popper's criterion for identifying scientific statements. He set out a series of rules of procedure for framing theorems for testing. First, theorems should be put forward on the basis of 'bold conjecture' rather than observation. The remaining procedural rules concentrated on precluding defensive strategies on the part of those scientists attempting to ensure a non-falsification result. For example, if a macroeconomic theory failed to account for the 1930s Depression, it was not legitimate then to exclude the Depression years from the theoretical statement. (See Hendry and Ericsson, 1983, for a critique of Friedman and Schwartz, 1982, along these lines.) If theories are to explain and predict, Popper urged that a falsification should provoke a modification of theory to incorporate this new evidence; science thus progressed by new theories (dealing with these anomalies) which of necessity conflicted with old theories. If tests were strictly specified, then an absence of falsification could be taken as corroboration (though still not proof) of the validity of the theory, although the problem of induction remained. Ultimately, a scientist should specify precisely what evidence would lead her to reject the theory outright.

For economics, this is a particularly exacting criterion for scientific behaviour, since observations are rarely if ever available in controlled circumstances. So many features of the economy are liable to unpredictable change of some degree that the range of possibilities is difficult to anticipate before a theory is tested. Nevertheless, some form of Popper's falsification principle is widely put forward in economics as the preferred method of testing. The relevance of the Duhem–Quine thesis, which questioned the ability of falsification procedures to deal with a complex body of theory, has been sufficiently strong to limit even further the applicability of Popper's principles to economics; Popper provides inadequate guidance outside the realm of falsifiable statements. Indeed, as a result, economic practice has diverged markedly from what is *professed* to be the preferred methodology (Blaug, 1980).

Popper's thought reflects elements of the Cartesian/Euclidean tradition, specifying a demarcation between science and non-science, and viewing the philosophy of science as normative, setting out a code for acceptable scientific practice, in terms of formulating theorems for testing, if not the formulation of theories themselves. His notion of scientific progress is internalist, and rational; progress occurs according to scientific rationality (although hypothesis-by-conjecture raises questions about how far the source of conjectures is rational). Further, Popper (1944, 1945) developed the case for situational logic. In the case of the social sciences, this required axioms with respect to rational individual behaviour which would be immune from falsification; then each situation could be analysed on the basis of the axioms. Popper thus reinforced the deductivist approach in economics, apparently immunizing it from his falsificationism.

However, Popper's enquiries also led him in a direction which influenced others approaching the philosophy of science in a new way. First, he arrived at his code of behaviour in reaction to his observation of how scientists actually behaved, in particular that they were strongly motivated to protect their theories from falsification in a way which could inhibit the growth of knowledge. Second, part of that code of behaviour was that different scientists should maintain several competing theories at any one time as possibilities not yet falsified, on the grounds that the incentive to falsify competing theories would speed up the process of arriving at theories which resisted falsification, i.e. were closest to the truth.

Before proceeding to discuss the subsequent developments in methodology, it is perhaps useful at this stage to summarize in point form some of the features of the philosophy of science as it developed under the influence of the Cartesian/Euclidean mode of thought. These points can be regarded as the views of a 'representative' traditional methodologist (although each point has been a source of considerable debate). (The list is based on Hacking, 1981, pp.1–2.)

(1) A line of demarcation can be drawn between science and non-science.
(2) Science is cumulative, adding to knowledge over time (whatever counts as knowledge).
(3) A distinction can be drawn between observation and theory.
(4) Scientific concepts are precise in the sense of 'susceptible to mathematical expression' and scientific terms have fixed meanings.
(5) The logical basis for justifying acceptance of a theory can be distinguished from the circumstances in which the theory was formulated.
(6) There is one scientific method, so that in principle all sciences are part of a single scientific structure.

The final three features below refer to the connection between theory and observation. As we shall see in the fifth section, this relationship is of a different nature in the social sciences than in the physical sciences. But, since economics has been influenced so much by criteria set for the physical sciences, it is worthwhile to note these three features:

(7) There is one best description of any aspect of the real world.
(8) Observations and experiment provide the foundations for and justification of hypotheses and theories.
(9) Theories have a deductive structure in their expression, if not in their discovery (which may be inductive); they are tested by deducing observation reports from theoretical postulates.

It should be noted that the philosophy of science, within this mode of thought, is itself frequently regarded as a science – or at least as a metascience, science on a different level. By principle (6) above, if it is part of the unity of science, it must itself display the other features listed above; any other type of methodology must be classified as unscientific.

3.3 Issues in the New Methodology

The 'new methodology' can be defined relative to the traditional methodology, differing from all the above features of the traditional methodology, both as a prescription for scientific behaviour, and as a description of it. It is argued that the induction–deduction dual is subject to serious logical problems. But, in addition, the scientist cannot be separated from her environment and thought-conditioning either to form universal general laws *a priori*, or to observe real-world events other than in terms of her mode of thought in general, and theoretical stance in particular. Finally, the complexity of evolving systems is such that it is unlikely that universal laws can actually be identified, even in principle.

The scepticism from which this methodological approach emerged was fuelled by non-Euclidean developments in mathematics and by developments within physics which seemed to overthrow what had been taken as general laws: Einstein's theory of relativity, and Planck's quantum physics (see Canterbery, 1976, Chapter 8). These new theories not only demonstrated that what seemed to be general laws at one time could be superseded by more general laws at a later date. But also their content raised questions about relativism in theory-formulation itself. Laudan (1977) identifies the resulting change of view in the theory of knowledge (epistemology) as dating from the 1920s, due to the perception which became widely held, that knowledge was not certain or immutable. (The perception itself was not new, having been held by Hume and Adam Smith, for example.) At a sociological level, in Western Europe, the First World War initiated a new questioning of traditional ideas, particularly the notion of cumulative progress across a variety of spheres.

But it was not until the 1960s that a distinctive methodological approach developed out of the older notion of 'theory-laden facts' (Hanson, 1965). The central figure in this group (who in turn stands on the shoulders, as it were, of Duhem and Quine) is Kuhn (1962), whose *Structure of Scientific Revolutions* sparked off further work in the area. Some writers sought to develop his ideas, others attempted to reformulate them within the traditional methodological framework, i.e. to contain them (see also Kuhn, 1974). Kuhn's theory is addressed to the observation, unexplained by traditional theory, that falsification does not in practice lead to theory rejection. Indeed any individual theory is part of a theoretical structure; it is not separable as a testable entity. And yet, historically, theory structures have been overthrown, and replaced with new structures, for reasons other than falsification, which Kuhn undertook to explore.

Kuhn's style of reasoning has Babylonian features. He took a broad, 'system' approach to the questions at hand, exploring not only the 'internal, rational', scientific environment, but also the sociological, and above all historical 'external' environment, in which scientific discoveries were made. He showed in the process that the traditional duals (rational/irrational, and internal/external) are in fact inappropriate distinctions in this context. In other words, the process of scientific discovery, or of changing theoretical structures, is inherently a part of its broader environment. Approaching methodology more as a historian of science than as a philosopher of science, Kuhn emphasized the historical particularity of scientific developments, and concluded that it was not possible to identify any necessary trend of scientific progress over time, other than from the viewpoint of any one school of thought.

The central concept he employed was the paradigm, or 'disciplinary matrix'. This was a concept broad enough to encompass all aspects of a theoretical structure, ranging from practical techniques of analysis to the underlying world-view and mode of thought of the scientist. Indeed, his conception of a paradigm is commensurate with the definition we are using here of methodology. Its strength lies in its application simultaneously to several levels of a theoretical structure. Kuhn explained the paradigm concept by means of historical examples, demonstrating the range of possible applications. He was as a result widely criticised for ambiguity (see the debate in Lakatos and Musgrave, 1970). According to the principles of traditional methodology listed above at the end of section 3.2 (particularly item (4)), the paradigm concept could not be scientific. But the reaction to Kuhn, extending well beyond questions of pure logic, has amply demonstrated the power and range of the paradigm concept. Kuhn's reply to his critics itself provides an example of the necessary initial stage in a debate, of separating arguments of substance (expressed within a common framework) from arguments arising from lack of communication across frameworks.

Paradigms are identified with the community of scientists who practise them (although individuals may participate in more than one group; Kuhn's psychology is social rather than atomistic). The common mode of thought and theoretical structure allow communication among members of the group, as well as a means of appraising scientific discoveries within the paradigm. The paradigm is transmitted by 'exemplars' or examples; far from relying solely on the persuasiveness of logic as laid down in traditional methodology, scientists in practice employ such means to convey the paradigm's way of approaching questions without necessarily making the underlying theoretical structure explicit. Activity within the paradigm consists of 'normal science', which involves incorporating new discoveries which are compatible with the paradigm.

'Extraordinary science', which involves questioning the basis of the theoretical structure, occurs as a prelude to crisis, when a new paradigm may supersede the old as a result of a revolution. This crisis occurs, not because of the falsification of any part of the old paradigm, but as a result of a widespread perception that it has failed to address an important problem. Because the new paradigm, by definition, consists of a complex structure based on a different world view from the old paradigm, using different techniques and language, there is no basis on which the two can be compared, or on which any decision can be made as to whether scientific progress has occurred or not. The process of revolution is not discontinuous in that the anomalies within the old paradigm must have been the subject of communication in terms of the language of the new paradigm. The discontinuity refers rather to the absence of a neutral 'paradigm', by which to compare the old and new paradigms.

Kuhn's position was rendered ambiguous, however, when he set out five criteria by which theories may be appraised, referring to the following characteristics of theories: accuracy, consistency, breadth of scope, simplicity and fruitfulness (Kuhn, 1977, p.297). Although he provided no rational justification for these criteria, the fact that they were put forward as something transcending individual paradigms appears to weaken the incommensurability of paradigms and at the same time open the door to the development of a rationale for universal criteria. Implicit also in Kuhn's work is the perception of a universal goal for science which transcends paradigms. On these grounds, Newton-Smith (1981, chapter 5) argues that Kuhn is not so far from being a rationalist (who adopts a universal goal of science and appraisal criteria) as he had at first seemed.

No matter how far Kuhn himself recognized any ambiguity in his own position, it is possible still to present a Kuhnian methodology which is both distinctive and internally consistent. First, it is possible (and indeed probable) that several paradigms will hold some appraisal criteria and goals in common. But as long as some criteria and goals differ, or are employed with different weights or with different interpretations, the paradigms are incommensurate; there is no extra-paradigmatic basis for comparison. Second, any methodologist will have her own preferred set of goals and appraisal criteria; any discussion must be coloured by that fact. The best that can be done is that these preferences be made explicit, with recognition that they are paradigm-specific. Kuhn has misled readers, to the extent that he had not always displayed that recognition with respect to himself. Johnson (1983) has pointed out that the features which define a paradigm should explicitly include a 'purposive function', or set of goals, to highlight this important feature of incommensurability. To recapitulate, Kuhn's theory suggested that scientific practice has thrown up a multiplicity of scientific methods. One supersedes another for reasons other than what is traditionally regarded as scientific rationality, and it is impossible to identify objectively (i.e. independently of any paradigm) any one change as representing progress or regress. This latter conclusion was perhaps the hardest for many to accept, since it seemed to lead to relativism, or nihilism. Indeed, from the dualistic perspective of traditional methodology, Kuhn's philosophy of science was misunderstood as being the dual of traditional methodology, i.e. replacing universal scientific criteria with no criteria. In fact his approach was addressed to the *universality* of criteria, while demonstrating the importance for the progress of science that it be organized within paradigms with shared criteria.

Lakatos's work can be interpreted as an attempt to bridge the gap between Kuhn and Popper, providing an empirical criterion for appraising theories. Lakatos's (1970, 1981) approach appears on the surface to have a lot in common with Kuhn. He explained the fact that scientists retained parts of their theories which had been falsified by Popper's criterion by means of the concept of 'research programmes'. These are theoretical structures, consisting of a hard core, the basic unquestioned principles of the programme, and the protective belt of theories derived from the hard core. Anomalies might persist until some new theory emerges to deal with them; activity within the programme is directed by its positive heuristic (its agenda of problems to be solved and the methods used to solve them) rather than by anomalies as such. New research programmes emerge, but rather than being incommensurable, they will generally incorporate much of the content of the previous one, allowing a more or less continuous evolution. The criterion by which one research programme is appraised is whether it responds to anomalies with new theories designed to explain them; thus a research programme is progressive if it deals with more novel facts than competing programmes, and degenerating if it protects the hard core from novel facts by *ad hoc* adjustments. The criterion is historically specific, in the sense that what constitutes a novel fact is historically specific.

Lakatos restored the traditional notion of continuity of scientific progress, which occurs by application of an internal criterion of scientific rationality. Checking Lakatos off against the list of features of traditional methodology identifies him as leaning towards it. He had moved towards Kuhn by accommodating the persistence of research programmes despite anomalies. But, by aiming to specify what ultimately determines the decision to reject an anomalous programme, he joined with Popper in envisaging some universal, neutral set of criteria which transcended individual bodies of research. (See Latsis, 1976, for a forum on Lakatos's approach as applied to economics.)

The Kuhnian approach appears still to be left with the problem of lacking a means of appraising different theories, i.e. of relativism. The absence of any universal criterion for appraisal was in fact welcomed by Feyerabend (1970, 1981) who also emphasized the significance of theory-laden observation for the philosophy of science. It is customary for Feyerabend to be dismissed as an extreme Kuhnian; Blaug, for example, refers to Feyerabend's philosophy as 'the philosophy of flower power' (Blaug, 1980, p.44). It is important, however, to understand Feyerabend's stance as that of an advocate of academic freedom. He was conscious of the power (in sociological terms) of the dominating paradigm, and its capacity to be perpetuated through the educational system. He rejected the notion of universal methodology as much as universal laws. His position constitutes a plea for tolerance, an advocacy of an alternative mode of scientific thought. But he lapsed into traditional dualism by equating the absence of universal scientific laws with complete scepticism. Rather than universal appraisal criteria he went to the other extreme of no appraisal criteria. It was only later that he modified his position to something closer to Kuhn which was something other than the dual of traditional methodology (see Feyerabend, 1978).

Rather than adopting the dual of relativism, Kuhn focuses on delineating those areas where scepticism is relevant and those where it is not. In Babylonian tradition, by accepting the inevitable difficulties attached to the traditional scientific method, he put forward a methodology which takes into account those difficulties in a constructive way. He set out to describe rather than attack (or support) the existence of paradigms; he certainly denies forcefully the interpretation that he advocates the supremacy of normal science over extraordinary science (Kuhn, 1970). Rather, he argues on methodological grounds that Popper's (1970) prescription of exclusively extraordinary science is unreasonable. If scientists were continually trying to falsify the entire range of assumptions underlying their hypotheses, there would be little scope for scientific progress – not because arriving at correct assumptions would not constitute scientific progress, but because 'correctness' is paradigm-specific, i.e. there is no universal, ahistorical criterion for correctness. In line with the Duhem–Quine thesis, falsification procedures, as Popper prescribes them, are not feasible.

While Kuhn, like Feyerabend, denied the feasibility of universal criteria for appraising theories or paradigms with a common set of weights, several paradigms' weighting of criteria could coincide in particular contexts. Kuhn (1970) quite explicitly emphasized the common ground of logical argument. But the metaphysics from which theories are logically derived are rooted in history, and are transmitted by forms of persuasion which include, but also go beyond, pure logic. The choice of premises, the interpretation of observations, even the choice of questions to be addressed all provide scope for disagreements which evade settlement on the grounds of logic alone, even though they are transmitted or justified by reasoned argument. An argument can be logically watertight but still unpersuasive. A market economist may find a logical Marxian argument unpersuasive, for example, until it can be expressed in terms of markets; but such a translation may not be possible.

The number of paradigms which emerge is limited by the necessity for scientists to belong to groups within which they may communicate; in Kuhn's world, Feyerabend's methodological anarchy would, in fact, be unlikely to produce a proliferation of paradigms. In order to function within a discipline, any practitioner must belong, however loosely, to one or another paradigm, which has its own language, techniques, metaphysics and basis for theory appraisal. It will also have its own perception of its aims, of what problems it should be addressing. But the perception of problems themselves cannot be ahistorical, nor, by implication, divorced from the concerns of the prevailing paradigm and its competitors. It is possible to have reasoned arguments about the existence of those problems and how they are dealt with; scientific revolution arises from conclusions being drawn that the prevailing paradigm does not deal satisfactorily with what is widely held to be an important problem for the discipline, and that an alternative, more satisfactory paradigm is available. Thus Kuhn does not suggest that scientific development by paradigm revolution is irrational, simply that the relevant rational arguments cannot be understood except in the context of the particular use of metaphysics, language and appraisal criteria of the relevant paradigms.

This Kuhnian approach, as interpreted above, is useful for the general task at hand here, which is to sort out the debates in macroeconomics according to schools of thought. In other words, since the primary aim is to classify and describe, the appropriate methodology is one which is designed to describe, rather than prescribe, and one which allows for different modes of thought.

Implicit in that description will be an element of appraisal, since that is implicit in any paradigm. But by recognizing explicitly the methodological basis for differences between schools of thought, the criteria for appraisal within any one school of thought can be addressed on a rational basis.

3.4   Application of Methodological Issues to Economics

In attempting to apply the discussions of issues in the philosophy of science to economics, the assumption is implicit that these issues are applicable to economics in some way. Before making such an application, therefore, we will consider in this section, in general terms, three questions. First, is economics a science like other sciences? If not, in what ways does it differ? Finally, what is the relevance of these differences?

The question of whether economics is a science begs the question of how science is defined. Within traditional methodology, the demarcation was drawn according to adherence to the principles laid down for acceptable scientific practice. These principles differed from time to time, depending among other things on the prevailing view as to whether the mind or observation of matter was the source of truth. But aside from that difference, which determined the source of the axioms, or general laws, the structure of scientific argument (if not discovery) followed the broadly defined Cartesian/Euclidean model of a linear system of logic. This system produced theorems, or predictions, which could then be compared with observations for confirmation of the truth of the axioms.

The problem of employing induction as a means of deriving general laws is common to all fields of empirical knowledge; no science can derive indubitable inductive general laws. The traditional methodological approach to economics thus posed the question as to whether economics qualified as a science in terms of how far it fell short of the ideal, relative to other sciences. There was, then, a perception that there were differences, possibly only of degree, between economics and other sciences, but not differences which justified necessarily an alternative code for scientific behaviour. Generally speaking, the consequence of acknowledgement of these differences simply strengthened resolve to approach as closely as possible the traditional scientific ideal.

Twentieth-century scepticism about traditional methodology raised the possibility of diversity of method for different disciplines. Within the field of scientific methodology itself, however, there was still need to specify its own scope, so that there was still a tendency to classify fields as science and non-science. Feyerabend (1970) was a notable exception, drawing parallels between reasoned argument in the structure of poetry and 'scientific' theories. While Kuhn suggested that method was paradigm-specific, he did discuss the degrees of scientific maturity of different disciplines. He identified maturity with the emergence of dominant paradigms, and with the specialization of knowledge (including language) within the discipline, precluding the participation of the lay person from its deliberations. While he has tended to exclude the social sciences from his enquiries, he has explicitly identified economics as having reached maturity in the second respect. There would seem to be little doubt that economics is 'mature' also on the grounds of generating dominant paradigms.

The reactions of economists to Kuhn's approach is determined to a considerable extent by their prior methodological stance. Thus an economist who views scientific progress as a continuing accretion of knowledge, according to rational criteria internal to the discipline, will find Kuhn's account of scientific revolutions with new and old paradigms incommensurate, an incorrect account of the history of economics; the account, in Kuhn's terms, does not fit into their paradigm (see, for example, Weintraub, 1979).

Among those whose methodological stance is receptive to Kuhn's approach, however, there is debate as to its applicability to economics, as against the physical sciences (see Dobb, 1973, Chapter 1; Coats, 1969; Bronfenbrenner, 1971; Blaug, 1976; Kunin and Weaver, 1971; and see Gutting, 1980, for papers dealing more generally with the social sciences). There is first the question of whether economics has in fact developed discontinuously, with periodic revolutions. In fact, Kuhn (1970) allows for continuity in the sense that individuals can be seen to have developed in their thinking from one paradigm to the next. The incommensurability of different paradigms stems from the fact that each paradigm uses concepts and language in different ways; once the new paradigm is established, the ideas of the old paradigm will be thought of in terms of the new paradigm, implying a continuity over time which disguises the fact of conceptual change. Even if this were not the case, the notion of a violent revolution is not essential to the application of Kuhn's theory to economics. As Deane points out:

> What the Kuhnian interpretation did bring out ... more effectively than any other, is the connection between the socio-historical development of professional schools of thought and the intellectual development in the theoretical content of the discipline... [I]t is scarcely in dispute that there have been ruling paradigms in economics in that the textbooks describe a related set of theories, concepts and analytical techniques accepted as authoritative (though not necessarily as beyond criticism) by a majority of economists; and that there have been radical changes in the structure of economic doctrines which determine the generally accepted problem situation. (Deane, 1978, pp. xii–xiii)

The second question raised, by Kunin and Weaver (1971) for example, is whether the differences between a social and a physical science affect the applicability of Kuhn's framework of analysis to economics. Kuhn's own method consists of demonstration by means of exemplar, taken almost exclusively from the physical sciences. The problem of induction rears its head again in employing a theory based on the observation of one set of disciplines to another set. We turn now, therefore, to the second question concerning the nature of the differences between economics and the physical sciences. The differences between economics and the physical sciences can be grouped into four categories: differences in source of observation, the significance of historical context, human will and purposefulness and the *verstehen* principle. We address each in turn.

Differences in source of observation

The standard difference to be pointed out in any methodological discussion is that the scope for experiment in economics is extremely limited. Certainly there is an increasing amount of experimental work aimed at refining the axioms of individual behaviour (Gerrard, 1993). Indeed some see this as pointing the way to the future (Buchanan, 1991, Fishburn, 1991 and Schmalansee, 1991). But the methodological issues involved in conducting experiments on human behaviour remain to be addressed; in the current experimental work, there is of necessity a presumption of atomism which would allow individuals, and their behaviour, to be separable. The difference, as Friedman (1953) points out, is one of degree; no physical experiment is truly isolated from its environment, and the application of the results of an isolated experiment to another environment requires additional hypotheses. But because the subject of economics (or any social science) is human behaviour, the difficulty in isolating particular features of behaviour and then applying the results within a complex social environment is so marked as to rule out experiments as a general source of information. The only source of information, then, is observation of actual economic behaviour in its social environment. Economics is thus at a disadvantage in not having one of the tools of the physical sciences which facilitates the construction of general laws on which predictions can be based. The problems of testing these predictions 'in the real world' are the same for each, but the experimental physical sciences have access to short-cuts for deriving the initial axioms.

The significance of historical context

Even if experimental observation were available to economists, the capacity to generate predictions is hampered by the fact that the historical context in which theories are tested is necessarily different from that in which the axioms, or general laws, were formulated. A social science like economics must incorporate structural change in its theories, or at least arrive at a measure of structural change which can be used for adapting particular theorems or predictions to the environment in which they are to be tested. The basic subject matter of most of the physical sciences does not change historically (medicine being a counter example), whereas economic institutions and behaviour do change historically.

This difference has two important consequences. First, the scope for universal laws in economics is restricted by the capacity of the economic system to evolve over time; the majority of general statements must be conditional on the environment in which they are formulated. In particular, as Hicks (1979a) points out, the time element in statements of cause and effect becomes important if structural change can occur during that time period. In order to retain the causal statement, therefore, it must incorporate a statement about behaviour reacting to the structural change, as well as the initial cause. This requirement to account for historical developments further impedes the ability of an economist to conform to the traditional rules of scientific enquiry.

The historical dimension of economics alters also the application of the Kuhnian concept of scientific revolutions. If economics must adapt to take account of changes in the economic system, then there will be a continual source of fresh anomalies, and thus impetus towards paradigm shift for that reason alone. Rather than weakening the applicability of Kuhn's approach to economics, however, this additional feature of economics would seem to strengthen it. Paradigm shifts have perhaps been more frequent in economics than in the physical sciences. But, as Deane suggests, there have been identifiable shifts rather than continual evolution. This indicates that the dominant paradigm at any one time has been resistant to change, whether that change was warranted by its own shortcomings or by changes in the economic environment.

Human will and purposefulness

Human beings as an object of study differ from physical objects in having their own will, and by acting purposefully rather than being passive. At one level, the capacity to conduct experiments is limited by the capacity for human subjects to behave purposefully in experiments, possibly wilfully subverting proceedings. At another level, human beings are so complex in their behaviour, particularly in reacting to different economic environments, that it is very difficult to encapsulate that behaviour in a few axioms which define 'economic man'. The representation of human beings as deterministically following set rules of behaviour appears to conflict with a generally-held view as to the nature of humanity, which combines stable behaviour patterns with creativity. But if economics is to conform to the traditional criteria for science, reductionist axioms depicting the universal features of human behaviour must be formulated, and, given the argument of the previous section, formulated in such a way as to incorporate the human impetus to institutional change and the behavioural reaction to such change.

In addition, the human content of economics influences the scope of the discipline. The conscious attempts around the turn of the century to make economics more scientific focused on the distinction between normative and positive economics, advocating concentration by economists on the latter.

Political economy was thus replaced by economics, moral science by mathematical science. (It is significant that the terms 'moral' and 'science' were used together, implying that they were viewed at that time as not necessarily incompatible.) But the question of how far economics can be made value-free is central, given its subject-matter.

The verstehen *principle*

While the differences noted so far have impeded the conformity of economics to the traditional view of science, this last difference provides some counteracting assistance. The *verstehen* principle (from the German 'to understand') refers to the capacity for an economist to have knowledge of human behaviour from introspection. A physical scientist cannot have an innate understanding of her subject-matter in any comparable way. Indeed, if one takes the results of introspection as indicators of 'true' human behaviour, then economics is rescued from the problem of induction. Like Kant's *a priori* ideas, which have independent existence in our minds, but require observation to bring them to the surface, these ideas can be used to formulate axioms. If these ideas are indeed true, and the deductive logic is correct, then economics is a purely deductive system to rival mathematics.

A Kuhnian approach would question the universality of application of observations of oneself, on the grounds that each individual is at least partially a product of her environment. Indeed, if introspection is simply detailed observation of one person, and does not tap the essence of human behaviour, then it too comes up against the problem of induction. On these grounds, Mises (1949) argued that the predictive power of economics was limited to individuals' own prediction. Nevertheless, it would be accepted that this additional source of observation generates further understanding of the individual input into economic relationships, within a particular economic environment.

While we saw that perceptions of methodology within the physical sciences underwent something of a revolution during the early years of this century, the above discussion still suggests that there are some significant differences between economics and the physical sciences. The final question we must address, then, is what significance these differences have. Do these differences preclude economics from the sciences? Or is economics a science requiring an alternative scientific method? Indeed, the case has been made that, if the unity of science is rejected, then economic methodologists should not be concerned with the history of scientific methodology (see, for example, Boland, 1982, Introduction).

Interpreting the differences between economics and the physical sciences from the standpoint of traditional methodology, the first three differences are differences of degree, and do not preclude the retention of the Cartesian/Euclidean ideal of scientific behaviour. Only the last difference, in its extreme form of relying exclusively on introspection, breaks with the empirical element in traditional methodology. Yet this *a priori* approach can be viewed as consistent with an older element in this tradition, on a par with mathematics. From the Kuhnian standpoint, the greater problems facing economists in interpreting observations place even more weight on the conceptualization process, and thus on the metaphysical, linguistic and metaphorical content of a paradigm. The paradigm concept thus seems to be even more powerful when applied to economics.

But it has been the result of attempts to apply traditional scientific principles, as developed for the physical sciences, which has governed much of the development of both the methodology and content of economics. It is still the case that alternative schools of thought are judged within the orthodoxy by the standards of traditional methodology (whatever actual methodological practice is within the orthodoxy). It is therefore necessary to understand that background, and to understand the particular problems economists have faced in attempting to conform to those standards. The tenacity of traditional methodology as an ideal within economics is contrasted by McCloskey (1983) with a practice which, as he describes it, has more in common with what we call here the Babylonian mode of thought. But McCloskey falls into a traditional dualism by arguing that an awareness of the divergence between principle and practice would put an end to concern with principles. Rather, if economists were more aware of the principles which implicitly govern their practice, and of those which govern the practice of economists within other schools of thought, the constructive discussion of principles would be possible. However, McCloskey has been influential in methodological developments in economics in the 1980s and 1990s which have arisen within economics, or at least within social science, quite independently of the physical sciences.

3.5 Constructivism

The relativism inherent in the dualistic interpretation of Kuhn, as the dual of the traditional foundationalist approach to philosophy of science, attracted an increasing degree of support in the 1980s and early 1990s. The rejection of authority characteristic of the 1960s translated into a rejection of methodological authority in science. But in what Backhouse (1992) terms constructivism, this moderate relativism was taken to the extreme of an absolute rejection of methodology. The two main forms of constructivism are postmodernism and rhetoric, both of which have had a significant effect on economic methodology and on economics.

Postmodernism involves the dualistic rejection of modernism, where modernism is identified in very similar terms to those which characterize traditional methodology (Klamer, 1995). Postmodernism is an intellectual development which has emerged in a wide variety of fields, identified first within architecture. But it takes on a different character in different fields, so we will focus on its character within economics. By rejecting modernism, postmodernism also rejects the validity of general laws and general theories in economics; the preference is for context-specific analysis. As a corollary, postmodernism rejects humanism, and thus a role for government intervention; as in neo-Austrian theory, then, economics is denied its role in informing policy-making. The emphasis is on fragmentation, of knowledge and of the economy. Even the self is fragmented (Amariglio, 1988), so that postmodernism goes beyond the methodological individualism of neo-Austrian economics.

As yet, most postmodern literature in economics is at the methodological level, although attempts at addressing specific theoretical issues are emerging (Amariglio and Ruccio, 1995). However, its influence as a cultural and intellectual undercurrent has been felt in the rise of neo-Austrian economics and in the path taken by mainstream economics (Dow, 1991). The reductionist drive arising from the traditionalist, axiomatic methodology has been reinforced by the postmodern rejection of aggregation and aggregative relationships. Within methodology, the greatest influence of postmodernism has been the dualistic rejection of prescriptive methodology. This has encouraged the rise of descriptivism among economic methodologists (de Marchi, 1991, and Weintraub, 1989). It should be made clear that this is intended as pure descriptivism, whereby the methodologist applies no external criteria to their descriptions of bodies of theory. Even the notion of classifying economics into schools of thought is regarded as being too judgemental and divisive (McCloskey, 1994).

This descriptivist role for methodologists has been encouraged by the other main strand of constructivism: the rhetoric approach. McCloskey spearheaded this approach with his influential article (McCloskey, 1983, and subsequent books, McCloskey, 1986, 1994); the other standard-bearer has been Klamer with his influential volume of conversations with economists (Klamer, 1984), a technique subsequently widely copied. McCloskey emphasized the difference between the official discourse of economics, which corresponded to traditional methodology, and the unofficial discourse, which we would classify as corresponding more to Babylonian thought. The purpose of the rhetoric approach is to promote tolerance by avoiding a judgemental application of methodology to each other's economics, and to promote an understanding of the rhetoric economists actually use to persuade others to accept their theories. The outcome has been an increasing body of work addressed to understanding the methodology actually employed by economists.

This body of work has been most constructive, potentially improving mutual understanding between methodologists and economists. But there is evidence of unease among some methodologists with a purely descriptivist role. This unease arises from the relativism which partly spawned this approach in the first place. Just as economists do not have external criteria of appraisal by which to appraise each others' theories, nor do methodologists have external criteria by which to appraise other methodologies. Just as pure descriptivism is not open to economists, nor can it be open to methodologists. Pure descriptivism is thus unsustainable. Thus, having initially advocated a pure form of pluralism (the non-judgemental acceptance of a range of methodologies), Caldwell (1989) subsequently advocated a more critical approach. Even McCloskey (1994) has moved towards considering appraisal criteria, the preferred ones being those which are the most persuasive.

Just as traditional methodology proved unsustainable in its attempts to establish universal criteria for appraisal, the dualistic reaction of constructivism seems to be proving unsustainable in its absolutist rejection of any criteria of appraisal. The direction methodology is taking is thus one which can be understood dialectically. Traditional methodology as the thesis was replaced by constructivism as the antithesis. The search is on for a synthesis which moves beyond this duality. Babylonian thought provides the foundation for such a synthesis. We explore a development in the next section which offers a methodology along these lines.

3.6   Critical Realism

Methodological debate in economics has thus for a long time been between the positivist position on the one hand and the constructivist position on the other. An important recent development which has rejected both sides of this debate is critical realism. Like positivism, it accepts that economics can be a science in the sense of a natural science. But like constructivism, it rejects the positivist conception of science, and insists on development methods specific to the nature of objects of the social sphere.

This approach to economic methodology has been pioneered by Lawson (1989, 1994, 1995a), building on the philosophy of transcendental realism as developed by Bhaskar (1978); it is also strongly influenced by Keynes's philosophy. This approach combines the insights of the 'new' methodology with respect to the complexity of knowledge and the limitations of traditional methodology. The economic system is understood to be organic, with interdependencies which are evolutionary and which cannot be represented formally. These interdependencies operate at the level of 'deep structure' of economic process, as opposed to the surface appearance of events which are the normal focus of attention of economists. (Critical realism thus clearly also has roots in Marxian analysis.) Further, the 'realism' refers to the level of the nature of reality as understood by the economist; it goes much further than the traditional discussion of realism of assumptions, which is more a matter of what Maki (1989) refers to as 'realisticness'. Knowledge too is understood as organic, on

the part both of economists and of their objects of study, requiring an openness
to other disciplines. Although the deep structures of reality are understood to
have objective existence, there is no mechanism for establishing true knowledge
of them in any absolute sense.

Critical realism can be said to be founded on a Babylonian mode of thought.
Although some dualism was apparent in the early, rejectionist, statements of the
approach, critical realism is increasingly being expressed as containing traditional
methodology (see Lawson, 1995b). The latter is seen as seeking statistical
correlation of 'events' in the Humean tradition. Thus traditional theory is designed
to allow statistical correlations between, for example, changes in the money
supply and the rate of inflation, with a view to prediction, but at the expense of
explanation. The critical realist view is that explanation should refer to the
underlying structural forces of which events are simply a manifestation. Thus,
in the case of a money supply increase, it would be regarded as important to
understand the processes by which the increase took place, and the forces
underlying price-setting behaviour, in order to predict tendencies, rather than
predicting the values of variables. Not only are there limits to predicting
tendencies with respect to any one process, since this is open to behavioural and
institutional change, but any one process is generally organically interdependent
with other processes which set up their own tendencies. Again taking the example
of a money supply increase, attention would be paid by a critical realist to the
forces which instigated the increase, to the forces for competition and innovation
in the financial sector, for changes in liquidity preference, and for expectations
and competitive structure of industry, domestically and abroad. An understanding
of these forces requires recourse to a wide range of (incommensurate) methods
and an openness to the insights of other disciplines.

The focus of attention in methodology had shifted since the 1960s towards
epistemology, or questions of knowledge. Critical realism has now shifted the
focus of methodological attention to the ontological level, i.e. the level of reality,
or being. It was argued earlier that it is difference in vision, or world-view,
which underlies differences in methodology; vision refers to both of these levels:
reality and our understanding of it. Critical realism provides a new methodological
development in the mode of synthesis, following the thesis of traditional
methodology and the antithesis of anti-methodology. But in addition, it serves
to improve our understanding of methodological differences.

3.7   Pluralism

Critical realism has been discussed here as an important example of the evolution
of a synthetic approach to economics arising from the thesis of traditional
methodology and the antithesis of constructivism. This dialectic may be discussed
more generally in terms of the concept of pluralism. The confusion caused by

the increasing appeal to pluralism over recent years seems to illustrate well the distinction between constructivism and the synthetic approach.

Traditional methodology may be characterized as adopting a unitary vision of reality: nature is unitary and subject to universal laws which it is the object of science to discover. Similarly traditional methodology adopts a unitary theory of knowledge: there is one best way of knowing the nature of reality. As we have seen, however, economic methodology has failed to settle on a universal set of rules of enquiry by which this knowledge should be generated. In the absence of such rules, methodologists have fallen back on methodological pluralism, i.e. the shift of methodology from a prescriptive to a descriptive role (see Caldwell, 1982), or the advocacy of pluralism of method, i.e. the use of a range of methods without criteria for choice (see Boland, 1982). This pluralism lacks foundation given the underlying unitary vision of reality and theory of knowledge; it is not surprising that the hope is retained that a unitary methodology will emerge in time (see Caldwell, 1989).

The shift of methodology towards descriptivism was encouraged notably by the rise of constructivism. Constructivism represents the rejection of foundationalism. Thus there is a marked reluctance to discuss vision of reality and theory of knowledge. In fact both may be seen as pluralist in constructivism: reality and knowledge are both seen as fragmented. The approach to methodology, and the methods of economic enquiry are also pure pluralist in that there is a refusal to appraise methodologies and thus also to advocate one method rather than a plurality. This pluralism is unfounded, unless pluralism is made explicit at the level of vision of reality and theory of knowledge. But if reality and knowledge are pluralist in a pure sense, then there is no scope for scientific (or indeed any) discourse.

The synthetic approach entails pluralism in modified form, i.e. not pure pluralism. The synthetic approach may be identified with the general category of political economy, of which neo-Austrian, Post Keynesian and Marxian economics are particular cases. Political economy sees a unity in nature which generates regularities which are the subject matter of science. Each school of thought however has its own distinctive vision of reality. Knowledge is regarded as pluralist in the sense that reality can be understood as an open system. Then no one system of knowledge can claim to have captured reality; each is partial, reflecting one vision of reality. Each school can support its approach to knowledge with reason while recognising the legitimacy of alternative approaches. This provides the foundation for a modified pluralism at the methodological level and at the level of method. If no one school of thought can present a true account of reality as an open system, then methodologists cannot derive universal criteria by which to appraise particular schools of thought. Any methodologist however will have her own preferred set of criteria by which to appraise schools of thought. World-view and theory of knowledge cannot be eradicated; yet recognition of differences at this level allows for more reasoned debate over appraisal criteria and analysis of different methodologies.

It is this modified pluralism which underpins this particular volume. The effort has been made to present alternative schools of thought and methodologies in their own terms, while accepting that this cannot be done independently of the author's own views. The open system foundation also supports pluralism of method, but again this is not pure pluralism. We shall see that the three political economy schools of thought to be explored here adopt a range of methods (as opposed to the unifying equilibrium method of mainstream economics). But the range of methods for each school, in turn, is determined by the vision of reality on which each is founded. Thus, for example, the methodological individualism of the neo-Austrian approach rules out particular macroeconomic methods, while the class-based Marxian approach rules out particular microeconomic methods.

3.8   Conclusion

The traditional methodology of science has conformed to the broadly-defined Cartesian/Euclidean mode of thought, setting standards for good scientific behaviour. The eventual overthrow of what had been regarded as universal laws in mathematics and physics, combined with the recognition that inductive logic was incomplete, posed a threat to the validity of those standards. The outcome was, on the one hand, scepticism of any attempt to impose standards, and on the other, a tenacious holding on to the traditional standard as the only other possibility allowed by this mode of thought.

Nevertheless, it is compatible with scepticism about universal objective scientific standards to develop methodological principles to suit the particular problems faced by any one discipline, such as economics, and to suit the historical context within which problems are selected and addressed. Kuhn's paradigm concept captures the process by which theoretical structures are built on a particular methodological base, and then replaced by another paradigm when that structure fails to deal with what is perceived as a major conflict between theory and observed reality.

Kuhn has been widely dismissed as relativist, in the sense of removing any universal criteria for theory appraisal, i.e. he has been dismissed for falling short of scientific criteria established within the Cartesian/Euclidean mode of thought. Rather, by stressing the uncertainty attached to knowledge noted by Russell in the quotation which introduced the previous chapter, Kuhn provides an alternative framework to prevent the 'paralysis of hesitation' which extreme scepticism brings about. It is a relativism which allows for reasoned argument (which may not be conclusive) rather than nihilism. By promoting awareness of the significance of world views for determining the inputs to logical arguments, Kuhn points to the boundaries of reasoned argument on the one hand, and the feasibility of the co-existence of incommensurate paradigms on the other. The observational problems in economics, and the pervasiveness of its moral or normative content, pose particular problems if economists insist on striving for the traditional scientific ideal. In economics, a Kuhnian starting-point can lead to a conclusion in favour of methodological diversity. Kuhn in effect presents a 'second best' argument: if the 'first best' of traditional methodology is unattainable, the 'second best' need not be to strive to come as close as possible to the first best outcome.

Relativism has however been adopted by the constructivist approach to methodology, which denies any prescriptive role for methodology, and even the usefulness of the concept of schools of thought. This has constituted a dualistic rejection of traditional methodology and Cartesian/Euclidean thought, which is at the same time at odds with the Kuhnian approach and with the Babylonian mode of thought. The latter mode of thought offers a synthetic solution to the opposition of prescriptive methodology and anti-methodology. Critical realism is a particular methodology which promises progress along these lines.

In the next chapter we explore how economists have interpreted scientific methodology for application to economics. By rejecting the fifth postulate of traditional methodology (noted above), that justification can be isolated from the context of discovery, we will consider developments in economic theory in terms of the environment in which they occurred.

4 The Historical and Methodological Development of Schools of Thought in Macroeconomics

4.1 Introduction

The dominant ideal methodology for economics has generally been that which has prevailed for the physical sciences. This ideal has influenced the way in which the discipline of economics has responded to the problems which it has addressed, as well as the choice of problems to address. But, in turn, the particular features of economics outlined in the last chapter have required a particular interpretation of the 'ideal' methodology, and indeed have meant that economics has often had policy-related problems thrust upon it, whether or not they were regarded as falling within the scope of economics as traditionally interpreted. Thus the development of economics has reflected the continuation of ideals as represented by traditional modes of thought, in combination with the historical environment in which economists have found themselves.

According to traditional methodology, scientific development consists of an inexorable accretion of knowledge which brings scientists closer to objective truth about general laws. There is thus no history of science, only a history of pre-science; science is encapsulated in the current stock of knowledge (see Canterbery, 1976, Chapter 2). In contrast, according to the more recent understanding of the role of methodology which we employ here, the current state of knowledge cannot be understood without an appreciation of the environment which generated particular ideas in the past; such knowledge is indeed essential for an understanding of the current coexistence of several schools of thought. It is with a view to contributing to that understanding that this chapter is devoted to tracing some of the main features of the historical development of ideas which underlie the major schools of thought within contemporary macroeconomics.

Again, as with the last chapter, the aim is to provide only a framework for analysis of the issues involved; there is a wide range of excellent histories of thought to provide full accounts of the evidence relevant to these issues. It is necessary at this stage, however, to emphasize the influence of schools of thought on the perceptions of historians of thought (as much as on the economists they discuss). Historians give different interpretations to others' thought; they must also be selective in choosing the elements of economists' ideas to be conveyed in verbalizing their interpretation. The unwary explorer in the history of thought field will be as bemused and confused by the seemingly contradictory representations of economists' ideas, as is the unwary explorer in macroeconomics as such. Any two interpretations may be as incommensurate as any two theories of unemployment arising from different schools of thought.

An important factor governing interpretation of the history of thought is the degree to which the historian adheres to traditional methodology. The greater that degree, the more emphasis is put on the continuity of the history of ideas than on its discontinuity. No historian of thought would deny the existence of both continuities and discontinuities in economic thought; it is a matter of emphasis. Since we are concerned here with identifying the source of ideas of the different contemporary schools of thought, we will focus on the discontinuities in the history of thought, the forces behind splits which sent bodies of theory off in different directions.

The chapter thus follows, roughly chronologically, the way in which macroeconomics has developed, both methodologically and in terms of theory content. We start with Adam Smith as the first major Classical economist, both because he is generally regarded as the father of modern economics, but also because his work is still an important contemporary influence on economists. The subsequent developments selected for discussion are those which appear to have been major influences on contemporary thought. Such a selection, particularly presented in one chapter, inevitably represents a limited account of the history of economic thought. In order to formulate her own views, the reader is encouraged to follow up this overview with detailed reading of histories of thought, and, better still, of the original texts themselves.

4.2   The Classicists

Economics began to emerge as a distinct discipline with the Physiocrats in France. Quesnay, the founder of the Physiocrats, combined induction with deduction and avoided a deterministic representation of human behaviour. The Physiocrats did not attempt clearly to distinguish their economic analysis from political and ethical analysis. But even at this stage, methodological differences were already becoming apparent. Quesnay's followers, influenced by Descartes' deductive method, shunned 'the facts' and employed deductive logic to derive economic, or 'moral' laws on a par with natural laws (Neill, 1949).

Modern economics can be said to have started with the Classical period, which found its first major expression in 1776 with the publication of Adam Smith's *Inquiry into the Nature and Causes of the Wealth of Nations*. But, while the Classicists were the first to develop a systematic approach to economics as a distinct discipline, they still retained its connections with politics and ethics. Indeed, the Classical period can be distinguished from later developments by its treatment of economics as political economy, a moral science. Whatever the method employed (and there were methodological differences among the Classicists too), the predominant starting point was policy questions. Indeed, the contemporary environment was one of major changes in the political, economic and social order, as the Industrial Revolution followed on agrarian reform. The agenda for political economy which this environment spawned emphasized the questions of value (as the measure of the product), of growth of the national product, and of distribution, both as a social concern and as a determinant of capital accumulation to promote further growth. In short, the aim was to understand the laws of motion of the newly-emerging industrial capitalist system.

While Smith established this agenda which was to occupy economists for the following century, underlying his own work is a prior and more fundamental question. How do individuals co-operate within a specialized market economy in such a way as to create a cohesive system? Just as Newton's laws of planetary motion laid to rest the fears of cosmic disorder aroused by the revelation that the earth was not the centre of planetary motion, Smith laid to rest fears of social disorder aroused by the experience of rapid social change. He demonstrated that self-interested individual behaviour (tempered by social conventions) had positive externalities which benefited society as a whole. Further, competition enhanced this process by encouraging efficient production which benefited consumers. But, since there were inherent tendencies for market power to become concentrated, Smith advocated institutional measures designed to curb monopoly power.

While Smith identified with developments in the physical sciences, his own methodology did not employ the deterministic application of natural laws to human behaviour characteristic of Quesnay's followers. In particular, Skinner (1979) has argued that Smith (1759, 1795) perceived theories not as general laws with an objective esistence, but as subjective constructs which were psychologically satisfying to the scientist. Certainly Smith himself appears to have found the construction of a logical system psychologically satisfying. But his method of arriving at that system, as well as of employing it for policy questions, was not restricted to linear chains of reasoning. Across the range of his publications, and also within the *Wealth of Nations* itself, Smith brought together arguments from a broad range of disciplines: philosophy, psychology, sociology and history. Economists in the Cartesian/Euclidean tradition trace their approach back to Smith. But in fact it is only Book I of the *Wealth of Nations* which reflects that method; taking his work as a whole, Smith's method conforms more to what we have classified here as the Babylonian tradition. Indeed this is not surprising given the environment of the Scottish Enlightenment within which he formulated his ideas (Macfie, 1955).

Smith's eclectic methodology was invoked as an ideal by several major figures in the Classical tradition: Malthus (1824), Sismondi (1819) and Say (1803) and John Stuart Mill (1848, pp. xxvii–xxviii). Both Malthus and Mill, through his father James Mill, had been influenced by enlightenment thought, and particularly by Hume's empiricism together with his wariness of induction. (Malthus' wariness did lapse, however, when he predicted a doubling of population every twenty five years on the basis of evidence from the United States.) But the dominant Classical figure in the nineteenth century was David Ricardo, who initiated a methodological change of direction, even though James Mill was his mentor. According to Sowell (1974, p.113), '[t]he historical, the institutional, and the empirical faded into the background, and explicit social philosophy shrank to a few passing remarks'.

Ricardo's approach was primarily deductive, simplifying macroeconomic relationships into formal statements about a specific range of variables, and deriving by deductive logic a complete analytical system. Although the deductive method applied to abstract concepts precluded empirical verification, he still applied this method to policy questions (see Deane, 1978, Chapter 6). It is arguable that this was, in Ricardo's case, a change in emphasis rather than a revolution in mode of thought; John Stuart Mill, for example, although much more eclectic than Ricardo in his own method, was a great promoter of Ricardo's work, and explicitly justified the deductive method in his methodological treatise (Mill, 1836). In spite of widespread objections to Ricardo's method, the completeness of his analytical structure was welcomed at the time as representing progress from Smith's work, producing a satisfactory theoretical account of the determination of rent, the rate of profit, and value (see also Dobb, 1973, p.66). But, according to Sismondi (1819, Chapter II, p.115):

> That habit which tends to simplify everything, to classify everything, to generalise everything is no doubt the most essential course of the progress of various sciences. It is not necessary, however, to abandon oneself to it in an unreflecting manner.

Ricardo took as the principal aim of his work '[t]o determine the laws which regulate this distribution [of income]' (Ricardo, 1817, p.49). The first task was to establish a measure of the value of output to be distributed. The notion that labour was the origin of value suggested that the standard measure of value was a given quantity of labour embodied in a commodity produced with a socially-average composition of capital; it was thus determined by the technical conditions of production. Ricardo never solved the problem of how to identify this standard. (The issues raised by the labour theory of value are very complex; for a full discussion, see Dobb, 1973.)

The distribution of the product as wages, profits and rent, and its long-run trend, were subject to a set of 'tendencies'. Wage rates were generally stable, as determined by institutional factors (a tendency for improving standards of living being offset by population growth). But diminishing marginal returns to labour and capital in agriculture would require an ever-increasing share of the total product being devoted to rent. Progressively more labour would be devoted to agricultural production, as agricultural improvements were overtaken by population growth. As agricultural production became more intensive and extensive, the share of rent would thus increase. The technical conditions of agricultural production at the margin would determine the minimum rate of return in the agricultural sector (all other land earning rent), setting a floor also for acceptable manufacturing profits; this rate of profit in turn would gravitate to a uniform rate across industries due to competitive forces. As the rate of profit fell in line with the return on marginal land, the incentive to accumulate would fall, and growth would cease.

A corollary of this determination of the rate of profit as a residual was that it was independent of aggregate demand. As long as all savings were invested, there was no reason for aggregate demand to fall short of whatever level of output was supplied. There could be a mismatch between the composition of output supplied and that demanded, giving the *appearance* of overproduction, but the cure was increased output in the sectors experiencing excess demand. This expression of Say's Law within Ricardo's comparative static framework supported the notion that there was no unique equilibrium level of output (or employment); at all levels of output, demand would accommodate supply. Among non-Ricardian Classicists like Malthus and Sismondi, however, Say's Law was employed within a dynamic framework of analysis which suggested that there was an equilibrium level of output to which the economy gravitated over time. For them, Say's Law was a denial of the possibility of general overproduction, which they viewed as inconsistent with the evidence. For them the important question was whether there was a mechanism for increasing consumption in aggregate to meet increased supply. Say himself came round to using this dynamic framework and consequently eventually denied the validity of his law. The debate over the meaning and validity of Say's Law reflected the confusion arising from two different frameworks being employed simultaneously. (See Sowell, 1974, Chapter 2, for a discussion of the Classical interpretations of Say's Law.)

It is important here to recall the context in which Say's Law was adopted. Empirically, saving was feasible only for the land-owning and capitalist classes. The former's saving was limited by the degree to which rental income was used for current consumption; any saving would generally be employed in making agricultural improvements, or construction of buildings. Capitalist saving, however, was carried out specifically to finance investment, firms at that time being owner-managed. Certainly, not all finance was direct, or self-finance, since banking and thus indirect finance had developed on a widespread basis in the eighteenth century. But in a steadily-growing economy, funds were unlikely to remain idle, and indeed the expansion of the banking system, which generated finance in excess of prior savings was primarily demand-led and was thus capable of neutralizing the effect of any hoarding (Cameron, 1967). There was thus some justification for the widespread Classical acceptance of Say's Law, provided by the economic conditions and industrial structure of the time. But, although Ricardo (1809–23, volume III, p.172) admitted the possibility of hoarding in the short run, he did not admit the long-run implications of any resulting contraction in investment not met by increased bank finance.

Ricardo's influence has been as significant and as diverse as Smith's, with important echoes in contemporary thought. First, he was a direct influence on Marx's economic theory, which we consider next. Second, he is an acknowledged influence on those within the Post Keynesian school of thought who focus on long-run analysis (see section 4.11 below). Third the deductive method he pioneered in political economy encouraged a narrowing of the discipline into 'economics', under the influence of the marginalist revolution, which had largely ousted Ricardian economics by the turn of this century. The change in methodological emphasis in Ricardo's hands became a change in methodology in the marginalists' hands. (The continuity or discontinuity between Ricardo and the neo-classicists is a matter of fierce debate, with Hollander, 1979, the major advocate of continuity. See Walsh and Gram, 1979, Roncaglia, 1982, and de Vroey, 1980, for the counter-position.)

A final major Classical figure whose influence is still important in contemporary economics is Marx. His methodology reflects a quite different background from the British, French, Swiss and American Classicists (Marx, 1975; Sayer, 1979). Marx came to political economy from philosophy, first that of the German Romantics, then that of Kant and Hegel. From Hegel particularly, he acquired the dialectical interpretation of the development of ideas, whereby a thesis is counterposed by an antithesis, out of which emerges a synthesis. While Hegel regarded the struggle for synthesis as the struggle of 'spirit', Marx saw the absolute to be approached by this struggle as being material. He shared the subjective view of knowledge, but saw objective reality as resting in material things rather than in the mind. The aim of science was to identify as closely as possible the objective physical reality, which he defined as economic reality.

In general terms, then, he emphasised disharmony in thought, arising from disharmony in economic relations; he revelled in the revolutionary aspect of Hegelian thought within philosophy. His doctoral thesis dealt with the Stoic/Epicurean basis of Christianity (tracing the influence through Roman thought), drawing on the parallel between the discontinuity between Stoic/Epicurean thought and Aristotelian thought, on the one hand, and that between Hegel and the Romantics on the other. Not surprisingly, perhaps, Marx's professed method of analysis conforms more to the Babylonian than the Cartesian/Euclidean mode of thought (Deane, 1978, Chapter 9). At the same time, the elements of historical necessity in his arguments and indeed the orthodox interpretations of his theories suggest strong axiomatic/deductive leanings.

Marx's method is profoundly historical, not only because of his detailed historical studies, but also because of the historical foundation of his theory of dialectical materialism. While he drew much of his analysis from Ricardo, Marx criticized the Classical school for generating natural laws which in fact only applied to one phase of historical development, the stage of early capitalism. He explained the Classicists' error as arising from reliance on appearances, rather than on the underlying objective reality of economic relations, as they are expressed at each successive stage in the dialectical process. It was in this sense that he castigated Ricardo for not taking his abstractions far enough (Sayer, 1979, pp.119-22).

Marx's concern was, like the Classicists, with long-term developments, with production and distribution, and with the laws of motion of capitalism; Marx employed Ricardo's labour theory of value, and his determination of the rate of profit. But he brought to these concerns the view that capitalism involved disharmony of interests between labour and capitalists. The Classicists focused on the generation of surplus as the means of financing further investment and thus growth, and thus emphasised the conflict between landlords, whose rent surplus was expended on consumption, and capitalists whose profit surplus was expended on investment. Marx focused on the conflict between workers and capitalists, between wages and profits: resolution of this conflict in the face of a declining rate of profit could eventually bring about the end of capitalism and its replacement with socialism. As well as looking back to the preconditions of capitalism, Marx looked forward to the possibility of financial crisis, the concentration of industry and thus the demise of free competition, and increasing capital–labour ratios as technological changes were introduced in attempts to delay the falling profit rate, with the outcome of increasing unemployment. He saw these developments ultimately as potentially producing sufficient social unrest to arouse workers to wrest ownership of the means of production from capitalists. At the same time, he noted countervailing tendencies (such as the growth of imperialism) which could stave off the tendency for the rate of profit to fall.

Marx's theory has been subject to differing interpretations, which can in part be traced to different interpretations of his method. As with Smith, Marx's eclectic method included a formal component which some have taken to be the essence of his theory; Marx has accordingly been interpreted by some in terms of the

Cartesian/Euclidean method. By focusing on his formal model, it seems that all history is predetermined; while it is worth studying for its own sake, greater understanding cannot alter history. A complete, formal model would then seem appropriate. But by adding Marx's philosophical perspective, a greater understanding of the material reality is seen to allow a more speedy approach to synthesis; workers who realize sooner the material reality of their exploitation will take action sooner. Going one step further, and accepting the difficulties Marx himself faced in identifying objective reality, Marx's theory may be reinterpreted for application to different historical contexts; in particular, the theory can be seen to require reinterpretation to deal with the unpredicted rise in real wages and extent of technological advance.

In summary, Marx had changed the whole tenor of Ricardo's labour theory of value. What to Ricardo had been a convenient mental construct for analysing value and distribution, for Marx captured the objective reality of labour's economic exploitation. For Marx, profit was surplus labour value extracted, by the power conferred by ownership of the means of production, from the working class. This politically charged direction to Ricardian theory (which was not exclusive to Marx) was a factor in the rejection of Ricardo's theory in the Marginalist Revolution (Dobb, 1973, p.98).

4.3   The Marginalist Revolution

While some turned away from Ricardo's theory because of the type of radical political implications associated with Marx, others turned away from it because it provided a case against reform. Whether wages were kept inevitably at subsistence level because of Malthus's theory of population or because of capitalist exploitation, there seemed to be little scope for alleviating the plight of workers in the short run at least. Walras in Switzerland and Marshall and Jevons in England, for example, were not unsympathetic to social reform. However, the other major participant in the 'revolution', the Austrian Menger, can be seen as the founder of what is now known as the neo-Austrian school of thought, which makes the general case against government intervention in the economy.

There are indeed three distinct traditions within this 'revolution': (a) the English tradition emphasising utility theory and preserving (particularly under Marshall's influence) some features of Classical thought: the neo-classical school; (b) the general equilibrium school led by Walras and Pareto, a more strictly formalist approach; and (c) the Austrians whose subjectivist approach involved a strong attack on empiricism. The directions adopted by these traditions hold sufficient in common to consider them together at this stage, but we will consider their modern descendants separately.

Most of the path-breaking works which turned the tide of Classical economics were published in the 1870s, although marginalism did not become the orthodox approach until shortly before the turn of the century. Turning away from the Classical approach which raised uncomfortable class-related political issues, the marginalists attempted to create a complete analytic system encapsulating economic relationships deduced from axioms depicting a universal pattern of individual behaviour exemplified by some form of 'economic man'. (This notion of economic man had already appeared in Mill's, 1836, essay on method.) The method was (with notable exceptions, like Menger) predominantly mathematical, employing calculus to incorporate the powerful notion of the margin. The field of enquiry also changed, reflecting the maturing of European economies. Growth and the distribution of income were no longer the prime concern; emphasis now was placed on the efficient allocation of resources, and thus more on exchange than on production. Value, which was the outcome of a social process in the Classical school, was now perceived as arising from the subjective preferences of individuals acting atomistically in markets. Along with the identification of value with utility (already apparent in Say's writing, see Hunt, 1979, pp.118–21), labour, which had formerly been regarded as the source of value, became a factor whose use was to be rewarded in the same way as land and capital, according to its marginal product. Further, beyond the psychological basis for the behavioural assumptions regarding 'economic man', there was no longer any need for reference to other disciplines, or arguments, than could be found in the calculus (Jevons and Marshall were exceptions.)

The main focus of marginalism was at the micro level, i.e. at the level of the determination of relative prices. Activity at the macro level was still implicitly seen to be governed by Say's Law. The Walrasian theory of equilibrium involved the equation of demand and supply in every market, implying the equation of aggregate demand with aggregate supply. Within this framework, the lack of concern with aggregate demand (and supply) had different origins from the Classical Say's Law (in either its static or dynamic interpretations). In the Classical school, Say's Law was the outcome of long-run tendencies, which referred to equality between total quantities demanded and supplied. It arose from the equality between wages and purchases of wages goods, and profits and investment, and the response of population growth to wage levels; it was the outcome of a particular historical organization of society. In the marginalist framework, system solutions were ahistorical; they referred to positions of static equilibrium, and they arose from a representation of economic relationships designed to be universally applicable. These relationships were the outcome of actions based on demand and supply schedules aggregated over all individuals for application to any range of possible prices and quantities. The equality of demand for and supply of labour was ensured by competition in the labour market.

The equality between saving and investment was ensured by the movement of their price, the interest rate, to the market-clearing level. In spite of the growing sophistication of the financial system by that stage, no scope was given for the interest rate to have a monetary role (except possibly in the short run). The money supply, which provided the only focus for theory at a macroeconomic level, simply determined the general price level; as long as money was not 'hoarded', relative prices were independent of the general price level. This Quantity Theory of Money was put forward as a generalization from microeconomic study of payments systems by Fisher (1911).

The methodology of the marginalist school was primarily axiomatic/deductive. It relied on a finite set of axioms as to individual behaviour; the rest of the theoretical structure could then be derived using deductive logic. The purpose of the study of economics had become to establish a complete logical system, rather than to answer policy questions. For the reformers, normative questions of social reform could be separated from positive economic analysis. Income distribution was no longer viewed as being class-related, but determined by the marginal product of the relevant factor. Indeed, welfare economics, developed by Pareto within a Walrasian general equilibrium system, and by Pigou within a Marshallian partial equilibrium system, was designed to generate value-free conclusions on policy questions, particularly those involving questions of income distribution. This excising of what were viewed as normative, and thus unscientific, components of political economy gave economics the appearance of conforming more to the requirements of a science. Consistently with their mode of thought, participants viewed alternative approaches as by definition unscientific.

This opinion was apparent in Menger's arguments with the German empiricists, particularly with Roscher and Schmoller (Schumpeter, 1954, pp.814–5). Menger saw the marginalist approach as taking advantage of social scientists' powers of introspection to generate 'exact laws', thus avoiding the logical impossibility of deriving general laws or axioms using induction. The German empiricists' method was to gather data in the hope of identifying general laws; their method too was a reaction against Ricardian economics, but in this case his deductive method. The debate, however, reflected the questions addressed by each group, as much as the method employed: Menger was concerned with allocative efficiency, while the empiricists were concerned with the Classical issues of growth and distribution (Hutchison, 1981, Chapter 6).

This debate had an important outcome in the publication of John Neville Keynes's (1891) *The Scope and Method of Political Economy*, which was designed to restore methodological consensus to economics. It was published at the same time as Marshall's (1890) *Principles*, which attempted to express marginalist theory as a progression from Ricardian theory, i.e. to restore a theoretical consensus; and indeed Marshall's partial equilibrium framework (contrasting with Walras's general equilibrium framework) was designed to preserve the capacity to relate theory to developments in historical time. While setting out to advocate a combination of the deductive and historical approaches, Keynes was popularly interpreted as coming down more in favour of the deductive approach already dominant in Britain. The method he actually advocated was the hypothetico-deductive method, whereby hypotheses are generated by observation (including introspection), and results derived by deductive logic, which could then be verified against observations. Keynes was also concerned to re-establish economics as a credible science. First, he identified the hypothetico-deductive method as being in the Classical tradition, thus implying a continuing tradition of scientific progress. Second, he identified economics as being positive, or value-free; by implication the demarcation between positive and normative enquiry corresponded to the demarcation between scientific and non-scientific economics (Deane, 1983).

The support which Keynes's book was (incorrectly) interpreted to provide for the axiomatic approach was further reinforced by Robbins's influential *Essay on the Nature and Significance of Economic Science*, first published in 1932. The essay concludes that 'economic analysis consists of deductions from a series of postulates, the chief of which are almost universal facts of experience' (Robbins, 1932, p.100). Robbins also provided a definition of the scope of economics which is still widely adopted: 'Economics is a science which studies human behaviour as a relationship between (a given hierarchy of) ends and scarce means which have alternative uses' (ibid., 1932, pp.16–7).

The anti-empiricism of Robbins's stand was identified with the Austrians, as was his emphasis on human action as the subject matter of economics, rather than the categories of activity: he did not specify the ends of human action. Nevertheless, neo-Austrians distance themselves from Robbins's definition because it encourages economists to employ what they see as an artificial, technical analysis of action; and indeed it is maximizing behaviour which is conventionally understood to be implied by Robbins's definition (Kirzner, 1976, Chapter 7).

4.4 The Institutionalist School

Meanwhile, the historical school survived in various forms, although excluded by the positivist definition of science. It survived in the discipline of economic history (Deane, 1983). It also survived in empirical research for policy issues in the tradition of the London School of Economics in Britain and in the National Bureau of Economic Research in the United States. Finally, it survived in the institutionalist, or 'evolutionary', school in the United States; their objections to the axiomatic orthodoxy arose from their preference for inductive analysis, but also from their insistence that the axioms chosen by the orthodoxy did not conform with their world-views (Canterbery, 1976, Chapter 10; Ekelund and Hebert, 1975, Chapter 17).

Neither the Classical nor the neo-classical systems of thought had taken such firm root in the United States as in Britain and Europe. (Cairnes, an important Classical figure, was not at all averse to the combination of empirical and historical work with theory.) Indeed, historicist dissenters within Britain had argued that what was put forward as universal theory was not in fact easily adapted to different economic environments. Particularly influential in the promotion of historicism were developments within biology which focused on the development of systems. (A parallel influence is found in Marshall.) Veblen (1898, 1900a; 1899a, 1899b, 1900b) adapted biological theory to the analysis of social systems along evolutionary, rather than deterministic, lines.

Veblen's method was multi-disciplinary (Veblen, 1899c). In particular he brought anthropological and psychological ideas to his analysis of human behaviour; he reacted strongly against the mechanistic behaviour ascribed by the marginalists to 'economic man'. He concluded that individual and group (or institutional) behaviour are governed by technological conditions; in particular these conditions influenced both demand and supply. He foresaw that the attempts by large corporations to maintain profit rates and large unions to maintain wage rates would lead to contraction of output and eventual collapse of the capitalist system. There are strong parallells with Marx's thought in Veblen's analysis. The institutionalist tradition was carried on by Commons, Perlman, Copeland, Mitchell, Ayres, and Galbraith. Eclecticism of method, however, meant that the tradition for a long time lacked cohesion. Brady and Dowd, for example, pursued Veblen's approach of theoretical and social criticism, while Copeland pursued the evolutionary aspect of Veblen's work and joined with Mitchell, Moore and Kuznets in the strong empirical tradition associated with many of the institutionalists.

Institutionalist or evolutionary economics, like the Post Keynesian and neo-Austrian schools, has in recent years achieved increasing support, and, with the aid of journals such as the *Journal of Economic Issues* and the *Review of International Political Economy*, and organizations like the European Association of Evolutionary Political Economy, achieved a greater degree of coherence. A comprehensive account of the modern form of Institutionalism can be found in Hodgson, Samuels and Tool (1994): see also Samuels (1995). This school of thought is sometimes referred to as Old Institutionalism to distinguish it from the New Institutionalists who, following the lead of Williamson (1985), study institutions in terms of atomistic, optimizing behaviour. Old Institutionism, rather, continues in the Veblenian tradition, rejecting methodological individualism and focusing on irreversibilities, in knowledge acquisition and in evolutionary change in institutions and behaviour, all analysed in terms of an open system (as theoretical system and as subject-matter).

Although institutionalist economics is a distinctive school of thought in terms of understanding of the economic process and theory of knowledge, it has much in common with Post Keynesian economics, and indeed has drawn influences also from neo-Austrian, Marxian and mainstream economics. It is thus an example of a school of thought which has much in common with a range of other schools of thought yet is incommensurate with them. While this is true of all schools of thought, the overlaps in the case of Institutionalist economics are relatively greater. Since the purpose here is to emphasize distinctiveness rather than commonalities, Institutionalism has not been singled out as one of the schools of thought for elaboration of its conceptual foundations. In other words, the selection of schools of thought made here reflects the particular need to illustrate the importance of differences in methodological foundations, rather than to represent macroeconomics in its entirety.

4.5 The Keynesian Revolution

It was Neville Keynes's son, John Maynard Keynes, who galvanized the growing dissent from the neo-classical paradigm in his *General Theory of Employment, Interest and Money* (Keynes, 1936). Keynes's main interest when he joined the academic profession was in mathematics, particularly in the area of probability theory. He was concerned with the formation of inductive statements on the basis of information held with varying degrees of uncertainty. Starting out with a dualistic view of rationality adopted from Russell and Moore, Keynes approached probability as a possible basis for rational argument. But probability estimates based on frequency distributions could rarely be established. He thus extended the meaning of probability to encompass knowledge which was uncertain, but which nevertheless provided a rational basis for decision-making and action. In the process, he developed a logic (human logic) to be applied to uncertain knowledge, which was offered explicitly as an alternative to Cartesian, or classical, logic, where certainty as to the truth-value of premises is required (Gerrard, 1992). In the 1907 dissertation which was the basis for his *Treatise on Probability*, Keynes wrote (as quoted in Skidelsky, 1983, p.184):

> The idea of a premiss's having some weight to establish a conclusion of its lying somewhere between cogency and irrelevancy, is altogether foreign to a logic in which the premiss must either prove or not the alleged conclusion.

Keynes (1972c) himself used the term 'Babylonian' to refer to Newton's actual scientific methodology, which was an exercise in human logic. The origins, nature and implications of Keynes's philosophy have been the object of study in a burgeoning literature (Lawson and Pesaran, 1985; Carabelli, 1988; Fitzgibbons, 1988; O'Donnell, 1989, 1991; Bateman and Davis, 1991; Gerrard and Hillard,

1992; Dow and Hillard, 1995). In particular, it has now been generally accepted that the methodology employed by Keynes in his economics derives directly from his philosophy, so that his economics is an exemplar of the application of human logic, or Babylonian thought.

Keynes viewed his *General Theory* as an alternative to what he called Classical theory. In fact, the names of 'classical economists' he lists suggest that he meant what we call neo-classical theory, plus Ricardo; he lamented the influence of Ricardo on economics at the expense of Malthus, because Ricardo appeared to have argued against the possibility of a general glut (not against persistent unemployment), while Malthus's dynamic analysis had raised the possibility of insufficient effective demand. However, the theoretical basis for Ricardo's advocacy of Say's Law differed radically from that of the marginalists. Keynes was probably misled by Marshall and his own father's insistence on the continuity between Classical and neo-classical thought. Keynes may also correctly have identified Ricardo as the initial impetus behind the mathematization of economic theory, a trend about which he voiced marked reservations. These reservations stemmed from his work on probability, which suggested that most probability estimates rested on judgemental factors. 'Mathematical reasoning now appears as an aid in its symbolic rather than its numerical character' (Keynes, 1973a, p.340).

All the indications are that Keynes was striving to maintain an alternative mode of thought to the orthodoxy, one which employed a variety of methods. (The environment which generated this unorthodoxy in Keynes is explored in Skidelsky, 1983 and Bonadei, 1994.) Indeed Keynes described the composition of the *General Theory* as a 'long struggle of escape ... from habitual modes of thought and expression' (Keynes, 1936, p.viii). The *General Theory* itself represents that alternative mode of thought, with arguments presented in a variety of ways, ranging from formal mathematical models to 'purple passages' (see Chick, 1983, Chapter 2, and Harcourt, 1987, for an account of that method). Because of the diversity of method within the *General Theory* and in prior and later writing, there has been considerable debate about the degree to which, and senses in which, Keynes departed methodologically from the orthodoxy. The recent understanding of Keynes's philosophical foundations has however brought to light the underlying unity of Keynes's distinctive methodology.

The *General Theory* itself, and the eagerness with which it was received (among some), were prompted by the apparent divergence between orthodox theory and the emergence of persistent unemployment in the 1930s. This unemployment did not falsify orthodox theory, in that the marginalist version of Say's Law could be expressed as stating that market forces, if free, would eradicate any unemployment; persistent unemployment was thus an indicator of the absence of free market forces. Rather, Keynes's rejection of the orthodoxy arose more from the judgement that its concentration on the micro level had unduly diverted efforts from pursuing important macroeconomic issues.

Keynes certainly at times used the language of rejection. But the logic of his economics (as his philosophy) was one of containment; the emphasis was on the strict conditions necessary for the orthodox results to hold (or for orthodox philosophy to apply). Keynes's approach was to demonstrate the minimum changes to orthodox assumptions which would generate a result of persistent unemployment which would not be eradicated by market forces. This choice of approach was attributable in part to Harrod's arguments as to the best strategy for providing new ideas (Keynes, 1973b, pp.526–65). This put the onus on orthodox economists to justify their choice of assumptions (Carabelli, 1994). Thus he demonstrated that the failure of money wages to fall when aggregate demand fell would prevent labour market clearing. But then even if money wages did fall, there would be no assurance that planned output would settle at the full employment level; there was no automatic mechanism whereby aggregate demand would be at the full employment level of output. (See Chick, 1983, Chapters 7 and 8, for an excellent exposition of Keynes's labour market theory.) He then proceeded to demonstrate that the other major market price of the orthodox theory, the interest rate, could not be relied upon either to promote the full employment level of output; once the interest rate is influenced by monetary factors, it cannot play the role of equating planned saving and investment. Most important, Keynes redirected attention to aggregates as something other than the summation of the outcome of individual behaviour, and particularly to aggregate demand. Keynes followed in Smith's footsteps by demonstrating paradoxes between individual intentions and macroeconomic outcomes.

Further, he placed his theory within its historical context, in a way which had much in common with the institutionalists. First, he incorporated the growing division between ownership and control into his investment analysis, the relative absence of hiring halls for labour and exchange halls for goods into his labour and goods market analysis, and the growing sophistication of financial markets into his monetary theory. At an early stage, Keynes (1926, pp.32–3) had castigated orthodox economists for failing to reflect in their theory the implications of production being organized by large firms. Second he posited historical norms which would prevail during a given period (although not immutable in the face of structural change): norms in wage differentials, norms in consumer behaviour, interest rate norms, and so on. Finally, within that historical context, he focused on the (necessarily) speculative behaviour of entrepreneurs and financial investors, and the consequences for the level of output and employment.

The outcome was a revolution at both the academic and policy levels. Indeed, it was to a large degree the active role for government supported by Keynes's theory which spawned much of the new work in macroeconomics. In particular, the development of econometric macroeconomic models was a direct consequence of Keynes's work, although the original impetus for data gathering as such had come primarily from the institutionalists in the United States. Further, the emergence of the modern discipline of macroeconomics, as distinct from microeconomics, dates from Keynes. As we shall discuss further in Chapter 5, this micro–macro split was as much the outcome of a misunderstanding of Keynes's microeconomics as of any positive decision to separate the two levels of analysis.

There is no doubt that Keynes's work marks a turning point in modern macroeconomics. What is in doubt, however, is how far macroeconomics turned in the direction Keynes intended, and how far he simply provided a focus for other forces for change. It is in the nature of paradigms that new ideas are understood differently according to different paradigms; not all economists at the time or since have interpreted Keynes as he is interpreted here. We will, therefore, explore now the ways in which Keynes's ideas were adapted and developed by different schools of thought.

4.6   Hydraulic Keynesians and the Neo-classical Synthesis

Because Keynes introduced his new theoretical approach by showing how little it would take to change the orthodox results, it is not surprising that much attention should be focused on the minimum alterations he made to the orthodox assumptions for this purpose. As Kuhn suggests, it is the natural reaction of an orthodoxy under attack to revise their theories in such a way as to incorporate what have been put forward as anomalies. Thus great efforts were expended to demonstrate Keynes's theory as a special case of the orthodoxy, interesting because it explicitly dealt with the actuality of persistent unemployment, but an embellishment of, rather than an alternative to, the prevailing orthodoxy. These efforts were directed at containing Keynes's theory.

The process of expressing Keynes's theory as a special case of the neo-classical model was one of applying traditional methodological principles. Only those parts of his analysis which conformed to, or could be interpreted within, the orthodox pattern of a unified system of axiomatic logic were recognized as 'scientific'. Everything else could legitimately be ignored, including the entirety of his alternative methodological framework, since this was presented as a holistic, rather than piecemeal, alternative to the neo-classical framework.

It was Hicks (1937) and Modigliani (1944) who led this effort by demonstrating that the Keynesian result of persistent unemployment could be generated within the neo-classical model if one of the following three conditions held:

(1) investment demand is insensitive to the interest rate, preventing the interest rate from bringing investment to equality with savings at the full-employment level of income.

(2) the liquidity trap case, where the demand for money is perfectly elastic at a rate of interest above the full employment rate of interest, preventing the rate of interest from falling.

(3) money wages are rigid downwards, preventing the labour market from clearing.

Without any of these conditions, the neo-classical model could generate the traditional result of full-employment equilibrium. Pigou (1941) further argued that the first two conditions, which could cause aggregate demand to fall below the full employment level, would be neutralized by the fall in the general price level which would accompany such a situation. The real value of money balances would rise, increasing wealth and thus consumer demand. The only remaining condition which could then be agreed on within the neo-classical school was the third; *persistent* unemployment could thus be explained only by rigid money wages. Pigou had posed the real balance effect as a theoretical point, showing that the first two conditions were insufficient to explain *persistent* unemployment. But the real balance effect might take some time to work through, and indeed there might be impediments to price reductions, as to money wage reductions, in the short run. Pigou himself maintained that there still remained scope for government action to boost aggregate demand as a short-run measure as an alternative to the real balance effect. The major source of debate, then, was about the degree to which conditions (1) and (2) above were present, and thus the need for government intervention.

This interpretation of Keynes's theory has been dubbed by Coddington (1976) 'hydraulic Keynesianism'. As this name suggests, it presents a picture of the macroeconomy as a mechanical system whereby various categories of expenditure flow according to stable relationships; if the flow was insufficient to call for full employment, then it could be topped up by government expenditure. Although it was still in the neo-classical tradition, this approach shifted analysis away from *a priori* axiomatic theory, towards empirical analysis. This occurred for two reasons. First, because the driving force was the policy application of macroeconomic analysis, empirical estimates were necessary of effective demand deficiency. Second, macroeconomics had been cut adrift from microeconomics with its axioms of individual behaviour. Now the basic axioms were of the form 'consumption is a stable function of income', i.e. they were more easily testable statements than 'individuals maximize utility'.

The resulting constant reference to data posed new methodological problems for economists. First, since data derived from economic conditions which were not necessarily in equilibrium, some explicit treatment of disequilibrium was necessary, showing how observations related to a path towards equilibrium, i.e. how the actual dynamic process corresponded to the theoretical equilibrium model. It was Samuelson's (1947) major contribution to develop the correspondence principle, specifying the parameters of the adjustment process by which the economy moved from one static equilibrium to the next; this in theory allowed 'correspondence' between theoretical comparative static arguments, now augmented by the dynamic adjustment from one position to the next, and observation. Samuelson's aim was explicitly in line with the principle of falsifiability, which had become the dominant scientific principle within traditional methodology (Boland, 1982, Chapter 8).

By far the bulk of methodological discussion within macroeconomics since the 1940s has centred on the relationship between theory and observed reality. The Austrian influence during the marginalist revolution had allowed such issues to be avoided, but now theory purported to make statements which corresponded to actual economic events, and the development of econometric tools for analysing that correspondence were at the leading edge of the profession's activities. Most orthodox methodology during this period can be classified as 'conventionalist' (see Boland, 1982, for a discussion of this methodology). Given that the logical problem of induction prevents the discovery of truth from data, conventions are established to determine whether or not a theory is 'better' or 'worse' than another, i.e. how closely it corresponds to the 'true' theory. The chosen conventions are those held by the most influential (implicitly, the most able) individuals or bodies in the profession. Since the choice of conventions is presented as a rational process, it follows that conventionalism is consistent with unidirectional scientific progress.

Because this was the dominant professed methodological position within macroeconomics during the 1950s and 1960s, and some way into the 1970s, it also followed that developments within macroeconomics over this period represented progress. Indeed, there was a general perception of synthesis. While Keynes had put forward his theory as revolutionary, as an alternative to the orthodoxy, his theory had been remoulded in such a way that it no longer conflicted with the orthodoxy, except in ways which were amenable to empirical testing. It is for this reason that the body of theory which developed over this period is known as the neo-classical synthesis.

4.7 The Monetarist Counter-revolution

The leader of the Monetarist counter-revolution, Friedman, played a major part in the methodological discussions of the post-war period. The initial statement of his position, in Friedman (1953), caused a *furore*. This position, known as instrumentalism, was that the sole purpose of theory is prediction; theories should thus be constructed in such a way as to generate the best predictions. As a corollary, realism of assumptions was not a relevant criterion for choosing between theories; indeed, since the purpose of theory is to simplify reality (for the purpose of prediction), a good theory is likely to have unrealistic assumptions.

In fact, the way in which Friedman *practices* instrumentalism is simply a special case of conventionalism. In other words he takes care to construct theories which appear reasonable (this is discussed explicitly in Friedman and Schwartz, 1963b). The *furore* was caused, not because Friedman had proposed an alternative to conventionalism, but because he was interpreted by conventionalists as advocating an unconventional set of conventions. As Wong (1973) demonstrates, the foremost counterattack by Samuelson (1963) was descriptivist, simply providing different conventions for realism than predictive success. The *logic* of instrumentalism is strictly distinct from conventionalism, since no attempt is made to aim for a better theory in the sense of being 'closer to the truth'. But neither Friedman nor most of his followers who profess instrumentalism is true to the logic of instrumentalism.

Friedman's methodological position took on particular significance because of the theoretical significance of his monetarist theory. In his mammoth study, with Schwartz, of United States monetary history (Friedman and Schwartz, 1963a), and in subsequent work, Friedman employed induction from the observed correlation between the money supply and nominal income to develop a theory of nominal income determination. Thereafter, the theory was developed in such a way as to generate predictions of nominal income from money supply data. By combining this theory with the neo-classical theory of output determination, Friedman produced a theory of inflation. He was apparently instrumentalist in allowing predictive success to determine the precise formulation of this theory. Nevertheless, he consistently embellished the resulting formulation with a theoretical explanation which accorded with accepted conventions for good theory: generality, grounding in maximizing behaviour, and so on.

It is difficult in fact to perceive a real distinction between this use of econometrics, and its use in falsification tests; many professed conventionalists would in practice use instrumentalist criteria. It was generally accepted, for example, that the monetarist-(hydraulic) Keynesian question could be settled empirically, by measuring the interest elasticity of the demand for money function. In practice, participants in this debate would rarely be seen to change their positions on the basis of falsifying evidence against their prior positions. Indeed, this whole period of monetarist-(hydraulic) Keynesian debate saw a series of contradictory positions being taken on both sides, both within their methodological positions, and between their stated methodologies and their application.

If Friedman's methodology in practice was not so different from the prevailing orthodoxy, why was his work regarded as counter-revolutionary? It marked a turning-point in several respects. First, Friedman's theory of inflation coincided with the emergence of persistent inflation as a policy problem. Keynesian theory had dealt with inflation in terms of a Phillips curve which implied that there was a trade-off between inflation and unemployment. This theory was perceived to be unsatisfactory in the light of co-existing inflation and unemployment, and Friedman's alternative theory filled the need for an alternative explanation. It also threw up a new set of policy proposals, as well as new avenues for economic theory.

But, most important, Friedman signalled the return to pre-revolutionary orthodoxy in inflation and unemployment theory. He explicitly grounded his monetary theory in the Quantity Theory of Money, the pre-Keynesian orthodoxy. (In conventionalist tradition, he did, however, represent the Keynesian episode as allowing the development of embellishments to that earlier orthodoxy, so that Friedman's theory was put forward as a synthesis, part of the march of progress.) Further, having arrived at this theory ostensibly by instrumentalist means, he justified it by referring to the axioms of rational behaviour. Keynes's theory had been perceived as a system separable from microeconomics, based on alternative axioms. But this flouted the traditional Cartesian/Euclidean requirements for a unified deductive system. Friedman's theory of consumer behaviour, as well as financial behaviour, was explicitly presented as deriving from the axioms of rational behaviour. Previously only separable parts of Keynesian macroeconomic theory had been reformulated in terms of the neo-classical axioms of rational behaviour: monetary theory by Tobin (1958) and investment theory by Jorgensen (1963), for example.

Friedman's theory was thus counter-revolutionary in the sense that he signalled the way for the orthodoxy to develop a complete macroeconomic system, which both appeared to be empirically testable, and which also started from the same axioms as orthodox microeconomic theory. Friedman did not himself achieve this development (and indeed he distances himself from those who have made this achievement), but his partial success encouraged those who have taken up the challenge of general equilibrium macroeconomics for empirical application. A parallel development of general equilibrium theory by Arrow, Debreu and McKenzie, stemming from Hicks (1939) (discussed in section 4.9, below), was not designed for empirical application or testing. The conflict between the neo-classical and pure general equilibrium theorists on grounds of correspondence of theory with observation has continued to create a rift within mainstream macroeconomics.

4.8 Reconstituted Reductionists

A second major influence on modern mainstream macroeconomics has been the group dubbed by Coddington (1976) the 'reconstituted reductionists' because of their return to concern with individual behaviour, but in a disequilibrium setting. Their starting-point was quite different from Friedman's. Clower (1965) first focused attention on the issue of the market behaviour implicit in macroeconomics, and sought the basis of Keynes's contribution at this level.

This marked the first step in the concern with the microfoundations of modern macroeconomics. Clower judged the issue at stake to be whether or not Keynes had accepted Walras' Law of markets. He concluded that Keynes had argued in effect that Walras' Law did not hold, because it was possible for the labour market not to clear even when all other markets cleared. This situation could arise from the inability of unemployed workers to signal to producers the product demand they would express if only they were employed. His analysis thus focused on positions out of equilibrium, and on the information requirements of agents in different markets. He had shown that Keynes's result of persistent unemployment was consistent with behaviour which was rational by the criteria of neo-classical microeconomics, and that the result did not rely on wage rigidity.

Strongly influenced by Clower, Leijonhufvud (1967, 1968) further examined the orthodox representation of Keynes's theory and demonstrated its divergence from the *General Theory*. Hicks (1976, 1980–81) himself was later to take the courageous step of pointing out the limitations of his IS-LM apparatus as an expression of Keynesian theory. Both Leijonhufvud (1968, 1981) and Hicks (1974) developed micro-foundations for macroeconomics by examining the behaviour of markets with both price adjustment and quantity adjustment to non-clearing.

After Clower, however, the most influential theoretical exposition of the reconstituted reductionist position has been that of Barro and Grossman (1971). It has been influential, in the sense of influencing orthodox economists, because it is expressed in terms of a formal model, expressing individual behaviour in markets out of equilibrium in a deterministic way. It was also Barro (1979) who proceeded to reject the *ad hoc* elements in his early work on market behaviour, and thereafter grounded it exclusively in the axiomatic logic of general equilibrium theory. From Barro and Grossman's work developed a whole range of deterministic models of behaviour in markets out of equilibrium. This has now been incorporated into general equilibrium theory and constitutes a major area of activity in macroeconomics. We turn now to look at the development of modern general equilibrium theory, and how it came to be influenced by the reconstituted reductionists, as well as by the monetarists.

4.9 General Equilibrium Theory

Modern general equilibrium theory traces its roots from the marginalist revolution, and particularly from Walras. Some general equilibrium theorists perceive a continuity from the Classical school (see, for example, Koopmans, 1957). This is particularly true in Britain where the neo-classical tradition stemmed from Marshall who departed much less radically from the Classical tradition (and indeed did not embrace the *general* equilibrium framework). We use the term 'general equilibrium', however, in its most general sense, to cover any closed system of simultaneous equations. The solution to that system of equations, if it exists, is the position of general equilibrium. Any solution may not be unique, and it may represent a stable or unstable equilibrium; some adjustment mechanism must be included to cover movement to and from an equilibrium position.

The Walrasian system is simply a particular example of general equilibrium, where the system of equations refers to demand and supply in individual markets, and their simultaneous interaction, with the auctioneer managing the process of adjustment, or approach, to the equilibrium position in each market. This tatonnement process ensures the stability of equilibrium, though not necessarily its existence. Edgeworth (1881) put forward an alternative system, whereby equilibrium is approached by recontracting whenever a price fails to clear the market.

In the neo-classical synthesis macroeconomics, the system is one of 'hydraulic Keynesian' expenditure flows between aggregated markets, with Samuelson's correspondence principle providing the dynamic connection between static equilibria. The neo-classical synthesis is thus in the general equilibrium tradition. But since that tradition is quintessentially Cartesian/Euclidean, it is antithetical to have parallel systems of equations, one set referring to the micro level, and one to the macro level; the latter should be derivable from the former. And indeed, many of the major developments within general equilibrium macroeconomics over the last thirty years can be seen as an attempt to develop a consistent micro–macro system, with macroeconomic relationships derived from the same axioms of rational behaviour as neo-classical microeconomics.

The starting point for modern pure general equilibrium theory was the mathematical appendix to Hicks (1939). From this base, Arrow and Debreu (1954) developed the concept of Walrasian equilibrium in terms of production sets and preference structures (rather than fixed-coefficient technologies and marginal utility functions). This led to the establishment of conditions for the existence of simultaneous clearing in all markets with non-negative prices, and for the uniqueness of that set of equilibrium prices. Since market activity is influenced by plans for the future, the system must include forward markets to take account of deferred demand and supply, and a set of forward prices referring to the range of contingencies (states of nature) in which future trades could take place. Drawing also on Hicks's (1939) analysis of sequence economies, the notion of temporary equilibrium has been developed to distinguish an equilibrium based on incomplete information from a position of final equilibrium from which no impetus for change is present. The relative completeness of information has assumed increasing importance; but all information is in principle knowable.

Temporary equilibrium and disequilibrium analysis went beyond traditional neo-classical microeconomics in considering unstable market clearing, and market non-clearing positions, respectively. The impetus for this development came from attempts to accommodate an absence of clearing in the labour market within a general equilibrium system grounded in maximizing behaviour. As long as Walras' Law holds, then the labour market must clear if all other markets clear, even if money wages are rigid. To deal with unemployment, then, there must be some way of analysing positions other than full Walrasian general equilibrium. But it is still a necessary feature of such analysis (reviewed in Chapter 5) that it be expressed in terms of a closed system of equations; the system is extended to include trading at non-Walrasian prices, but this trading behaviour must derive from the assumptions of maximizing behaviour.

The argument however gained strength that general equilibrium theory is not equipped to deal with disequilibrium behaviour because it is inconsistent with maximizing behaviour; the only alternative framework to full general equilibrium is temporary equilibrium. For some, like Hahn (1973b), this consideration imposes limits on the applicability of general equilibrium analysis to real situations. (Since general equilibrium analysis alone conforms to strict Cartesian principles, Hahn equates it with economic analysis.) Hahn's approach is consistent with the early Austrian position that economic theory should be a system of deductive logic, derived from axioms in terms of abstract concepts. He denies that the Arrow–Debreu system is a description of reality, yet values a theory which is more rather than less descriptive (Hahn, 1973b); theories are to be tested by falsification procedures (Hahn, 1973a). His position is thus a conventionalist one, where the conventions favour an axiomatic deductive system. This system is advocated for its logical properties, and its precision, where precision refers to the specification of the system; since the correspondence between the system and the real world is not clearly set out, the precision cannot refer to the system as a description of reality (Coddington, 1975).

Others than Hahn, who rejected the validity of disequilibrium analysis get round this correspondence problem by defining each observation as deriving from an equilibrium position (possibly temporary). This is the only possible logical outcome of a general equilibrium system where the axioms of maximizing behaviour are taken to be true representations of individual behaviour (even if they are only 'as if' representations). Individuals who always engage in maximizing behaviour cannot be in disequilibrium; all mutually advantageous trades must have taken place. The economy can only depart from full general equilibrium as a result of constraints (on information, for example).

It is this focus solely on equilibrium positions which underlies the rational expectations hypothesis of New Classical Economics, that individuals make optimal use of available information. The corollary is that there is no truly involuntary unemployment; the unemployed have chosen to be so on the basis of a rational assessment of available information, and rational choices as to how much information to obtain.

The rational expectations hypothesis received considerable acclaim in academic and policy circles in the wake of Friedman's success with monetarism. Rational expectations theory builds onto a monetary theory of inflation a theory of expectations formation more consistent with the axioms of individual behaviour than Friedman's adaptive expectations. While it is presented as being an advance on earlier theory, by being more rigorous and complete, and more coherent as an equilibrium model (note the conventionalist criteria), the primary convention put forward by rational expectations theorists is in fact the instrumentalist convention (see Lucas and Sargent, 1981, for example). The value of the theory depends on its predictive success.

Laidler (1981) discusses the theoretical significance of the New Classical theorists' exclusive focus on market-clearing compared with the neo-classical disequilibrium focus on adjustment from one equilibrium to the next. He expressed the difference as follows:

> The (disequilibrium) approach ... does *not* differ from the clearing market view in denying that individuals perceive and then engage in all available mutually beneficial trades. It simply denies that they do so infinitely rapidly. (Laidler, 1981, p.13)

Pure general equilibrium theorists like Hahn (1981) similarly do not quarrel with the underlying representation of individual behaviour or about the theoretical structure, but with the one-to-one correspondence presumed between theoretical positions of equilibrium and observation. New Classical theory for a time thus occupied a middle methodological ground between disequilibrium theory and pure equilibrium theory, making direct empirical applications like the former but analysing only equilibrium positions like the latter. But this methodological position was weakened by a growing acceptance of the Lucas critique (Lucas, 1976) of econometric modelling practice. Lucas pointed out that, if agents adjust their behaviour to new information, then the behavioural structure of models cannot be presumed to be stable, casting doubt on the capacity of econometrics to predict succesfully. (This represented a revival of Keynes's, 1973c, pp.285–320, more general critique of Tinbergen. Logically, in fact, the Lucas critique also casts doubt on the representation of agents' expectations formation by econometric modelling.) Finally, the key prediction of New Classical Economics, that only unanticipated money supply changes could cause deviations of output from the full employment position, did not seem to stand up well in relation to empirical evidence.

The same impetus for finding choice-theoretic foundations for macroeconomic results motivated the development of New Keynesian Economics, which offered a series of explanations for deviation of output from full employment. This approach built on the foundations laid by the reconstituted reductionists, attempting to explain non-market clearing in equilibrium terms (introducing imperfect competition in product and labour markets), and to explain rigidities in prices, money wages and credit supply in choice-theoretic terms. (See Gordon, 1990; Mankiw and Romer, 1991; Greenwald and Stiglitz, 1993; and Romer, 1993.) The resulting macroeconomic models produce Keynesian conclusions in terms of the possibility of involuntary unemployment and scope for government policy to reduce unemployment. While the starting-point of this approach was a critique of New Classical economics with reference to observed non-market-clearing, some of the empirical work in New Keynesian economics has absorbed the Lucas critique of econometrics, taking the form of simulation models. But the underlying mode of thought is shared with New Classicals, with their focus on closed equilibrium systems, so that New Keynesian Economics, methodologically, still fits within a broad mainstream school of thought.

In the meantime, market-clearing theory shifted its focus from New Classical models, where the money supply was the key causal variable, to the development of real business cycle models, where change in technology is the key causal variable (Kydland and Prescott, 1982, being the seminal paper which provided the impetus for the approach). In fact, real factors such as changes in technology have been part of the business cycle literature for a long time, and the analysis of the business cycle as the process of unwinding over time the consequences of changes in technology owes much to Austrian theory. There is further a strong emphasis put on inter-temporal optimization, with Frank Ramsey's work in the 1920s providing the starting-point. What distinguishes modern real business cycle theory is the features it has in common with other forms of modern mainstream theory: a grounding in choice-theoretic foundations, a reliance on exogenous factors to initiate change in a closed system, and a move away from traditional econometric techniques, the preference being for calibration techniques. The real business cycle theory approach is influenced by the same motivation as critical realism, to identify 'deep structure'; but the outcome is very different given the Cartesian/Euclidean principles that govern the real business cycle theory approach.

While there is thus diversity among the bodies of thought discussed in this section, we shall still treat the entire general equilibrium school of thought as a separable entity, unified by important methodological principles. In order to avoid confusion with the common, narrower, usage of the term 'general equilibrium', we will use instead the term 'mainstream'; this term is less methodologically descriptive, but conveys better the broad *corpus* of thought included in the category. (The implications of methodological differences within mainstream theory will be brought out as we go along.)

The main unifying principle is that Cartesian/Euclidean thought is the correct basis for scientific enquiry. This mode of thought requires that theory be exclusively constructed within a closed, formal framework, deriving theorems from a set of axioms, delineating rational individual behaviour. The methodological debates within mainstream theory arise from differences of opinion as to the appropriate conventions to be adopted, given the difficulties of establishing correspondence between this theoretical system and reality. The reassertion of neo-Walrasian general equilibrium theory within macroeconomics, and the success, first of rational expectations theory, then of New Keynesian theory and real business cycle theory, have resulted from the persuasiveness of the relentless pursuit of the logic of Cartesian/Euclidean thought.

Since the divisions within mainstream theory are the focus of a large proportion of economic research, it may seem antithetical to emphasize the principles held in common. But, as we consider now the other three schools of thought on which later chapters will focus, it should become apparent that there are equally important divisions within each of them as in mainstream theory. Yet they too each have their own distinctive conceptual foundations, and it is on these grounds that the subsequent categorization is based.

4.10   Neo-Austrian Theory

The theoretical pre-occupation with the micro-foundations of macroeconomics, together with the growing political concern with allocative efficiency rather than unemployment in the 1970s and early 1980s, have focused attention also on neo-Austrian economics. The Austrian tradition stemming from Menger (1883) was still alive in Hayek's work in the 1930s; indeed Hayek was one of Keynes's most noted sparring partners during that period (Hayek 1931b, 1931c and 1932; Hicks, 1981). With the preoccupation with macroeconomic aggregates thereafter, Austrian theory went out of fashion. It is now enjoying a resurgence, however, based on the work of Hayek and Lachmann, the major current participants including Garrison, Lavoie, O'Driscoll, Rizzo and Rothbard.

There is a strong methodological consciousness among neo-Austrians, since they perceive their work as a methodological departure from a unified orthodoxy in the Ricardian tradition (Dolan, 1976). This alternative methodology, based on methodological individualism, derives from Mises's (1949) praxeological view of economics: economics as the science of human action. The *a priori,* or self-evident, truth on which economic theory should be based is that humans act, and act purposefully. If economics is to explain objective events, then it must concentrate on the subjective motivation for action: the formation of plans of action, rather than the outcome of action. As a corollary, since data can only refer to objective facts at a particular historical juncture, they have no relevance for the analysis of the subjective choice of behaviour by individuals. The resulting theory is regarded as true in the sense that it is derived by deductive logic from the unchanging essence of human nature.

Hayek accordingly rejects positivist orthodox theory as 'scientist', on the grounds that formal models, and their subjection to empirical testing, cannot deal with the subjectivity of knowledge, or with the complexity of social phenomena (see Barry, 1979, Chapter 2). In particular, neo-Austrians reject the orthodox theory of costs as a reflection of the physical conditions of production, in favour of a subjective theory of cost, where cost is a foregone utility (Buchanan and Thirlby, 1973; O'Driscoll, 1977).

But this strong position against allowing any connection between abstract theory and empirical reality has imposed severe limitations on neo-Austrian theory. Hayek (1937) in particular modified his stance significantly, embracing the falsification criterion for accepting or rejecting theories. Barry (1979, Chapter 2), looking for the continuity in Hayek's thought, argues that Hayek's advocacy of empirical testing is prompted by his rejection of the particular general equilibrium form of abstract theorizing. The general equilibrium framework conflicts with the neo-Austrian abstract framework which is grounded in the subjectivity of knowledge and the imperfection of information. General equilibrium, while a useful abstract reference point, is limited in its capacity to make the economy more intelligible since it cannot allow for human action of an unsystematic sort. To provide explanations, then, theory must refer to situations other than equilibrium, i.e. to actual (empirical) situations. While some (Kantor, 1979; Laidler, 1981) have emphasized the Austrian roots of rational expectations theory, there is a fundamental difference between their views as to whether observed situations can or cannot be equated with equilibrium.

Hayek's position on the value of falsification can, however, only be seen as inconsistent with the position outlined in the previous paragraph with respect to the exclusivity of *a priori* theorizing (Hutchison, 1981, Chapter 7). On the other hand, within the neo-Austrian school there are those, such as Rothbard (1976a), who still consistently deny an objective empirical content.

There is a further difficulty associated with basing market analysis on axioms of individual motivation, which account for the ambiguous role of equilibrium in neo-Austrian theory. In particular, problems arise from attempts, advocated by Hayek, to study the unintended consequences of human action. Indeed, Popper (1963, pp.124–5) identifies this as the subject matter of the social sciences (in a volume dedicated, incidentally, to Hayek) (see Kirzner, 1976). Unintended consequences confound expectations. If action is at all unsystematic, however, then learning cannot be totally systematic, and so the choice of plans of action in response to falsified expectations cannot be predicted, except partially, on a case-by-case basis. The equilibrium concept, which requires the assumption of systematic learning (which is a complete process in itself, although not necessarily complete in the sense that all information is known and used), is irrelevant. Certainly, developments can be explained after the event, but the scope for generalizations about market behaviour are very limited. The only logical conclusion is that economic theory itself is very limited.

Within neo-Austrian thought there is a conflict between an approach akin to Babylonian thought and elements of Cartesian/Euclidean thought. The aim of constructing an all-encompassing theoretical structure on the basis of self-evident axioms with respect to purposeful human action is Cartesian/Euclidean. But Hayek, for example, stresses the complexity of social phenomena (Barry, 1979, Chapter 2); and indeed Hayek is associated particularly with seeing praxeological theory as transcending the conventional disciplinary divisions within the social sciences. Further, the rejection of logical positivism given the historical particularity of economic events focuses analysis on explanation rather than prediction. The differing historical, political and sociological contexts of particular events requiring explanation call for a certain diversity of method; their vision of market processes is holistic, but their analysis is particular. Many neo-Austrians have thus rejected the Cartesian/Euclidean ideal as impractical for social science and adopted instead what we call a Babylonian approach. The methodological conflicts which persist among neo-Austrians can be explained partly in terms of conflict between those who retain the Cartesian/Euclidean mode of thought, and those who do not. Rothbard's (1976a) insistence on maintaining the theoretical system separate from observation of objective reality, for example, reflects an adherence to the pure axiomatic approach.

An important influence on modern neo-Austrian thought is Shackle, who clearly conforms to our definition of Babylonian thought. In one paper, for example, Shackle (1966) characterizes general equilibrium theorists as attempting 'to see the whole economic scene as the manifestation of the free operation of self-interest within a frame of law and order' (Shackle, 1966, p 31). But, because of the necessary assumption of perfect knowledge (requiring probability estimates of uncertain events), mainstream theory has:

> renounced the endeavour to reach down to the deep roots of human conduct. Thus it is from the outset precluded from the search for any unifying principle in that conduct. What can be done? If we cannot have a *system*, we can have a *scheme*, an orderly array of theories differently grounded in basic assumptions, some acknowledging uncertainty, some concerned with progressive, irreversible evolution, some with mechanical, insulated, deterministic repetition; an outfit of tools, not an ultimate philosophy. (ibid.)

4.11　Post Keynesian Theory

Shackle is also an influential figure among Post Keynesians (other than those concerned exclusively with long-period analysis). His influence has been felt primarily in the area of methodology, in the sense of theoretical treatment of the concepts of time, expectations and uncertainty. It was with respect to these concepts in particular that many felt that the neo-classical synthesis had departed most seriously from Keynes's theory.

What is now known as Post Keynesian macroeconomic theory arose from the work of those who rejected the neo-classical synthesis either as seriously misrepresenting Keynes, or because of its departure from Classical principles and concerns. The main mouthpieces for these two groups within Post Keynesian theory are the *Journal of Post Keynesian Economics* and the *Cambridge Journal of Economics* respectively. Three recent accounts of Post Keynesian theory are found in Arestis (1992), Lavoie (1992) and Davidson (1994).

The neo-classical synthesis was viewed as an attempt by those within the general equilibrium orthodoxy to contain any tendency towards Kuhnian crisis by proving that persistent unemployment was not an anomaly within their framework. On conventionalist grounds, those within the orthodoxy who were reasonably satisfied that the anomaly had thus been dealt with were content to continue to accept other features of their framework which Post Keynesians argued were unsatisfactory (see for example Weintraub, 1979, p.37). Post Keynesians, however, continued to insist that persistent unemployment *is* an anomaly within the mainstream framework, because that framework itself prevents the accommodation of persistent unemployment. This position has been vindicated by those within the mainstream school of thought who themselves have taken it to its logical conclusion that persistent involuntary unemployment is inconsistent with the optimizing behavioural assumptions.

Post Keynesian theory has been conditioned by the two requirements of a Kuhnian crisis. First, an important anomaly must be shown to be present in the orthodox theory. The anomaly of persistent unemployment, even in the long run, which Keynes had highlighted, is still the main focus of Post Keynesian macroeconomic theory. But, while economic conditions in the late 1970s and early 1980s bore a strong resemblance to those in the 1930s Depression, there was not the same groundswell of opinion in favour of Keynesian expansionary measures. First, orthodox theory had built a stronger case this time for the argument that much of the high unemployment is in fact voluntary. More important, the co-existence for a time of inflation and unemployment reinforced arguments for monetary tightness; this contrasts with the 1930s, when even some Chicago economists presented monetarist arguments for monetary expansion (Tavlas, 1977).

As long as a Kuhnian crisis is not perpetrated at the political level, the orthodoxy can preserve the logical consistency of their theory by, in effect, defining away persistent involuntary unemployment. The second aspect of the Post Keynesian position, then, is to argue that there are shortcomings within a framework which allows unemployment to be defined away in this way, and to present an alternative framework without these shortcomings. As a result, much Post Keynesian work is presented at the methodological level, i.e. emphasizing the differences in methodological framework. Because the Post Keynesian framework derives primarily from a Babylonian style of thought, however, it cannot accord with the Cartesian/Euclidean criteria for scientific activity. It is, therefore, straightforward for orthodox theorists to reject Post Keynesian theory in dualistic fashion as unscientific, and to argue that the inability of the general equilibrium framework to deal with certain phenomena does not justify rejecting that framework, given the absence of a preferable 'scientific' framework (see, for example, Hahn, 1981, pp.128–9).

Post Keynesians share neo-Austrians' concern with the role of historical time (Robinson, 1978), the importance of problems of knowledge (particularly with respect to the future), and of institutions (Davidson, 1981, p.158). They also share the goals of making the workings of the economy intelligible, and understanding the unintended consequences of human action (Bausor, 1982–83). But they choose a different theoretical approach based on different views as to the central concerns of economics and the nature of the economic process (Dow, 1990b). While neo-Austrians are concerned primarily with exchange, and its capacity to promote the efficient allocation of resources, Post Keynesians are concerned primarily with production and distribution. Both are concerned with the causes and consequences of structural change, but with respect to exchange and production respectively. These Post Keynesian concerns reflect their focus on the Classical antecedents of Keynes, and the influence of Kalecki who, starting from Marxist theory, arrived at a similar theory to Keynes about the role of effective demand failures. Indeed some regard Kalecki as the more important of the two (see Eichner, 1979, p.7; Sawyer, 1982). How far Keynes's and Kalecki's methodology are compatible is a matter of active debate.

The role of exchange in Post Keynesian theory requires some elaboration. Exchange necessarily features in any economic theory. In neo-Austrian, as in neo-Walrasian general equilibrium theory, exchange is the mechanism by which consumers exercise their choices in an economy, while prices are the parameters of that choice. The Post Keynesian position is that individual choice is limited. It is determined much more by income and class and the technical conditions of production than by relative prices, while the incidence of monopoly and oligopoly power in product markets confers the power to administer prices (where power refers to the socio-political role of large corporations as much as power in any one market as such). Capacity to administer price (as well as product preferences) relative to power over input costs (particularly labour costs) determines the surplus earned by corporations. How far that surplus is translated into new investment depends on long-term expectations with respect to the product market in question, and on short-term expectations with respect to the prices of financial assets. Since these latter expectations and the institutional structure of financial markets simultaneously determine the supply of, as well as the demand for, financial assets (particularly money), orthodox supply and demand analysis again is not applicable. Social relations are of importance here too, determining the relative power of financial institutions (Minsky, 1980; Kregel, 1980b).

Institutional structure and industrial organization are thus of considerable importance, since they determine the distribution of income, the level and composition of output, the capacity for generating surplus, and the degree to which that surplus is expended in such a way as to increase output and employment. The abstract mainstream model presumes an institutional structure (based on perfect competition) which essentially remains fixed. Post Keynesian theory, in contrast, presumes that institutional change is the norm, and indeed makes the historical development of economies (as societies) the main object of analysis. The starting point, then, rather than introspection, is observation of economies (albeit necessarily theory-laden), both to understand the process involved, and to facilitate a view of the current structure of particular economies, in order to address policy questions. Further abstraction is then employed to simplify that structural view, in order to reach conclusions. For example, it may be accepted as a simplification of reality that firms price according to mark-up procedures; if an increase in an input price is expected, then a mark-up pricing model allows some predictions as to the outcome for product prices.

There is an emerging consensus that the Post Keynesian approach is consistent with much of critical realism, with open-system theorizing applied to an economy understood as an organic, open system (Dow, 1990b and forthcoming, e; Arestis, 1992, pp.94–100; Lavoie, 1992, pp.7–10). Different forms of abstraction are relevant to different questions, and different economies; and indeed the study of actual economies required before abstraction can occur involves the application of different disciplines. This is the essence of the Babylonian method. There is no presumption as to theoretical truth; the only truth rests in actual events, which can only be observed imperfectly in the light of theoretical preconceptions, and only understood imperfectly by abstract theorizing. There are, nevertheless, conventions as to how best to promote understanding given these imperfections. Conventions unite any community of 'scientists' within the paradigm they adopt. This does not prevent Post Keynesians arguing that their collection of theories and methods is the best, on rational grounds, given the conventions of the paradigm. In other words, admission of lack of full objectivity does not require theory to embrace the dual, complete subjectivity, given Babylonian conventions.

Interpreted broadly, the Post Keynesian school of thought incorporates a diversity of approaches. There is for example a strong tradition in long-period analysis combining Classical concerns with value and distribution with Keynes's principle of effective demand (that it is income, not relative prices, which brings about equality of *ex ante* saving and investment). Of great influence is the work of Sraffa (1960), whose critique of the marginalist theory of value and distribution was enhanced by a model which used a standard commodity as an invariant measure of value (Harcourt, 1972; Hunt, 1979, Chapter 17). Among those who engage in this type of long-period analysis there are some (notably Garegnani, 1978, 1979; Eatwell, 1979; Milgate, 1983) who argue that Keynes's methodology is more akin to the neo-classical synthesis, than to Classical political economy, in that he postulates a marginal productivity theory of distribution (Hunt, 1979, pp.382–3); the principle of effective demand can, however, be incorporated into a Classical framework. In particular, short-run analysis is regarded as detracting from the study of long-run forces of gravitation which govern the underlying trends in the level and distribution of income.

It is certainly true that, for all its underlying unity, Keynes's own method *appears* to many as confused; some of his arguments were couched in neo-classical terms in order to show how little it would take to confound the neo-classical results of full-employment general equilibrium. Keynes had a keen understanding of the force of rhetoric (Dow, 1988). But, whatever Keynes's own intentions, contemporary Post Keynesians do not in general employ neo-classical market analysis, and in particular do not posit a negative relationship between employment and the real wage, or between capital and the rate of interest. Further, the short-run results are perfectly compatible with the long-run result of less than full employment, while explaining the level of investment and rate of interest over the cycle – and thus on average over the cycle. Thus, it is the *form* of short-run analysis which is important for determining compatibility with particular long-run analysis. The monetary role of the rate of interest, however, prevents it from averaging out at some long-term norm which is independent of the short run; it is the determination of the rate of interest by the short-term conjuncture of expectations which acts as the connecting link between the short run and the long run. This connection is made explicit notably by Davidson (1972) and Minsky (1975, 1982).

Finally, since Post Keynesian theory starts with observation, the position on empirical matters must be discussed. First, rejecting the subjective/objective dual, Post Keynesians regard observation as involving both subjective and objective elements. 'Facts' can be observed with some degree of objectivity; the primary subjective element enters necessarily into the grouping of 'facts' according to theories. Thus economists, like individual economic agents, are viewed as arranging thought by means of theories, within paradigms. Since the group of theories includes formal models which are susceptible to empirical application, Post Keynesians do not (unlike most neo-Austrians) reject econometrics. It is the way it is currently practised and its results employed which is rejected (see Lawson, 1995b). Keynes's arguments concerning econometrics referred to exclusive reliance on econometric results, with a lack of recognition of the limited domain of techniques which presume a given structure of relationships. The particular form of econometric analysis employed by Post Keynesians, however, is diverse and context-specific, in accord with theory which is diverse and context-specific (Lawson, 1983). In addition, the capacity to predict with econometric techniques is regarded as limited, given the inevitable fluidity of economic structure which Keynes had emphasized in his critique of Tinbergen (Keynes, 1973c, pp.285–320). Rather, the primary task of econometric analysis, as practised for example by the Cambridge

Economic Policy Croup, is to capture structural change in models continuously revised in the light of the evidence.

4.12 Marxian theory

Modern Marxian theory is derived directly from the works of Marx. But Marx's method was explicitly historical in the sense that it focused on the changing structure of social relations as the result of the historical unfolding of capitalism; the object of study is the 'laws of motion of capitalism'. To the extent that capitalism in the 1990s differs from a particular form anticipated by Marx, new theoretical developments are necessary. Herein lies one feature which gives scope for diversity – the interpretation of the form and consequences of contemporary social relations. Of particular importance is the question of how to analyse advanced capitalist economies, like the United States, where issues of gender, race and relations with developing economies now appear to many to be at least as pressing as issues of class. The shift in focus to consideration of mixed economies rather than planned economies which began in the 1960s has gained added force from the relative demise of state planning in the 1990s.

More fundamentally, the nature of Marx's method lends itself to different interpretations. Consistent with a Babylonian approach, Marx employed different methods of analysis at different stages of his enquiry. Thus he began (Marx, 1857–58) in the *Grundrisse* with a methodological statement (the main elements of which are outlined in section 4.4). In *Capital* itself, Marx (1867) starts with a simplified analysis of the most abstract categories, which referred to the most important feature of objective reality, setting out the labour theory of value and the General Law of Capitalist Accumulation. Volumes II and III consist of a progressive breaking down of abstract categories, to allow the analysis to be related to the real-world categories of prices, profits, etc., which themselves offer only the appearance of the underlying realities. His theoretical analysis started and ended with detailed study of the actual conditions of capitalism in Victorian England (see, for example, Sweezy, 1942, Chapter 1).

It has therefore been open to Marxian scholars to select only part of this method. In particular, if the formal method alone is employed, it is hard to resist a presumption of determinacy which was absent in the entirety of Marx's own work. Althusser (1968, pp.17–25), for example, likens Marx's effect on the science of history to Plato's effect on mathematics and Descartes' on physics; he proceeds to advocate rigour in identifying the objective dividing-line between truth and falsehood, as between classes. Orthodox Marxism can be classified as a deterministic interpretation of Marx, an interpretation which has communicated relatively well to the deterministic non-Marxist orthodoxy, inviting dualistic rejection on the part of both. Marxist theory, taken as Volume I of *Capital,* has offered an easy target to the extent that events have not conformed to this abstract model. Non-orthodox Marxists, whom some classify as 'radicals', reject the deterministic account of Marxism. Some prefer an overdeterministic interpretation which combines a focus on social structure with a focus on human characteristics (Resnick and Wolff, 1992); others interpret overdeterminism in terms of a dialectical process (Sherman, 1992). This approach, employing a mode of thought other than Cartesian/Euclidean thought, is more difficult to comprehend from a Cartesian/Euclidean perspective; writers in this tradition have been classified by some as radicals rather than Marxists (Scott, 1991).

Marx's writings are in fact notoriously difficult to understand, particularly since significant portions were actually written by Engels from Marx's notes. Indeed Marxists have if anything been too successful in persuading others of the incommensurability of their methodology with 'bourgeois' methodology. Thus Althusser (1968, pp.69–94), in a Preface to Volume I of *Capital,* warns the reader that 'a real revolution of consciousness' is necessary for an understanding of Marx. It is thus easy to read into Marx thoughts which were not his. What is important, however, is the direction taken by modern Marxian theory in the light of the events of a century since Marx's death. This direction has four main features which are explicable by structural changes which have occurred, but which are still grounded in Marx's theoretical approach.

First, at the political level, this century has seen not only the Russian revolution, but also the election elsewhere of social-democratic governments with a mandate to pursue the interests of the working class within a capitalist system. On the one hand, the conflict between the working class and the capitalist class have brought about 'legitimation' crises for these governments, attempting to act legitimately in the interests of the first, but within a power structure favouring the second. Capitalism left to itself would undergo periodic purgatory crises, whereby asset values would fall, industry would become more concentrated, and the profit rate could be (temporarily) increased; at the same time unemployment would permanently be increased. Marxists thus explain stagflation by the attempts of social-democratic governments to prevent such crises (see, for example, Chernomas, 1983).

Second, the outcome of crises in the past which have not been prevented by government policy has indeed been the growing concentration of industry. Marx's analysis, while predicting concentration, focused on the extent of free competition extant in the nineteenth century. Modern Marxian theory presumes a high incidence of monopoly (see in particular Baran and Sweezy, 1966).

Third, following Hilferding (1910) and Lenin (1916), there has been a growing concern with issues of globalisation. The spread of multinational corporations, as well as the interdependence fostered by international trade, has required a broadening of the concept of class struggle to apply internationally, as well as a focus on exchange as much as production. The result is a concern with imperialism as such, and the development of an analysis of global crisis (see, for example, Harvey, 1982, Chapter 13). In addition, a Marxist analysis of international patterns of trade and investment has been developed, under the lead of Frank (1967), as dependency theory, to explain the persistence of underdevelopment in some countries and regions.

Finally, while Marx did theorize about money and financial markets, his work requires development to take account of financial development this century. Now a significfnt area of Marxian research is in the area of monetary theory, exploring the role of money as integral to Marx's theory of crisis, i.e. in bringing together monetary and value theory (Mandel, 1968; de Brunhoff, 1973; Panico, 1983). This will be explored in Chapter 8.

These new areas, particularly the legitimation question and the development of global crisis and dependency theories, do not lend themselves readily to formal analysis, so that much of modern Marxian theory remains in the Babylonian mode. But there remains a hard core of traditional Marxist theory which is expressed, deterministically, in terms of a complete formal model. The conflict between these different views as to what constitutes acceptable theory accounts for some of the deep differences of opinion within Marxian economics. Roberts and Feiner (1992) identify this conflict as being the product of external pressures which challenge radical economics politically, as much as internal difference of opinion. But the outcome is that the current state of radical economics (defined as economics taking Marxism as a starting-point) is 'clearly marked by fragmentation and experimentation' (Roberts and Feiner, 1992, p.2). As with other schools of thought, the clearest potential for crisis lies in the exclusivism of orthodox, deterministic theorists; an open system approach in contrast can tolerate some degree of fragmentation. For fragmentation to be sustainable, there must be a common vision to provide a commmon structure of thought. There does seem to be such common vision, in terms of political, theoretical and epistemological comitments (see Roberts and Feiner, 1992, pp.2–3), so that a synthesis is likely to emerge in due course.

4.13 Conclusion

Ideas do not arise in a vacuum. It has been one of the purposes of this chapter to promote some understanding of how we have arrived at the current state of macroeconomic theory, both in terms of the 'real' economic environment in which economists have worked, and in terms of the influence of each generation of economists on the next. A Cartesian/Euclidean interpretation would be one of more or less steady progress, while a Babylonian one would be one of incommensurability between succeeding or indeed co-existing, schools of thought.

The other purpose of this chapter has been to arrive at a categorization of modern schools of thought in macroeconomics. The four categories on which we will concentrate from now on are: neo-Austrian theory, mainstream theory, Post Keynesian theory and Marxian theory. These are widely recognized categories, although they are by no means the only possible categorizations and there are still notable disparities (both methodological and theoretical) within each school of thought. Nevertheless, we shall treat each as a separate entity on the grounds that, by and large, they each represent identifiable positions on methodology, particularly in the sense of the methodology they profess (even if it diverges from what is used in practice). It is professed methodology which is often the object of debates between schools of thought, and the rationale employed for accepting one body of theory rather than another. Thus, for example, Post Keynesian theory may be rejected by a mainstream theorist as unscientific, although much mainstream theory does not conform to the professed criteria for scientific behaviour. (The same would of course be true if any developers of exclusively formalistic theory within the Post Keynesian school of thought were to reject mainstream theory for being formalistic.)

Having selected these categories, we now proceed to consider in turn particular features of macroeconomic theory which illustrate the general methodological distinctions drawn in this chapter. The differences between groups within each school of thought will be discussed, but the general coherence of each school's professed methodological stance should become apparent. The following four chapters will compare the four schools of thought in their treatment of four important concepts in macroeconomics: micro-foundations, equilibrium, expectations and money.

5 The Micro-foundations of Macroeconomics

5.1 Introduction

The question of the micro-foundations of macroeconomics refers to the relationship between theory expressed in terms of aggregates and the underlying behaviour of decision-making units. It raises fundamental issues concerning co-ordination of behaviour, the response of decision-makers to unintended consequences of their actions, and the meaning of equilibrium. But the formulation of these issues varies among the four schools of thought to be considered, according to their focus of attention, the units chosen for microeconomic analysis and their use of the equilibrium concept. Indeed, the micro-foundations issue provides an immediate illustration of the principles held in common *within* each school of thought, in spite of their other differences.

The fallacy of composition is a central feature of any discussion of micro-foundations; according to this fallacy, individual actions, if common to a large number of individuals, will generate an outcome different from what was intended by each. Thus, in Keynesian economics, a general increase in the propensity to save reduces total income, and thus the absolute level of saving. In competitive markets, attempts by entrepreneurs to achieve super-normal profits are thwarted if other entrepreneurs act likewise. The outcome cannot be an equilibrium one in the sense that all expectations have been fulfilled; some further reactions can be anticipated. How then can an equilibrium situation, and the approach to that equilibrium, be modelled?

The co-ordination of individual behaviour has been a matter for concern ever since Smith attempted to analyse the new configuration of individual behaviour along the lines of specialized production. But the emergence of macroeconomics as an enquiry separable from microeconomics was the outcome of the Keynesian Revolution. Neither Classical nor neo-classical economics had explicitly separated the two fields of study, most participants regarding the economy as a harmonious system whereby activity at the microeconomic level generated the outcome at the macroeconomic level captured in Say's Law. Certainly, after

Smith, the Classicists had concentrated attention at the macro level, i.e. they were concerned with the determination of the rate of growth of activity and its distribution by class. The neo-classicists concentrated their attention on the micro level, i.e. they were concerned with the efficient allocation of activity. But neither viewed the two levels as being necessarily incompatible. Similarly, those, including Marx, who employed theories of systemic disharmony provided a holistic account incorporating individual behaviour and economy-wide outcomes in terms of the fallacy of composition.

The apparent anomaly of persistent unemployment during the Depression of the 1930s, and Keynes's explanation of it, raised questions as to how far individual self-interest could be relied upon to produce socially-desirable outcomes at the macro level. Expressing his alternative theory in a manner inconsistent with neo-classical micro-foundations, Keynes encouraged renewed attention to be given to macroeconomic aggregates. But the basis of this attention was the conclusion drawn within the orthodoxy that there must be reasons for microeconomic behaviour, as analysed within the neo-classical paradigm, not to satisfy Say's Law, not that there might be some inadequacy in neo-classical microeconomics itself. The macroeconomic problem studied by Keynes was thus interpreted by others as a result of a logical problem in aggregating from the micro to the macro level, not a result of the problem with the type of microeconomics employed. On this basis, it was regarded for some time as legitimate to study aggregated variables within a separate framework, while retaining neo-classical microeconomics in its traditional form. The predominant macro problem was persistent unemployment, the inability of the labour market to clear. This contrasted with the market-clearing framework of neo-classical microeconomics. It became conventional, as a result, to view macroeconomics as dealing with co-ordination failure and microeconomics with co-ordination success (see Leijonhufvud, 1981, pp.104–6; Shackle, 1972, p.334; Loasby, 1976, p.171).

This inconsistency between analysis at the two levels of aggregation, initially justified by conventionalism, was further encouraged by Friedman's instrumentalism, which released macroeconomists from any requirement to use realistic assumptions; in particular this stance justified the use of assumptions in macroeconomics which differed from those employed in microeconomics, quite apart from any question of realism. But inconsistency within an analytical system goes against the fundamental principles of Cartesian/Euclidean thought; indeed by the neo-classical definition of rationality it is irrational. And in fact Friedman in practice grounded his theory (of consumption and the demand for money, for example) in orthodox microeconomic principles.

It became imperative for conventionalist neo-classicists to demonstrate that the micro–macro inconsistency was indeed simply the outcome of the logic of aggregation, not an inconsistent use of microeconomic assumptions in the two fields and, understandably, not an indicator of any fundamental flaws in neo-classical economics. In fact, most of the major advances in neo-classical economics over the last thirty years have been adaptations to analysis at the micro level explicitly to address the logical problems entailed in translating microeconomics into macroeconomics (Weintraub, 1979). However, since different schools of thought employ different forms of microeconomics, and take a different methodological position on the micro–macro interrelationship, the micro-foundations issue is much broader in scope than is implied by the general equilibrium treatment (Harcourt, 1977).

In considering the position of each school of thought on the issue of micro-foundations, we look first at how the relationship between macroeconomics and microeconomics is viewed methodologically. We then examine the content of the assumptions as to microeconomic behaviour incorporated in macroeconomic theory: the choice of relevant microeconomic units, the motivation of those units, and the co-ordination of action. The discussion will focus on treatment of the labour market, since this has been the context of much of the recent discussion on micro-foundations. (The role of money has perhaps historically been more central to the micro-foundations issue; but since it is also central to the other conceptual issues to be discussed in Chapters 6 and 7, the whole of Chapter 8 is devoted to money alone.)

We start by examining the position of the neo-Austrian school, since it is most closely identified with the micro-foundations issue, and has indeed influenced other schools of thought in their treatment of micro-foundations. We then examine the attempts dating from the 1940s to extend the neo-classical synthesis in macroeconomics to microeconomics within one grand general equilibrium system. The neo-classical synthesis had deviated from Keynes by ignoring the micro-foundations of the *General Theory* and retaining only the aggregative results. (Indeed without such a separation, the neo-classical synthesis would not have been possible.) The logical outcome of adding neo-classical microeconomics to the neo-classical synthesis has been the restoration of Say's Law, albeit with much more sophisticated theoretical back-up. Meanwhile Keynesians have been pointing out the error involved in presuming that Keynes accepted neo-classical microeconomics and only objected to their aggregation in Say's Law. The fourth section deals with the Keynesian position on micro-foundations, and the different interpretations to which it has been subject. Marxians are described in section 5.5 as taking a position which is the polar opposite of that of the neo-Austrians on micro-foundations.

5.2 Neo-Austrian Theory

The neo-Austrian school has always taken the individual as the starting-point of theory, and in that sense has not been faced with a micro-foundations problem;

the problem has rather been the specification of the macroeconomic structure built on these micro-foundations. This problem has only recently been directly addressed, by Garrison (1984, 1989). Hayek explicitly set out to analyse the unintended consequences of human action (in accordance with Popper, 1945, pp.124–5), but without an apparatus for doing so in any systematic way. There is no theoretical necessity for individuals whose expectations have been disappointed to adjust their behaviour in such a way as to allow more rather than less co-ordination of their actions. The only possible solution is to focus all analysis on the subjectively-determined behaviour of individuals, at the expense of reaching any aggregative conclusions. Where such conclusions have been reached, the theoretical leap has been made of *assuming* that individuals' actions are co-ordinated harmoniously.

For neo-Austrians then, microeconomics is coterminous with 'economics'. Whether the result of indubitable *a priori* knowledge, or of fallible introspection, knowledge gathered by individuals is regarded as being the best knowledge available on which to base not only economic activity, but also economic theory. As a corollary, macroeconomic aggregates have no independent existence since they do not enter directly into decision-making at the market level; individuals have no objective experience of macro variables on which to draw for information. Information on general economic conditions may influence individuals' decisions, but the perception and interpretation of that information is subjective.

Market processes have traditionally been viewed (without proof) as harmonious, being the outcome of actions by individuals seeking their own self-interest. This view generates the strong result that centralized activity by government which alters market signals is by definition disharmonious. Since the government is the only agency whose decision-making is influenced solely by macroeconomic aggregates, measurement and use of these concepts thus serves no socially-useful function. The only purpose, then, in considering macroeconomic variables is for policy advice during a transitional stage while government macroeconomic policy is being phased out (Hayek, 1931a). Even then, the value of such advice depends on the view taken of the capacity to make predictions, which requires that observed aggregates can be treated as if representing an equilibrium position. In summary, there is a presumption that, whatever the level of aggregates, they are the outcome of a harmonious process; the important object of study is thus the market process which generates the aggregates, not the aggregates themselves. As a corollary, government *may* have a role at the microeconomic level of industry regulation (Littlechild, 1978, pp.38–43; Lachmann, 1973). Further, some neo-Austrians have been questioning the presumption of harmonious co-ordination, opening up new possibilities for the role of the state (Lachmann, 1986, and O'Driscoll and Rizzo, 1985).

The unit of study within neo-Austrian microeconomics is the individual, with particular attention paid to the entrepreneur. The individual is defined to be rational; rationality is thus equated with actual behaviour, rather than independently defined. Indeed, the absence of mathematical expression removes the need to be exact about axioms of human behaviour; in turn, it is because human behaviour is viewed as purposeful that mathematics is rejected as being an inadequate means of expression. The purposefulness of behaviour allows for a wide range of purposes; it also suggests creativity, and use of imagination. The speculative choices made by individuals in different markets, in their own interests, are the bricks and mortar of neo-Austrian economics. (See Alchian and Allen, 1974, for a textbook treatment of speculative micro markets from a neo-Austrian perspective.)

Rather than focusing on a (notional or actual) position of general equilibrium, neo-Austrians focus on the process by which individuals co-ordinate their market behaviour, i.e. the process of market adjustment. As in Schumpeter's analysis, entrepreneurs play a central role in profit-seeking behaviour, which requires alertness to new opportunities. The competitive environment is thus not seen as perfectly competitive in the neo-classical sense, since that leaves no scope for differential knowledge, or for originative action by individual entrepreneurs. As long as there is freedom of entry, then firms within any industry are threatened by the possibility of new competitors seizing opportunities within the industry. This behaviour ensures that excess profits do not persist. Competition is thus seen in the Classical terms of 'free competition'. More recent developments in the theory of the firm to take account of the management (rather than entrepreneurial) function draw on behavioural theory, in the sense of analysing the behaviour of individuals within the corporate system (drawing on, for example, Loasby, 1976, and Casson, 1982). In neo-Austrian hands, however, behavioural theory is subordinated to the prior concept of purposefulness.

The importance of alertness in recognizing opportunities implies that they are not perceptible to all. Indeed, lack of full knowledge is an important feature of this process analysis. It provides a role for advertising, which alerts consumers to new opportunities. The differences between knowledge available to different individuals is, on the one hand, the driving force of the competitive market system, and on the other, the factor that ensures that a static equilibrium analysis misses the essence of that system. Even more than Kirzner's (1973) concept of alertness to existing information, Shackle's (1979) concept of originative behaviour involves the *creation* of new knowledge which is even more eluded by static equilibrium analysis (see Loasby, 1983, for a discussion of these two concepts).

The neo-Austrian analysis of the labour market is conducted in the same way as that of any other market, being governed by the opportunity-seeking behaviour of firms and employees under conditions of incomplete knowledge. Viewed in terms of market process, the labour market clears only by coincidence, since perpetually-changing conditions in product markets generate changes in labour market conditions and perceptions of those changes. A worker who has been laid off engages in search activity, gathering information on job opportunities and on the terms and conditions that can be commanded within the market for her particular skills. Similarly, firms engage in search for the required skills, and gather information on the terms and conditions required to attract a worker with those skills. Because this process takes time, there will always be some frictional unemployment.

The level of frictional unemployment is influenced by the competitive structure of the labour market. The activities of strong unions restrict the choices open to the unemployed and to firms with job vacancies, by specifying the terms and conditions of job offers, and also influence the terms and conditions offered to the employed labour force in collective bargaining. Unions are thus seen as introducing rigidities into the labour market which inhibit the adjustment of relative prices required to emit the correct signals. Indeed it is the downward inflexibility of wages in strongly unionized sectors, which need not be the sectors where demand for labour is strongest, which introduces an upward bias in wage settlements in other sectors where demand for labour is strong, leading to wage inflation (Hayek, 1960, Chapter 18).

The level of unemployment does, however, fluctuate over time, reflecting fluctuations in the conditions of search activity. The neo-Austrian explanation analyses a fall or rise in total unemployment in terms of its sectoral composition. Income and employment fluctuations over the trade cycle are generated by fluctuations in investment activity, induced by changing monetary conditions (see section 8.2). Financial inducements to increase investment in excess of what the free market would have generated attract labour into the capital goods sector. But the resulting capitalization of industry, being excessive, reduces labour productivity and thus wages. Dislocated labour, discouraged from employment in the capital goods sector by low wages then engages in search for more attractive alternative opportunities. The change in relative wages is only accepted after some period of search and information gathering. With an excessive capital stock for current conditions, it takes time for normal conditions to be restored in the capital goods sector, with employment below expansion levels but above contraction levels. In short, any rapid sectoral shift, which is later reversed, creates additional difficulties for employers and employees in their attempts to identify the best opportunities for them, and thus prolongs the period of search on one or other side (Hayek, 1967, pp.270–6). Ultimately, however, if there are no further outside shocks, harmonious co-ordination is assured.

5.3 Mainstream Theory

The apparent inconsistency between microeconomics and macroeconomic analysis derived from Keynes has posed fundamental questions within neo-classical economics, spawning the development of a sophisticated analytical structure designed to deal with those questions. This structure has been built on the work of those such as Hicks (1939) who had already been grappling with the difficult task of modelling the *process* of co-ordination in market behaviour, i.e. market behaviour over time (Hicks, 1976). It is the resulting body of theory which we identify now as 'mainstream' economics. The judgement that this programme for resolving the micro-foundations issue has been successful can be measured by the fact that the issue is now (with few exceptions, such as Jenssen, 1993) seldom raised.

The issue of micro-foundations for macroeconomics, as expressed after Keynes, was perceived initially as arising from a deficiency in Keynesian macroeconomics as interpreted within the neo-classical synthesis; aggregative analysis had not been expressed in such a way as to provide an explanation rooted in individual behaviour. The pioneering work of Clower and Leijonhufvud, however, pointed out deficiencies in the neo-classical account of individual behaviour in market transactions, which could explain the micro–macro inconsistency. As a result, much of the neo-classical account of market behaviour has been developed along the lines indicated by Clower and Leijonhufvud in order to reconcile that inconsistency.

If the axiomatic, deductive method is employed by neo-classical theory, all analysis must be reductionist. In particular, all results should be derivable from axioms about the behaviour of the smallest economic unit, the individual (although the axioms *may* be applied to the household, or firm). For macroeconomics to be methodologically acceptable, therefore, it must be derivable from those axioms. Conventionalism allows modifications from the ideal theoretical system, but a blatant inconsistency is difficult to accept within any framework. This is particularly the case when the inconsistency arises from a glaring anomaly (apparently – involuntary unemployment). To the extent, however, that neo-classical economists persist with logical inconsistency between their macroeconomics and their microeconomics it is possible to question the truth of their analysis on logical grounds, without any need for qualification with respect to the problems of induction, subjective observation, etc. While serious differences persist between neo-classical and pure general equilibrium theorists over the type of micro-foundations to be employed (in the sense of representation of market behaviour as Walrasian or otherwise, for example), all are in accord as to the need for a consistent reductionist basis for macroeconomics based on a marginalist theory of value (Weintraub, 1979; Perry, 1984).

A further difficulty stemmed from the Marshallian practice of specifying axioms in terms of a 'representative' individual. This practice was a means of simplifying from an actuality of diversity in the conditions and behaviour of individuals. But when the focus is put on the micro–macro distinction, it becomes apparent that a representative individual is simply an average derived from an aggregation of participants in any market; it cannot deal with the co-ordination of transactions among individuals within that market who are diverse in terms of tastes, perceptions and information. With some help from neo-Austrian thinking, general equilibrium analysis became more truly reductionist in order to analyse co-ordination. Even so, the behavioural units employed are conventionally households, firms and government, each of which is a collection of individuals. However, work has been directed towards explaining the unified behaviour of the group in terms of the behaviour of their constituent individuals (Gale, 1982, 1983), and the firm as identified with the individual entrepreneur (Machlup, 1967). The reductionist analysis of social behaviour was spearheaded by Becker (1976).

The axioms of individual behaviour define motivation and rules for rational behaviour. Individuals maximize utility subject to constraints given by the structure of consumer preferences and the conditions of production (the production function). Rational pursuit of this goal requires the specification of (consistent and transitive) preference orderings by consumers and income–leisure preferences by workers. The axioms are thus expressed in such a way as to allow equilibrium solutions to be generated; auxiliary assumptions are similarly required as to the mathematical properties of the production function.

The co-ordination of individual behaviour generated by these axioms is traditionally captured in Walras' tatonnement process. The resulting law of markets states that the sum of excess demand across all markets is zero; alternatively, excess demand in any one market must be matched by an equal excess supply in one or more other markets. Put another way, demand for any good or service in a market is the mirror image of supply of a good or service to be given in exchange. The process by which excess demand and supply are eliminated is described in terms of an auction. An auctioneer calls out prices and takes supply and demand bids; if these do not match, then a higher price is called if there is excess demand, and a lower price if there is excess supply; a market-clearing price is reached by a process of iteration (or 'tatonnement'). This is the process by which the market approaches the intersection of the supply and demand schedules central to neo-classical microeconomic analysis. Co-ordination thus takes a rather limited form in Walrasian theory, since no exchange actually takes place until the equilibrium set of prices is reached. Alternative representations of the market process (particularly the sequence analysis of temporary equilibrium theory) attempt to model reactions to actual exchanges.

The applicability of this analysis relies on the existence of independent demand and supply schedules. Doubts about the validity of the consumer axioms encouraged Samuelson's revealed preference approach which served to verify the existence of downward-sloping market demand curves (independently of the axioms) (Samuelson, 1938, but for a critique, see Wong, 1978). Further, Becker (1962) showed that the existence of budget constraints was sufficient to generate downward-sloping demand curves under certain carefully-specified forms of 'irrational' behaviour. The supply curve also encountered difficulties on a range of counts: the logical inconsistencies arising from the constant returns to scale assumption of perfect competition, evidence suggesting increasing returns to scale, and evidence suggesting that industry was not, in general, perfectly competitive (Shackle, 1967). Without the perfect competition assumption, supply curves could not be derived. Some, notably Hahn (1973b), take the limited realism of the perfect competition assumption as limiting the applicability of general equilibrium results; realism of assumptions is regarded as necessary to the realism of results. However, Arrow and Hahn (1971, Introduction), and Hahn (1973a), emphasize that description is not the purpose of general equilibrium theory. So, until New Keynesian economics took up the challenge of developing equilibrium models based on imperfect competition, the majority followed Friedman's (1953) lead in treating perfect competition as an 'as if' assumption; verification of results implies that individuals and firms behave 'as if' the microeconomic assumptions were true.

But persistent evidence of involuntary unemployment required an explanation of the failure of tatonnement; how could the labour market persistently fail to clear? The first explanation, provided by Modigliani (1944) was that there was an impediment to the free movement of money wages (as Keynes, 1936, had indeed suggested); if the real wage were not allowed (as a result of union action, say) to fall when there was an excess supply of labour, then that excess could not be eliminated. In this way, a fall in the general price level following a fall in aggregate demand would cause real wages to rise, unemployment to increase and output to fall. Demand could thus affect supply (countering Say's Law) if wages were prevented from falling. Labour's behaviour could only be explained by money illusion; if only labour realized that a fall in money wages, when prices had fallen, did not represent a fall in real wages, the problem would not arise. In terms of Walrasian analysis, employment falls when the price level falls because the labour supply curve is (irrationally?) expressed in terms of the money wage, while labour demand is a function of the real wage

Clower (1965), however, argued that deficient-demand unemployment did indeed contradict Walras's Law, because there was no mechanism whereby the excess supply in the labour market could be mirrored by a *perceptible* excess demand in any other market. The problem arose from the fact that transactions are conducted in terms of money; money must be possessed for demand to be expressed. According to his dual-decision hypothesis, the decision to hire labour for money is separate from the decision of workers to buy output with money; in particular the capacity for the latter decision is determined by the amount of employment income available. Starting from a disequilibrium position, where a fall in demand has induced a fall in employment, Clower showed that there was no mechanism by which the unemployed could convey to employers what their demand would be if they were employed, i.e. what their notional demand was. Employers were only aware of effective demand, and, as far as they were concerned, there was no excess demand for goods at the new, lower level of output. Although the excess supply of labour was matched by an excess *notional* demand for goods, there was no excess effective demand to induce a market reaction by producers.

Clower had thus pointed out serious implications of the absence in the labour and goods markets of an auctioneer who persists until the market-clearing price is found; in practice, 'false trades' (trades at prices other than the equilibrium price) have income effects which have repercussions on subsequent market outcomes. This approach was further developed by Leijonhufvud (1968, 1981) who questioned the realism of the Walrasian assumption that adjustment would occur through price changes anyway. Rather he suggested that Keynes's analysis had assumed quantity adjustment. (He identified quantity adjustment with Marshall; see Leijonhufvud, 1974, for his further thoughts.) If in fact prices are slow to adjust, then the time-frame within which market reactions occur becomes important. Leijonhufvud envisaged situations arising where lagged price adjustment allowed a downward spiral of output and employment. If a fall in aggregate demand caused stocks to pile up, firms would lay off workers. While prices would eventually fall, to run down stocks, and wages fall to reflect labour market conditions, unemployed workers and workers with lower earnings would by then have contracted their effective demand, further adding to stocks, and encouraging further lay-offs. As long as the price adjustment lagged behind quantity adjustment, this process could continue, generating a recession (without any automatic mechanism for reversal).

The work of Clower and Leijonhufvud pointed the way to the necessary avenues of enquiry for general equilibrium theorists attempting to deal with the micro–macro inconsistency. They had demonstrated the problem as lying with the co-ordination of individual behaviour out of full Walrasian equilibrium. Dealing with this problem would allow an explanation for the market successes, where activity was co-ordinated in such a way as to propel markets back to equilibrium, and market failures, where activity was prevented from co-ordinating successfully. This disequilibrium analysis could thus focus on the problems of information flows within markets and the sequencing of market reactions. They are often classified as 'quantity-rationing models', because of the income effects of excess supply or demand; if employment (or demand for goods) is rationed, a simultaneous excess demand for goods (or labour) is only notional and cannot induce the Walrasian market response. These models are often described as Keynesian because of the fixed-price assumption (particularly when that price is the wage rate), although that involves a severe misinterpretation of Keynes's own framework.

The possibility of quantity-rationing (both in the labour and goods markets) was seen by disequilibrium theorists as driving a wedge between their theory and equilibrium theory. A quantity constraint is a market, rather than individual, constraint; it is the outcome of aggregated effects of individual behaviour, which generate involuntary unemployment and slow down adjustment to equilibrium (Malinvaud, 1977; Solow and Stiglitz, 1968). In Solow's (1979, p.345) words:

> The difference between the equilibrium view and the disequilibrium view is not that in one theory agents are assumed to optimise and in the other they are not. The difference is in the constraints they are assumed to take into account.

The fixed-price assumption, however, raised questions about the competitive structure which prevents prices from responding to supply and demand; why should rationed workers or buyers be price-takers? Following Arrow (1959), Grandmont and Laroque (1977), for example, conclude that industry must have a monopolistically-competitive structure. This possibility has been picked up by New Keynesians (see Dixon and Rankin, 1994, for a survey), as a way of analysing non-market-clearing in equilibrium terms. This development has gathered pace in spite of Malinvaud and Younes's (1977, p.95) argument that the perfect competition assumption might still be necessary if the mathematical existence of equilibrium positions is to be proved; firm and industry supply curves are necessary to the theoretical framework. Alternatives have been sought within New Keynesian economics: implicit contract theory, for example, posits that a fixed nominal wage contract represents an optimal sharing of risk between employers and employees, in the face of uncertain demand conditions (Baily, 1974; Azariadis, 1975; Gordon, 1974; Hall, 1980).

Implicit contract theory is only one of the developments within New Keynesian theory which have drawn on temporary, or short-period equilibrium models, which specified non-market-clearing equilibrium positions which could arise from the limited information available at a particular point in time (using concepts developed by Hicks, 1939). While the outcome of the actions incorporated in this equilibrium would produce new information in the next period, and thus a new temporary equilibrium, each equilibrium during the relevant short period involves no impetus for change. However, because of the sequential character of these equilibria, attention must be paid to expectations formation, which governs the conjectures on which individuals base their market bids (see section 7.3 below). New Keynesians have made most headway in developing a rich array of models of wage and price rigidity, and of credit rationing, based on stylized facts about limitations on information held by employers of goods markets and the labour market, and by creditors of debtors (see Snowdon, Vane and Wynarczyk, 1994, Chapter 7).

Developments in mainstream theory of the labour market have generally followed in neo-Austrian footsteps (following the lead of Phelps, 1970; see also Frydman and Phelps, 1984). The axiomatic approach required that persistence of, and fluctuations in, unemployed labour be explained by workers' plans which are compatible with employers' plans in any one period of temporary equilibrium. In other words an explanation was sought for this unemployment to be voluntary, an explanation which was found in search theory. Search theory in mainstream analysis differs from neo-Austrian search theory in terms of being modelled according to axiomatic rules for behaviour within an equilibrium setting; the significance of this difference in setting will be explored in the next chapter. Otherwise, the general rationale is the same, that it takes several periods for new information to be acquired and for bids to be adjusted. In each period, workers weigh up the opportunity cost of job search against the expected benefits of seeking alternative employment, just as employers weigh up the relevant costs and benefits associated with hiring or firing on the basis of currently available information on product prices and wages. This behaviour is symmetrical in the sense that a worker may give up a job in order to undertake job search.

The analysis conforms to the Walrasian supply and demand analysis, except that supply and demand schedules are based on conjectural information, and include search costs for employers and employees, and may involve some wage and/or price rigidity if competition in the relevant market is not perfect, or reflecting implicit contracts between employer and employee. Thus individual workers may be unemployed because of a fall in demand for their product which is beyond their control; but they remain unemployed only through their own choice. In this case in particular, once unemployment becomes an outcome of inter-sectoral adjustment, the focus is naturally micro rather than macro.

Another development of particular interest for econometric work has been to model constraints as being stochastically determined, since systematic constraints pose such difficulties for explanation in terms of rational behaviour. Stochastic constraints are characteristic of the New Classical approach of Lucas (1972), Sargent (1973), Sargent and Wallace (1975) and Barro (1976). Otherwise, their approach is distinguished from 'pure' general equilibrium theory by the presumed one-to-one correspondence between theory and reality, and the corresponding econometric treatment of expectations (to be discussed in section 7.3). This approach has been carried forward in the real business cycle theory approach initiated by Kydland and Prescott (1982), whereby the impetus for economic cycles is random changes in technology.

The trend in the 1970s was towards temporary or short-period equilibrium frameworks and away from disequilibrium analysis (Weintraub, 1979; Casson, 1981; Hey, 1981; Muellbauer and Portes, 1978). The Harcourt (1977) volume had demonstrated the *impasse* reached in mainstream economics with attempts to analyse macroeconomic issues in disequilibrium terms. The only choice for mainstream macroeconomists wanting to pursue the disequilibrium approach was to ignore the logical inconsistency between macroeconomics and neo-classical microeconomics or to sacrifice neo-classical microeconomics. But this does not accord with the professed aims of neo-classical theorists. In the words of Tobin (1981, p.36):

> The adjustment process itself has not, in general, been successfully described as optimising behaviour, the only paradigm that carries theoretical conviction in our profession. This failure, neither surprising nor discreditable in view of the intrinsic difficulties of the task, is the root of the chronic crisis in macro-economics.

In the 1980s the flourishing of equilibrium models addressed to market non-clearing based on choice-theoretic foundations has proceeded generally with an acceptance of the equilibrium status of observations. Some of the testing however is conducted by means of simulation models which demonstrate the consequences of choice-theoretic behaviour with different assumptions about information-availability and market structure. The results rather than the assumptions are then shown to be consistent with observations of cyclical behaviour in the economy and apparent market non-clearing. Similarly, the real business cycle theory approach has been pursued with calibration and simulation techniques rather than traditional econometrics. This has been encouraged by their acceptance of the Lucas critique, which throws doubt on the capacity of econometrics to capture behavioural responses by individuals, i.e. for equilibrium theory to be expressed in such a way as to find empirical counterparts. The doubt is not one about the equilibrium status of observations but about theoretical adequacy.

In the meantime, the attempts by New Classicals to introduce diversity of information sets into macro models tested econometrically (i.e. equating observation with equilibrium) took the analysis further and further from the capacity to reach macroeconomic conclusions. For some New Classicals (such as Lucas, 1988) interesting macroeconomic questions could only then be addressed in terms of growth theory. The resolution of the micro-foundations issue has thus taken macroeconomics away from considerations of disequilibrium and short-term macroeconomic behaviour and moved it towards stylized models and long-term growth models. The conclusion reached by several eminent mainstream theorists (such as Hahn, 1991 and Fishburn, 1991) in the special centenary issue of the *Economic Journal* was that the axiomatic approach had been taken too far and was unduly limiting the subject-matter of economics. According to this view, the micro-foundations issue had been successfully resolved in terms of the internal logic of mainstream theory, but at the expense of unduly limiting the scope of that theory's application.

5.4   Post Keynesian Theory

The issue of micro-foundations has been presented so far as following on the Keynesian Revolution; it represented primarily an attempt to reconcile Keynesian macroeconomic analysis with neo-classical microeconomics. Certainly there is a degree of optimism within general equilibrium economics that significant progress has been made in that direction. The remaining work to be done lies in the logical extension of this work in generating a complete system which yields macroeconomic results; much of the progress so far has been in the microeconomic analysis of market adjustment.

Keynes, however, can be interpreted also as having taken a holistic approach in the sense that the *General Theory* was a logically consistent combination of micro and macro analysis, but the micro-foundations were not equivalent to neo-classical micro-foundations. Keynes's own micro-foundations did include some elements in common with neo-classical economics. But the case is persuasively made by Chick (1983) that the argument of the *General Theory* was structured in such a way as to show, in some parts, the inadequacies of Say's Law even *with* neo-classical micro-foundations. This makes it difficult to state categorically what Keynes's own micro-foundations were. But we are concerned here with the micro-foundations analysis of present day Post Keynesians, who do not inevitably adhere to Keynes's choices. We shall, therefore, focus (where confusion might otherwise arise) on Post Keynesian micro-foundations, although referring to Keynes as an important influence on Post Keynesian theory. The other major influence on Post Keynesian micro-foundations is Kalecki (1937, 1971).

The first principle of micro-foundations within this paradigm is that macroeconomics refers to the aggregation of the outcomes of individual action, and thus should not be logically inconsistent with the analysis of individual behaviour. Second, given the complexities of constructing a complete micro–macro system (as discovered by mainstream theorists), it is nevertheless legitimate to analyse behaviour in terms of aggregates. Keynes was very careful in his choice of aggregates and in the means of measuring them (Chick, 1983, Chapter 3; Carabelli, 1994), so that, although any aggregation is problematical in suppressing conflict and co-operation within the aggregate (Green, 1977), these problems would be rendered as harmless as possible. Thus, implicit is the judgement that there are sufficient regularities between the chosen aggregates to allow useful analysis of policy questions, without grounding the analysis explicitly in individual behaviour. In other words, without the reductionist imperative of a Cartesian/Euclidean mode of thought, it is acceptable to have different chains of logic which do not necessarily stem from a common set of axioms which refer to the smallest unit of analysis

In any case (following Classical tradition), the individual is not necessarily viewed as the appropriate unit of analysis, to which all analysis can be reduced. There are several areas of Keynesian macroeconomics where the group (or class) is the basic unit of analysis; although groups are made up of individuals, it is the impact of group behaviour on individual behaviour which is the important factor in, for example, the formation of expectations. Rather than founding all analysis on axioms of individual behaviour, then, Post Keynesian analysis is in part based on postulates as to group behaviour. In this sense, it is the aggregate which governs the individual, rather than the other way round (Crotty, 1980). As a result, the problems of specifying co-ordination are limited to co-ordination between groups. Put another way, individuals can legitimately be treated as representative individuals to the extent that it is aggregate, or average, values which influence behaviour; scope must be left, however, for creative individual activity to instigate a shift in group behaviour

Finally, the micro–macro relationship is analysed explicitly in terms of the logical distinction between the two levels of analysis. Keynesian results frequently follow from the fallacy of composition, whereby the consequences of individuals' actions in aggregate thwart the individuals' plans. Thus, attempts by labour to increase employment by accepting lower money wages may be thwarted if that leads to a contraction in effective demand. Since this problem arises only if a sizeable proportion of the relevant group (of workers in this case) behaves in this way, the appropriate unit of analysis is the group rather than the individual. Indeed any theoretical system which deals with disharmony – in macroeconomic terms, crisis – *must* focus analysis at the macro level (Harcourt, 1982, p.9; Harris, 1975).

Given this position on the micro-foundations issue, then, what determines the view taken of individual or group behaviour? Keynes's own conception of rationality underwent some change during his lifetime. Under the influence of Russell and Moore, and no doubt also of his father, Keynes's early view was that all behaviour was potentially rational in the sense of 'justifiable by reason'. But his work on probability suggested that reason had to act on limited knowledge, and thus on subjective assessments of probability. Indeed Keynes came around to the view that reason and emotion cannot necessarily be treated separately (Keynes, 1972b, pp.433–50). This rejection of the rational/emotional dual is consistent with the perception that Keynes rejected a dualistic mode of thought. Within the more holistic view of human nature which Keynes adopted (stemming from his analysis of the consequences of problems wiht respect to knowledge), Shackle's concept of human imagination and creativity has been an important influence on Post Keynesian analysis of the individual. Human behaviour is thus conditioned by the environment in which actions are taken. In particular, Keynes emphasized the problems of decision-making under conditions of uncertainty (which will be explored in detail in Chapter 7). Lacking the capacity in many instances to form predictions, even in probabilistic terms, individuals employ conventions which rely heavily on group behaviour. Thus in some circumstances the conventional prediction is the group prediction.

Keynes perceived individuals' motivation within a capitalist society to be determined by the nature of its social arrangements: an important motivating factor was the accumulation of monetary wealth (Keynes, 1937, p.213; 1972a, pp.268–9 and 292). Far from questioning individuals' motivation, general equilibrium theorists present the accumulation of wealth as being rational, reflecting a choice in favour of future consumption, at the expense of present consumption. Keynes in contrast observed rather accumulation without any particular consumption plans in mind. This he viewed as irrational (Keynes, 1972b, pp.307–9); indeed he seemed to view it in Freudian terms (Keynes, 1971, p.290; see Winslow, 1986, 1995, for a full expression of this argument). It could be argued further that Freud's behavioural psychology (of which Keynes was certainly aware; see Keynes, 1925, pp.643–4) influenced Keynes to define consumption and asset-choice behaviour in terms of 'psychological laws'. Given the social conditioning involved both in individuals' motivation, and in their expectations formation, Keynes's use of psychology was not individualistic. By taking account of the diversity and creativity of individual behaviour, Keynes did not opt for the atomism of individualistic psychology, rather he opted for a combination of individualistic and social psychology. Keynes's views find a precedent in Smith (1759) who argues that individuals deceive themselves in imagining that greater wealth brings greater happiness; for Smith, this self-deception had the positive externality of creating the conditions for growth.

It was Keynes's conceptualization of human motivation and behaviour which determined the limits of his formal (deterministic and reductionist) economic analysis. If human behaviour necessarily includes the exercise of imagination and the expression of emotion, as well as reasoned action, then that behaviour cannot be captured in a determinate system, based on axioms or rules of rational human behaviour. Within a Cartesian/Euclidean framework, such a view of human behaviour would rule out scientific analysis altogether. But within the Keynesian framework, analysis is still possible, since the axiomatic approach is rejected. In particular, since several chains of reasoning are admissible, it is possible to form conclusions as to predominant features of economic behaviour in any one context on the basis of historical, sociological or psychological analysis. Keynes's concept of animal spirits (Keynes, 1936, Chapter 12), for example, as the moving force behind investment decisions, is a signal to the economic analyst to study indicators of investors' mood as a crucial variable in determining aggregate demand. If one understands how different moods are generated and what their consequences are, then actual economic events can be analysed more fully than any deterministic analysis would allow.

So far, all Post Keynesians would be in accord, with varying degrees of enthusiasm, with this characterization of micro-foundations. But by releasing analysis from a strict, unified axiomatic framework, and by using groups as well as individuals as the unit of analysis, there is scope for a range of different theoretical developments. The two major developments within Post Keynesian economics are represented by the long-run analysis in the Ricardian and Marxian traditions and the short-period analysis more directly influenced by Keynes, emphasizing the significance of uncertainty and money for macroeconomic outcomes (with Kalecki and Robinson providing a bridge between the two).

Both strands of thought have developed around the common theme that unemployment is the outcome of systematic forces at work in a capitalist economy which determine effective demand. The nature of these forces is thus of crucial importance, and Keynes's way of representing them has led to considerable confusion. In particular, his use of a competitive framework seemed to reinforce marginalist supply and demand analysis (although it was not the *perfectly* competitive marginalist framework, with demand and supply schedules); he did, for example, adopt the neo-classical demand curve for labour, and a downward-sloping marginal efficiency of capital schedule. Whether these devices were employed for expository reasons only, or not, they certainly eased the task of the neo-classical synthesis in viewing unemployment as the result of temporary phenomena rather than persistent forces. It has thus been a more difficult task for Post Keynesians to present a short-period analysis which could clearly be distinguished from the neo-classical synthesis, presenting the short-run choices between money, other financial assets and capital goods in a way which reflected the systematic forces behind unemployment. This difficulty has not been relieved by sympathizers with the long-period approach who reject short-period asset choice analysis as detracting from perceptions of the systematic long-run forces. (Garegnani, 1978, 1979; Eatwell, 1979; Milgate, 1983; c.f. Robinson, 1979; Nell, 1983; Barens, 1983; Harcourt and O'Shaughnessy, 1983).

The long-period analysis derives, methodologically, from Classical analysis, where expenditure and the determination of value are analysed by class, rather than the outcome of individual choices. While activity is conducted by individuals, that activity is determined by the class to which they belong. The framework is provided by production conditions rather than market conditions. The starting-point for the modern development from the Classical tradition was Sraffa's critique of the perfect-competition framework of marginal analysis. Sraffa demonstrated logical inconsistencies within the marginalist framework, and that it could not generate a logical theory of income distribution, and then proceeded to demonstrate the possibility of a system which determined value independently of market conditions. Reinforced by Robinson's work on monopolistic competition (and her logical critique of the neo-classical treatment of capital), and building on the independent work of Kalecki (1937), these developments encouraged a rejection of marginalist market analysis as being only tangential to the study of the questions of the level of output and employment and the distribution of income. Using the assumption of imperfect product markets within the manufacturing seetor, profits could be shown to be the result of mark-ups on cost, employed in such a way as to promote accumulation. Thus the major portion of saving is conducted by capitalists, with a view to investment; supply is priced to increase surplus value, not to meet demand (see Steindl, 1945, 1952; Ball 1964; Eichner, 1973, 1976; Wood, 1975; Harcourt and Kenyon, 1976; Shapiro, 1977). Finally, the level of effective demand need not be the full employment level; there is no automatic mechanism whereby the labour market clears.

The short-period Post Keynesian analysis refers more explicitly to individual behaviour, and to short-run fluctuations in economic activity. It focuses on Keynes's three 'psychological' factors: the propensity to consume, liquidity preference and the marginal efficiency of capital. Attention is thus paid to choices made by individuals (albeit group-determined) between consuming and saving, between holding money and other assets, and between new capital goods and other assets. As with the long-period analysis, however, demand and supply in any market (for consumer goods, money or capital goods) are, even if identifiable, not independent; indeed each is profoundly influenced by the current state of expectations, both short-run and long-run. Also in common with long-period Post Keynesians, from the common root of Kalecki's work, markets are not treated as perfectly competitive; in particular, product markets are sufficiently uncompetitive, and average costs sufficiently constant over the relevant range, that mark-up pricing is presumed to be generally employed. While a downward-sloping MEC curve suggests that Keynes himself postulated a U-shaped average cost curve, the result of diminishing returns to new investment can be shown to be consistent with constant average costs as long as demand is not perfectly elastic (Chick, 1983, Chapter 5; Sardoni, 1987). Indeed, since investment is determined by the marginal efficiency of investment rather than of capital, the relationship between investment and the rate of interest must refer also to elasticity of supply in the capital-goods sector. As long as that elasticity is less than perfect *in the short run*, even an elastic MEC schedule will generate a determinate demand for investment relative to the rate of interest. But, in any case, neither a downward-sloping MEC or MEI curve implies a negative relation between investment (and thus the capital stock) and the rate of interest *over time*. Two dominant factors posited by Keynes were the shifts in MEC due to changes in 'animal spirits' and the *interdependence* between financial markets and the capital goods market (and thus the expected rate of return on investment and on financial assets including money).

In spite of the protestations of some participants in different parts of the Post Keynesian group, their analysis can in fact be presented in a mutually-compatible fashion (see for example Reynolds, 1987, and Dutt and Amadeo, 1990, for synthetic presentations with respect to Kaleckian economics and Sraffian economics respectively). The insistence by some that only neo-Ricardian analysis is admissible, and others that only short-period analysis is admissible, reflects the pervasiveness of the Cartesian/Euclidean mode of thought, even among those who reject it in most aspects of their work; it encourages the notion of an exclusively-correct scientific procedure. Joan Robinson's work, in contrast, sets a fine example of consistent, synthetic, use of both short-period and long-period Post Keynesian analysis (Kregel, 1983).

The long-period analysis starts with general observations regarding behaviour: the accumulation motive, and the limited scope for savings out of labour income, relative to corporate or capitalist saving. By establishing the capital requirements of particular levels of output, given the state of technology, conditions are established for the equality of planned saving and investment. These conditions define a centre of gravitation to which an economy will be pulled in the long run.

Short-period analysis, on the other hand, analyses actual outcomes as determined by the state of expectations in asset markets. These conditions thus determine the depth and persistence of cycles and, cumulatively, the long run as a series of short runs. But actual (and perceived) long-run trends act independently on investment plans in the short run. The resulting actual outcomes can then be compared with the conditions established by the long-period analysis to assess the *nature* of the centre of gravitation to which the economy is moving. Joan Robinson's 'Golden Age' set out the conditions for balanced growth while demonstrating the contradictions involved in the process of accumulation, rather than a prediction of what an actual outcome would be (Gram and Walsh, 1983, pp.532–6). While the long-period analysis does not require micro-foundations to generate the aggregative conditions for particular long-run outcomes to arise, micro-foundations are required for the analysis of how an economy actually fares, relative to these conditions. For both Robinson (1965, p.101) and Kalecki (1971, p.165) the extrapolation into the long run of existing conditions is a significant benchmark for economic analysis and even as an influence on current behaviour, but it is an imaginary rather than concrete phenomenon.

Finally, developments within behavioural economics provide a firmer foundation for Post Keynesian short-period analysis; much of the rejection of Keynesian short-period analysis as 'neo-classical' stems from the invalid equation of microeconomic (and market) analysis with neo-classical microeconomics. Starting from the presumption of imperfectly-competitive markets, with supply and demand interdependent, behavioural analysis studies the actual behaviour of consumers and producers, with emphasis on the institutional environment, and employing a type of social psychology reminiscent of the *General Theory* (Loasby, 1976; Earl, 1983, 1984, 1995a, 1995b). Although the connection is not a straightforward one, this work can be fed into macroeconomic analysis by allowing a better understanding particularly of expectations formation, as well as the functioning of financial markets (Dow and Earl, 1982; Earl, 1995b). Behavioural analysis does not generate specific predictions of consumer, producer or investor behaviour, but it does promote the type of understanding which reinforces the role of the expectations formation to which Keynes attached such importance (Dow and Dow, 1985 and Chapter 7 below). But, for macroeconomic analysis, it must be used in combination with analysis of the institutional and social environment within which individual behaviour is conducted (Carvalho, 1983–84).

The (short-run) Post Keynesian treatment of micro-foundations can perhaps best be illustrated in terms of the labour market. We will follow Chick's (1983, Chapters 7 and 8) treatment, which is contrasted explicitly with the mainstream treatment which involves independent labour demand and supply schedules expressed with respect to the real wage, and conducive to clearing. (A more explicitly sociological treatment of labour market behaviour, emphasizing the segmentation of that market has been presented by Piore, 1979. This type of analysis moves even further from the marginalist framework.)

First, wage bargaining is conducted in terms of the money wage, not the real wage. Employers have control over the price of their own product (which is the particular price relevant for their real wage calculation) as long as they operate in imperfectly competitive markets (or indeed as long as competitive markets are not in long-run equilibrium). Employers thus have the capacity to translate a money wage into a range of real wages, determined by the feasible range of product price changes. Workers, on the other hand, have no control whatsoever of their real wage over the contract period, the relevant denominator being the general price level. (Wage contracts will influence the general price level only in aggregate.) Nor do they have any firm knowledge as to what price level changes will be over that period. Their wage claims will be *influenced* by expectations as to changes in the price level, as well as by observed trends in wage differentials between them and other trades. But the relevant variable for wage bargaining is the money wage.

Second, the supply of labour above some full-employment level (where there is no excess supply of labour at the going wage) is a positive function of the money wage. But, when firms anticipate sufficient demand for their products to justify an increase in employment above the full-employment level, they must take into account the institutional fact that any wage increase designed to attract new members of the labour force must also be paid to the existing work force; a very significant increase expected effective demand will be necessary before the firm will embark on such an action. During the initial period of anticipated rising demand, then, prices are rising but money wages staying constant, so that real wages are falling. Real wages only have a chance to rise once the demand increase is sufficient to justify attempts to attract additional labour.

When product demand starts to contract, however, there is no mechanism to reverse the money wage increase. It is easier for employers to lay off excess workers than to institute a fall in money wages. For those workers still in employment, there is no incentive, and no mechanism generally, to induce a wage cut. More important, the unemployed have no mechanism for signalling their willingness to regain employment at a lower wage. The contraction in employment, then, is off the labour supply curve. Nor has it been possible to specify a labour demand curve, if only because the marginal cost of hiring is determined by whatever the labour force happens to be before an expansion. (Indeed the absence of a demand for labour curve would follow from the absence of a product demand curve, see Asimakopulos, 1980–81, p.164.) Also, the money wage during the contraction, and during the early stages of expansion before full employment is reached, is whatever it happened to be at the peak of the expansion.

As Chick (1983, p.162) points out, the distinguishing features of this labour market theory are that:

(1) There is no unique relationship between employment and *either* money or real wages.
(2) The cyclical pattern of employment and wages is not reversible.
(3) The money wage level throughout all of the cycle except the later stages of the cycle and the point at which money wages are allowed to rise is the result of historical accident.

It is important to note also that it is anticipated effective product demand which determines the demand for labour, not labour's marginal product. The marginal product of labour is relevant only at the next stage, when employers work out the wage which they will offer the labour they have already decided to hire (Weintraub, 1956; Davidson, 1983a,b). Further, the distribution of income is determined once money wages are set; as we have seen, money wages through a large proportion of the cycle are determined by what they happen to be at cycle peaks.

This account of the determination of employment differs from that in the long-period Post Keynesian analysis. The latter focuses on labour requirements in a steady state given the capital-goods sector requirements determined by the aggregate demand for consumer goods, and given technological change. These labour requirements will in general fall short of full employment. Thus, within labour market analysis as such, no inconsistency arises between the two time dimensions of analysis: one sets out the path of short-term, cyclical fluctuations, while the other specifies the conditions for a long-run steady state, and both postulate a general condition of less-than-full employment. As we shall see in Chapters 7 and 8, however, the difference in treatment of expectations and money *could* generate inconsistencies arising from the two different positions on micro-foundations.

5.5 Marxian Theory

The Marxian position on micro-foundations is the diametrical opposite of the neo-Austrian position, but with a similar methodological foundation in *a priori* knowledge. While neo-Austrians see the individual as the appropriate unit of analysis, Marxians see class as the appropriate unit of analysis. (For non-orthodox Marxians, gender and race have been added as alternative units of analysis; in what follows, we will use the term 'class' to represent the range of collective units on which radical analysis is grounded.) While neo-Austrians have *a priori* knowledge of the individual, Marxians have *a priori* knowledge of class, given class consciousness (Hollis and Nell, 1975). For the neo-Austrians, macroeconomic aggregates derive their only significance from the individual behaviour which generates them; for a Marxist, individuals derive their behaviour from the social conditions of the class to which they belong. Not only is individual motivation class-determined, there is also the possibility of class consciousness, which promotes individual sacrifice in the interests of the class. Methodologically, class performs a role in Marxian theory similar to groups in Keynesian theory, although the former is applied more deterministically, and more comprehensively. Individuals can thus more generally be regarded as representative individuals in a Marxian framework, in the same way as the rate of profit is regarded as a representative rate of profit. This rejection of reductionism has been identified by Roberts and Feiner (1992, p.3) as 'one of the most striking points of agreement' among radical economists.

The *a priori* knowledge of class relations is prompted by observation, as Kant would suggest. Indeed, Marx and Engels (who edited much of Marx's writings) were both steeped in factual knowledge of industrial conditions in England. (This tradition is being continued by, for example, Lazonick, 1979.) In other words, their consciousness of class relations was derived from micro data. Evading any problem of induction, the *a priori* basis for knowledge allows generalizations to be *recognized* in the mind which were only stirred by particular observations. As a corollary, the generalizations at class level can also be applied at firm level or household level. Indeed attempts have been made to model Marxian theory along general equilibrium lines by making these micro-foundations explicit (see Roemer, 1981, for example).

This does not mean that there is no tension between the individual and class. Rather, competition (among capitalists and among workers) imposes a behaviour pattern on individuals according to their class; capitalists are induced to invest rather than to consume, while workers are induced to offer their labour at lower wages than others. Marx (1857–58, p.248) argued, with respect to the apparent individuality of exchange that 'entirely different processes go on in which this apparent individuality, equality and liberty disappear' because 'exchange value already in itself implies compulsion over the individual'.

In addition, Marxian theory rests heavily on 'paradoxes' derived from the fallacy of composition. Competition among capitalists induces increased capitalization which reduces the rate of profit, for example. Unintended consequences of action are, however, compatible with a theory which attempts to capture the 'laws of motion' of capitalism; there is no requirement, imposed by any need for a static equilibrium solution, to be able to model a resolution of the paradox which would halt motion.

Marx's view of individual rationality within capitalism had much in common with that of Keynes (Winslow, 1986), although he foresaw scope for increasing rationality within socialism. The social conditions of capitalism generated the motive of financial accumulation among owners of capital, and survival among workers (Marx, 1867, p.739). Marx viewed such motivation as fundamentally irrational, in the sense that it was the outcome of 'false consciousness'. A rational motive for behaviour would be self-fulfilment in some form, but wealth in itself could not provide the fulfilment of any rational need if it was simply accumulated in such a way as to increase in value as much as possible (Marx, 1857–58, p.162). Similarly, the acquiescence of workers in allowing their labour value to be exploited only allowed their survival in the sense of subsistence. If consciousness of their objective condition could be acquired, they would perceive their real interests as lying within a change from capitalism to socialism.

The level of employment is analysed in terms of secular trends in production, punctuated by crises. The competitive market structure of capitalism (in the Classical sense) encourages technological innovation and increasing capitalization, i.e. an increase in the organic composition of capital. Relative labour requirements are thus reduced, so that unemployment progressively increases. But, since labour surplus value is the source of profit, the rate of return on capital falls as this process proceeds. This process is offset by technological improvements and by imperialistic extensions of markets and of sources of labour. In addition, the increasing 'reserve army of the unemployed' can be used as a threat to workers remaining in employment, allowing subsistence wages to be lowered, and the fall in profit rates to be dampened. Say's Law is not in general satisfied since, although firms save only in order to invest, the timing and value of investment is dependent on expected profits as well as on conditions in financial markets. Say's Law would only be satisfied in a position of general equilibrium

Marx postulated that there was scope for firms' expectations to be mistaken. If wages are kept too low to satisfy the supply of consumer goods, or if workers succeed in increasing wages, then actual profits will fall short of expected profits and further investment plans will be shelved. Savings already made will be hoarded in money form to avoid capital loss, since a widespread cutback in investment plans will start a downward spiral in product and asset prices, and demand for credit will increase to cover the earnings shortfall. The resulting general overproduction crisis causes an addition to the reserve army of the unemployed. It also causes bankruptcy among the weaker firms, lowering the value of their assets which are then built up by the stronger firms. As a result the industrial structure becomes progressively more concentrated with every financial crisis.

The level of employment, then, is generally independent of the real, or nominal, wage, although attempts by labour to increase wages at the expense of profits may instigate increased capitalization of production, which neutralizes those attempts. Rather, the competitive forces in the process of accumulation are seen as the underlying forces, with wage rates and employment levels the appearance of these forces in exchange. Thus, while these underlying forces refer to relations between individual capitalists and workers, the forces are regarded as so generally applicable as to suppress individuality. The laws of motion of capitalism are not seen as capable of influence by any individual action. Thus, the micro-foundations of Marxian theory are such that the problem of co-ordination can be analysed at the level of class, i.e. at the macro level.

5.6   Conclusion

The relationship between the determinants of individual actions on the one hand and their co-ordination (or lack of co-ordination) as represented in macro outcomes, on the other, poses fundamental questions for all macroeconomic theory. But the discussion of micro-foundations has been dominated by the particular problems posed within the general equilibrium school of thought. At one extreme, neo-Austrians avoid the problem by arguing that there is no macroeconomic knowledge other than that generated by micro-foundations. The polar version of Marxian theory suggests that there is no microeconomic knowledge other than what derives from the macro, or class, level; by concentrating on production conditions as determined by the existence of competitive forces, Marxians can deal with the problem of lack of market co-ordination in terms of macroeconomic aggregates. (The analysis of crisis, however, does require more explicit reference to market behaviour.)

The Post Keynesian approach does not take either of these extremes, but is also a holistic approach which attempts to avoid any logical micro–macro inconsistency. First, some participants study conditions for long-run steady states, which need not contradict (even if they do not employ) the short-run analysis which explicitly recognizes its micro-foundations. Second, the unit of analysis is frequently groups, on the grounds that this provides macro-foundations for microeconomic behaviour. But group behaviour is not deterministic in that it is susceptible to shifts arising from diversity of behaviour, as well as unfulfilled expectations. The presence of unfulfilled expectations resulting from conflict between individual actions and the macro outcome are compatible with an analysis which does not require static equilibrium solutions.

Micro-foundations have constituted a continuing problem for 'Keynesian' macroeconomics within the neo-classical synthesis, because the latter does appear to contradict the principles of neo-classical microeconomics, which are the only recognized microeconomics within this school of thought. Indeed this acceptance of a common framework for microeconomic analysis is an important unifying factor in mainstream economics. A fundamental source of difficulty is the reference point of equilibrium, which precludes conflict between micro behaviour and macro outcomes, i.e. which requires successful co-ordination.

In so far as a logical micro–macro inconsistency was regarded as acceptable, neo-classical macroeconomics continued in purely aggregative terms, within a neo-Walrasian general equilibrium framework, by imposing constraints on individual behaviour. Increasingly, however, these constraints have been modelled in terms of optimizing behaviour. The driving-force has been the reductionist requirement of logical completeness, such that the aim is to eliminate as far as possible any micro–macro inconsistency.

The treatment of micro-foundations, and their relationship to macroeconomics, is conditioned significantly by the use of equilibrium within the framework employed. Indeed this concept seems to represent a crucial divide between neo-Austrians and mainstream theorists. In the next chapter we turn to the equilibrium concept to see how each school of thought deals with it.

6 Equilibrium

6.1 Introduction

In the last chapter, we saw how each school of thought chooses to represent the individual behaviour underlying macroeconomics. The problem facing each school of thought was how to relate that individual behaviour and its co-ordination to aggregative outcomes. In this chapter we turn to consider an important organizing concept which may be used to analyse the interdependence of the behaviour of individuals and groups within an economy: equilibrium. Indeed we have identified one school of thought precisely in terms of its use of the equilibrium concept: the mainstream school.

The equilibrium concept is pervasive in economics in some form or another because it imposes some order on complex relationships; it provides a natural point at which to look at the outcome of particular forces. Even if it is the process itself by which forces are exerted which is of primary interest, the end point provides a useful reference point, a benchmark for analysis. In its most general sense, equilibrium means a point of rest. That state of rest can arise in different ways: from a balancing of forces, or from complementarity of forces, for example. If an equilibrium position is stable, then any displacement from that position will lead to a return to the equilibrium position.

Employed in any body of theory, the concept of equilibrium can be interpreted in a variety of ways, depending on what has been abstracted from; this abstraction determines what factors are left free, as autonomous variables, to cause a displacement from equilibrium, and which factors are available to induce a return to equilibrium. For example, the equilibrium position of an egg (in its shell) in a bowl on board a ship in a storm is the bottom of the bowl, if we abstract from the storm; the storm provides scope for an autonomous displacement of the egg, and the strength of the storm will determine whether the equilibrium is stable or not. On the other hand, if the ship is a space ship, requiring a weightlessness model rather than a gravity model, the equilibrium position of the egg, if any, is certainly not the bottom of the bowl, stable or unstable, storm or no storm. In the same way, in economics, the conditions for equilibrium will be determined by the theoretical framework in which the concept is employed.

111

The notion of equilibrium is inextricably tied up with the treatment of time. A state of rest is contrasted with a state of change, which occurs in time; and '[t]here could be no Time if nothing changed' (Georgescu-Roegen, 1971, p.131). Time in turn can have different meanings. The two identified by Georgescu-Roegen (1971) and Robinson (1978) are historical time and mechanical time. The first is more 'realistic', its main distinguishing feature being that it is irreversible; history consists of succeeding states, each of which is the outcome of the last (but not vice-versa) (Carvalho, 1983–84). To return to the egg-in-a-bowl example, the storm may be so fierce that the egg breaks; there is now a new 'state' which cannot generate a return to the original state of a whole egg. Mechanical (or mechanistic) time in contrast is reversible, and independent of events; the transition from one state to the next can be precisely reversed.

Implicit in these two notions of time are different views on expectations formation. One aspect of the irreversibility of historical time is the significance of uncertainty at one point in time with respect to another. If this uncertainty cannot be modelled deterministically, and indeed since the particular set of expectations which prevails determines the next state to which the economy will move, there could be no parallel with the set of expectations which would prevail if, instead, the second state were the starting point. In mechanical time, since processes are reversible, expectations formation (if full knowledge is not assumed to prevail) must be reversible; further, any lack of full information must be incapable of altering the equilibrium end point of the transition process. The modelling of expectations formation is a large subject in itself, which is the focus of the next chapter. The expectations aspect of equilibrium and time will be left implicit for the rest of this chapter, but it will be useful to bear in mind the role of expectations involved in the two uses of time.

A third possible use of the time concept is as a denominator of causal sequence, rather than of temporal sequence. This allows a third notion of equilibrium, which rests on what we call logical time (following Termini, 1981). Logical time does not explicitly incorporate time at all. Rather, it uses logical precedence of variables to determine causality. Variables need not be dated, but some are taken as exogenous and the forces of causation analysed with respect to the endogenous variables. If variables are ascribed dates, these dates refer to the causal sequence rather than time as such. There is no attempt to trace the temporal process of transition from one state to the next. Within this framework, equilibrium can be a partial or a general concept. If partial, then variables endogenous to a particular piece of analysis may be either independent variables, or givens, which may be allowed to vary in another piece of analysis, all other variables being defined as dependent. In a general equilibrium framework, the distinction between endogenous and exogenous is strict. Once an endogenous variable can be explained within the model, it cannot return to being an exogenous variable; there is no distinction between independent variables and givens.

Finally, Shackle identifies a fourth notion of time, which he calls expectational time (Shackle, 1968, p.67). This notion refers to the subjective perceptions of time by individuals. It is in fact an atemporal notion of time, since it does not flow; it is a construct of individuals' minds. It is, however, the temporal framework within which expectations are formed and decisions made. It is a purely individualistic concept since it does not allow for analysis of processes, or interactions between individuals (Carvalho, 1983–84). But, to the extent that individuals' expectations formation is incorporated in macroeconomic models, this notional use of time must be incorporated into frameworks couched in terms of historical, mechanical or logical time. The abstraction incorporated in individuals' expectations then becomes a double abstraction within a theory which includes these expectations. Even without reference to expectational time, however, there are differences in the degree of abstraction applied to the equilibrium concept. All theories are notional, but within the theory, equilibrium may be an actual state within which the economy is studied, or it may be a notional state used as a reference point for the (modelled) actual behaviour of the economy.

With these distinctions in mind, we turn now to consider the diversity of uses of the equilibrium concept within the four schools of thought.

6.2 Neo-Austrian Theory

The neo-Austrian use of equilibrium is somewhat confused; there is an uneasy, simultaneous (and usually implicit) reliance on different notions of time. The primary concern is with market process, and institutional evolution, suggesting a historical notion of time. Yet the underlying presumption of co-ordination success under all circumstances might suggest a mechanical notion of time. Finally, the subjectivist neo-Austrian methodology might suggest that the only relevant notion of time was one of expectational time.

Hayek's (1937) definition of equilibrium is a situation where all individuals' plans are mutually consistent. Such an equilibrium need not be a state of rest; it simply requires that events do not force changes of plan on any individual. The information requirements of such an equilibrium are in fact very strong, on a par with those of a Walrasian equilibrium. The underlying source of equilibrium must refer to the formation of plans itself, since it is to this level of motivation that the Austrian aim of purposeful behaviour applies. Thus, ultimately, an equilibrium situation is one in which there is no impetus for individuals to change their behaviour; no new information can be acquired which would act as such an impetus. Rizzo (1979) expresses equilibrium in terms of co-ordination of plans; disequilibrium implies a lack of co-ordination, and thus the existence of unexploited opportunities. (The neo-Austrian influence is clear in Leijonhufvud's

(1968, Chapter 2) development of the implications of disequilibrium as the outcome of co-ordination failure.)

So far, this set of definitions would not be dissimilar from those for an inter-temporal equilibrium model within the general equilibrium framework. But neo-Austrian micro-foundations require that all analysis refer to the individual, not to aggregates. Hayek (1937) therefore doubts the tractability of a concept such as general equilibrium, which applies to the entire collection of diverse individuals in an economy. Consistency between the plans for action in different markets for any one individual can be observed, and thus has meaning; but then every rational individual would be, by definition, in equilibrium. Consistency between all individuals' plans, on the other hand, cannot be perceived objectively. First, plans refer to the future in historical time, and unfold over time. Second, the knowledge on which plans are based is itself generated by the market process, over historical time (Caldwell, 1988). Finally, Austrian subjectivism means for some that costs and values are subjective (Buchanan and Thirlby, 1973); there is then no way of identifying whether or not an economy is in equilibrium (Barry, 1979, p.43). This argument took on particular significance in the 'socialist calculation' debates of the 1930s. Hayek's argument suggests that it is impossible to construct an objective socialist plan for production, distribution and exchange, since costs and preferences cannot be identified or predicted.

Even if equilibrium could be identified, the question arises as to how such an equilibrium could be established. Disequilibrium is in part a state of incomplete knowledge, of unco-ordinated actions. Approach to equilibrium requires that more knowledge be acquired (assuming the equilibrium is stable) and actions become progressively more co-ordinated. This requires either a theory of behavioural adjustment to mistakes, and of information retrieval, or else that the unintended consequences of actions according to inconsistent plans somehow make those plans more consistent. The first goes against the basic Austrian tenet that individual behaviour is unpredictable; each individual has the set of information most relevant to her situation, and as long as new information is becoming available to her (i.e. as long as equilibrium does not prevail) an outside observer does not have the means to detect the underlying behavioural pattern. In short, behaviour is not systematic (Kirzner, 1976). Certainly, it is presumed that individuals learn from mistakes, but this learning process itself is not systematic. The second option, that actions have unintended consequences which propel the system to equilibrium, is also problematic. Since neo-Austrians do not recognize events other than in terms of individual behaviour, it is difficult to envisage a systematic movement to equilibrium independent of human action. Market process is the outcome of individual action, and must be explicable in those terms.

In fact, the concept of equilibrium is contrary to what neo-Austrians regard as the moving force of a market economy: entrepreneurial behaviour. This was at the core of Schumpeter's (1934) theory of economic development. To the extent that lack of knowledge and disco-ordination are overcome, it is the result of entrepreneurs seeking the most profitable opportunities. It is in their interests to acquire relevant information, and to seek mutually-advantageous trades. But what the entrepreneur seeks is not a situation of uniformly perfect knowledge, but knowledge which others do not have. There is a continual impetus for entrepreneurs to seek (or even create for themselves) differential information, preventing the establishment of equilibrium.

Yet the presumption of successful co-ordination requires some notion of equilibrium. Some thus justify the retention of equilibrium as a notional concept. Rizzo (1979), for example, points out that Mises (1949, p.22) advocates abstraction from change in order to allow study of human action; equilibrium is then a useful reference point. Kirzner (1973, 1976) also favours its retention as a notional concept. But those most influenced by Shackle restrict attention to the subjectivist notion of expectational time which precludes statements about economy-wide co-ordination. Lachmann (1977, pp.312–7), for example, does not view entrepreneurial behaviour in Kirzner's terms of alertness, whereby some entrepreneurs acquire information from a body of data more quickly than others. Rather, entrepreneurs are viewed as being creative, putting together available information in a novel way which creates new knowledge and new opportunities. But equilibrium rules out the exploitation of new opportunities, and thus creativity; it rules out precisely what many neo-Austrians see as the moving force behind competition.

Here we come to the basic methodological split between neo-Austrians and general equilibrium theory. Neo-Austrians set their goal as being to make the economy intelligible. They start with their *a priori* understanding of the purposefulness of human action in order to observe the workings of the economy. In particular, this observation identifies historical time as being inherent in market process, the process of acquiring information and creating opportunities. Thus, if equilibrium reflects a balance between the forces represented by individuals' plans as they unfold over time, responding to new information, then, Hayek (1937, p.36) argues, 'it is obvious that the passage of time is essential to give the concept of equilibrium any meaning'. Equilibrium, then, is seen as the outcome of a process which takes place in historical time, where the future is a function of the creativity and mistakes of the past. Where it is used, then, in neo-Austrian analysis, equilibrium is a notional concept describing the tendency of market processes in historical time, a tendency which never reaches an end point because of the continued creativity of human action.

The market context of equilibrium thus corresponds to that of general equilibrium theorists, but is employed as a notional concept within the theory, reflecting tendencies in historical time, just as in Classical theory. But the Classical definition of equilibrium in terms of the uniform rate of profit is rejected because it refers to macroeconomic aggregates (Lachmann, 1973, pp.35–6, 41). In fact, as Kirzner (1976) points out, the very notion of general equilibrium presumes that individuals learn from their mistakes in a way which promotes movement towards equilibrium; studying the unintended consequences of human action underlines the interdependence of micro and macro analysis. While Hayek (1937) resorted to arguing that the equilibrating nature of learning behaviour is a matter which can be settled empirically, this flies in the face of neo-Austrian subjectivism, and indeed requires that equilibrium be actual rather than notional. Ultimately, however, neo-Austrian use of the equilibrium concept implying the successful market co-ordination which underpins much of their theory, can be derived neither from observation nor from logical deduction from the axiom of human purposefulness; it can only rest on a view of how economies work held independently of the theoretical structure.

6.3   Mainstream Theory

Equilibrium is the primary organizing concept of mainstream theory (Arrow and Hahn, 1971, Chapter 1); according to Weintraub (1985) general equilibrium is part of the hard core of mainstream economics. The purpose of this body of theory is to provide a framework for analysing the interdependencies in a decentralized exchange economy, to explain how the self-interested actions of individuals can be in natural harmony. This purpose is derived explicitly from Smith's Invisible Hand concept, which had generated a faith in the involuntarily successful cohesion created by the forces of free competition; Walras perceived a need to prove rigorously the logic behind the faith. Walras' method, as that of his successors (see Debreu, 1959, p.viii), was to start with an abstract axiomatic model, which could later be modified to take account of differences between assumptions and observed reality. By positing a simultaneous, instantaneous clearing of all markets, general equilibrium theory had to be couched in terms of logical time, or, to the extent that variables are dated, mechanical time. The entire model is notional, i.e. abstract, but equilibrium is actually reached within the model.

There is seldom any claim that the assumptions of general equilibrium models are realistic; at best, the behavioural assumptions are 'as if' representations of actual behaviour. Nor is the institutional structure within which exchange takes place put forward as realistic, particularly if the model is Walrasian. What we have then is a logical structure built on *a priori* assumptions about behaviour, with ancillary mathematical assumptions employed which render the system potentially capable of yielding the solution of a unique, stable equilibrium position. The outcome is a specification of the set of conditions which would generate the result of harmonious market behaviour.

Within the model, there is an explanation of what causes this outcome. A

Cartesian/Euclidean mathematical framework requires a strict dual between endogeneity and exogeneity. Endogenous variables are those whose values are explained by the model. It is thus the values of the exogenous variables, in combination with the structure of the model itself, which 'cause' the equilibrium values of endogenous variables to be what they are. (In a mechanical-time model, the lagged values of dependent variables may add explanatory power to those of the independent exogenous variables, but even then the causal implications are not at all straightforward (Addison *et al.*, 1980). By definition, there is no explanation of what causes the exogenous variables to have particular values, while the structure of the model is determined by the *a priori* behavioural assumptions combined with the ancillary assumptions about the mathematical properties of functional relationships. The more all-encompassing the model, i.e. the more variables are endogenised, the less explanatory power it has. If an equilibrium position represents a simultaneous clearing of markets, then within the model it cannot be determined which variable affects which. The function of the model is rather to prove the existence and uniqueness of a stable equilibrium, given particular sets of assumptions, and to demonstrate the effect on the equilibrium position of changes in exogenous variables.

The notion of simultaneity can be modified if we consider the means by which the economy is modelled as moving from one equilibrium position to another, following a change in an exogenous variable. In order to model disequilibrium positions, there must be some theory as to the path of adjustment to equilibrium, and one which is consistent with the axiomatic logic of the general equilibrium model. One way of dealing with disequilibrium is to model it as a situation of imperfect information; the adjustment path traces the return to a position of perfect information. Consider the case where the money supply is selected as an exogenous variable. When the money supply first increases, the information conveyed by rising prices is initially perceived as rising relative prices for particular goods, inducing increased production of those goods. Equilibrium is restored when there is a correct perception of a rise in the general price level only. Similarly, unemployment might occur if workers interpreted a fall in the money wage as a fall in the real wage, although the general price level was also falling. Full employment would be restored as soon as labour acted on the basis of full information.

Time enters the analysis in that acquisition of information, and thus the approach to equilibrium, are modelled as occurring sequentially. But, as long as comparative static analysis is replaced by dynamic analysis along a reversible 'time-path trajectory', no additional explanatory power is given to the model (Boland, 1982, Chapter 6); it is still the exogenous variable which is the sole 'cause' of all that happens to the endogenous variables. In neo-classical models, although the trajectory traced (as a result of a money supply increase, for example) from position A to position B, may not be exactly reversed in the case of a money supply decrease, the end points, A and B, remain the same. As long as the equilibrium position is independent of the adjustment path in disequilibrium, i.e. the equilibrium is not path-dependent, then the nature of the path does not add explanatory power to a general equilibrium model (Termini, 1981, pp.65–72). However, following the lead of Phelps (1972), a class of models has been developed incorporating path-dependency, or hysteresis. In these models, the new equilibrium is jointly-determined by the exogenous shock and the (deterministically-modelled) adjustment path. Thus, for example, an increase in unemployment may not be reversed along the same adjustment path because unemployment has led to de-skilling and/or a lack of power among the unemployed 'outsiders' to make effective their offer of labour at reduced money wages (Cross, 1988).

The practice of defining adjustment paths in disequilibrium terms was widespread in the neo-classical synthesis (both monetarist and Keynesian) until the 1980s. It was justified on the grounds of realism:

> The disequilibrium approach, as its name suggests, is based on the view that the typical market spends more time out of equilibrium than in equilibrium ... The proportion of the time the representative market spends in equilibrium depends upon the relation between the frequency of disturbance and length of the adjustment lag. (Casson, 1981, p.33)

But New Keynesianism has absorbed the reductionism of the rest of mainstream theory in its dissatisfaction with disequilibrium explanations of non-market clearing; disequilibrium entails non-optimizing behaviour. The aim is to endogenize the adjustment path itself on choice-theoretic grounds, so that, given any model's parameters, again it is the exogenous variables which are the prime causal force.

The distinction between endogenous and exogenous variables is a matter of definition within the model. The most common exogenous variables in macroeconomic analysis have been the money supply, government spending and taxation, technological change, and events in the economies of trading partners; technological change has, in real business cycle theory, overtaken the money supply as the preferred source of cyclical disturbance. But few would argue that any of these variables is 'in reality' completely exogenous to the actual workings of the economy. The scope for explanation is thus only available if we abstract from this aspect of reality. Any model must make abstractions; but it is an extremely important abstraction which itself determines the causal explanation for the results of a model.

The attempts to endogenise the adjustment path between long-term equilibrium positions have involved an explicit introduction of mechanical time into equilibrium theory, which had previously been restricted to disequilibrium theory. Time has been introduced in two ways. First, since current decisions are conditioned by plans for the future, the choice set is extended to include goods in the future as well as current goods; goods are thus dated by the time period in which they are to be purchased. Equilibrium thus requires that futures markets in these goods clear, as well as current, or spot, markets.

Second, since futures markets do not exist for many goods, and so full general equilibrium for the entire future cannot be settled at once, Hicks (1939) divided time up into notional 'weeks'. During each week, all disequilibrium adjustments would take place in response to the outcome of events in the previous week, generating a new equilibrium position. The disequilibrium process is not analysed, only the weekly equilibrium, which changes as the range of goods for which there are spot and futures markets changes from one week to the next. From this concept stemmed the conjectural equilibrium analysis which grew with the micro-foundations literature. Being only temporary equilibria, these positions may involve employment at varying levels, giving the appearance of involuntary unemployment. But the definition of equilibrium has changed accordingly, to conform to the neo-Austrian definition, and also more explicitly with the behavioural axioms; an equilibrium is now a state in which all plans are met.

In both uses, time is mechanical rather than historical. Time comes in discrete periods. In the temporary equilibrium analysis, there is a reckoning at the end of each period, at which all mutually-advantageous trades (given available information) are made. Information is perfect (within a probability distribution) and uniformly available, to particular groups at least, subject to some specified exclusions; the main exclusion is the market-clearing prices for goods without futures markets. These models are fundamentally similar to the original Walrasian model; if only general equilibrium positions are studied, then the only source for involuntary change is change in exogenous variables.

In Hahn's (1973a) methodological statement about the correspondence between general equilibrium theory (excluding disequilibrium theory) and observed reality, he reaffirms the position that general equilibrium theory does not attempt to describe reality. Rather, it abstracts from intractable aspects of reality to provide a watertight rigorous framework for analysis of those aspects which are tractable. Further, the test for the theory's results are falsification tests; it is the advantage, he claims, of a complete, precise theory, that it yields precise propositions which can be falsified. In other words, although the theory can only, according to Hahn (1977), make statements about equilibrium positions, there is a correspondence between these equilibria and observed states of the world. But, as Coddington (1975) points out, it is not clear how one translates a statement expressed in terms of a general equilibrium model into a statement about a world which it does not describe. The precision refers to the model, not to economic events which reflect theoretically intractable elements. And indeed, Hahn throws doubt on the correspondence of equilibrium to reality (although not the framework itself) when he states: 'it is not true that in our present state of knowledge the notion of an equilibrium which may never be attained is not of very great help in doing the best we can' (Hahn, 1973a, p.10). The general equilibrium framework is in fact the only one which meets Cartesian/Euclidean criteria for scientific enquiry, so that 'the best we can' means 'the best we can within that framework'.

Although Hahn's positivist criterion of testability finds many echoes in the Popperian or Lakatosian professions of many mainstream economists, in practice theoretical and empirical work have increasingly diverged (see Boland, 1991 and Pencavel, 1991, for example). Indeed much of econometrics inspired by the Minnesota school is quite deliberately atheoretical (Johnston, 1991). The thorny question of the empirical counterpart to the theoretical focus on equilibrium is thus avoided. An alternative route to dealing with this question has been recourse to testing by means of simulation excercises. In one of the few contributions to the methodology literature to address this fragmentation between theoretical and empirical work, Mayer (1993) endorses the fragmentation. He advocates that theory continue to conform to the principles of deductive logic and the empirical work conform to the requirements of end-users. In the meantime, however, Hendry (1993) has developed what became known as the LSE approach to econometrics. This is a deliberate attempt to reverse the divergence between theory and empirical work by testing theoretical propositions along falsificationist principles. (See Gerrard, 1995, for a critical survey of the methodology of econometrics.)

Any theory must abstract from reality in some way, and indeed the major advances in general equilibrium theory over the last thirty years have been in the direction of removing abstractions. But the entire framework is governed by the necessity, increasingly perceived, to confine statements to positions of general (albeit temporary) equilibrium, in which each individual has done the best she can in full awareness of all the options. There is no presumption even that equilibrium is associated with permanence in the actual values of variables, i.e. that actual occurrence of equilibrium could be recognized; the regularity of behaviour postulated by equilibrium analysis in mechanical time by no means precludes changing preferences or technology in historical time.

6.4   Post Keynesian Theory

Critiques of the general equilibrium concept frequently include arguments about the realism of assumptions. For example, the existence of competitive equilibrium depends on the absence of global increasing returns to scale; increasing returns not only encourage the break-up of perfect competition, but also do not provide a point of rest until all production is monopolized and all economies of scale exploited (Kaldor, 1972). More generally unrealistic is the full (or optimal) information assumption (highlighted by Shackle, 1967, Chapter 11, for example). But general equilibrium theorists make no claim to be realistic, and it is difficult to argue conclusively about the relative value of realism of different assumptions when it is not at all clear how the results are to be compared to reality. Indeed Hahn (1981) admits freely the theory's shortcomings with respect to realism, but still maintains that it is the best we have.

The fundamental critique of general equilibrium theory put forward by Post Keynesians is addressed to the concept of competitive general equilibrium itself (Robinson, 1978; Kaldor, 1972; Davidson, 1972, Chapter 2; Shapiro, 1978). The fundamental objections are, first, to a theory requiring atomistic individuals to arrive at an optimal set of trades, at optimal prices, on the basis of given preferences, resources and technology, independent of a particular historical context, and, second, where the capacity to explain events is limited by the choice of exogenous variables; any situations which do not accord with these equilibrium states are beyond the purview of analysis.

The alternative formulation of equilibrium which deals with the first objection would be based on the historical notion of time. That which deals with the second could be based on the logical notion of time, but with a less strict dichotomy between exogenous and endogenous variables; the alternative categorization of independent, given and dependent variables allows for a richer causal explanation. There is some dispute as to the preferable use of time as between these two, not only in terms of interpreting Keynes's own use of equilibrium, but also in terms of the preferred method of Post Keynesian analysis.

Termini (1981) emphasizes the logical-time framework employed in the *General Theory*, while Robinson (1978) emphasizes the historical-time framework required by Keynes's emphasis on uncertainty, expressed most explicitly in Keynes (1937), although evident in Keynes (1936, Chapters 22 and 24). Kregel (1976) expresses Keynes's use of equilibrium for the purposes of deriving causal relations in terms of the treatment of expectations, implying a combination of logical and historical time (since expectations necessarily refer to time). In fact there is no conflict involved; Keynes used both frameworks (separately or in combination) for different purposes, and indeed he used a third, expectational time, in his analysis of behaviour in financial and capital goods markets. The logical-time framework provides a general analysis of causal forces. Historical time modifies the causal relationships for application to processes within historical contexts, by emphasizing the prevalence of institutional factors and uncertainty and their consequences. Expectational time allows analysis of individual behaviour under uncertainty and the resulting reliance on norms and conventions. Similarly, in contemporary Post Keynesian theory, analysis employing the three concepts of time can be seen to complement each other. The common position which differentiates Post Keynesian equilibrium analysis from that of general equilibrium theory is the rejection of mechanical time and the narrow conception of logical time equilibrium required by an axiomatic framework.

The rejection of the mechanical-time and logical-time equilibrium concepts (where equilibrium is to be used at all) is based on two judgements. The first judgement refers to the relationship between theory and reality. If theory is to have some correspondence to reality, then abstraction poses least problems if it is of the sort where a variable is presumed to be present, but is held constant for the purposes of a particular theoretical argument. It is, therefore, possible to assess empirically whether this variable was in fact constant, and if it was not then the theory must be complicated by allowing the variable to change if the theory is to have any applicability to that situation. This is fundamentally different from starting with a theoretical structure which automatically excludes consideration of variables (like money). Thus, for example, Keynes in the *General Theory* at times assumed long-term expectations to be constant; he did not assume they were not there, simply that they were given for the purposes of that particular argument (Kregel, 1976). Other assumptions are drawn from empirical observation: the relative stability of the consumption function, for example, or the instability of investment demand. They are not tied to axioms, and are thus not immutable. The equilibrium concept itself, when expressed in historical time in the Classical tradition, is notional and thus cannot in general be observed. In the long-run it refers to a position which the economy would reach if certain trends were to continue, or if certain conditions were to be met. Equilibrium could conceivably be observed if these trends did continue. Thus, for example, falling rates of profit in the post-war years can be seen to correspond to Keynes's predictions of a stationary state with a zero rate of profit (Chick, 1983, Chapter 19), but since this state is portrayed as the notional outcome of a process in historical time, the process is of as much theoretical and empirical value as (if not more than) the prediction of the equilibrium state itself. The important result is not so much the character of the equilibrium itself, but the causal forces which generate it; within Post Keynesian analysis, effective demand (particularly the investment component) plays the most important causal role. For most long-run analysis, particularly that in the Sraffian tradition, the process of causation is a logical one; it does not refer to historical time in the sense of addressing the indeterminacy of investment planning, for example, when faced with the uncertainty associated with historical time.

For short-run analysis which recognizes this indeterminacy, Kregel (1976) suggests that Keynes emloyed three different versions of the equilibrium concept, which allow indeterminacy of behaviour a successively increasing role:

(1) Static equilibrium, where long-period expectations are exogenous and short-period expectations are realized.

(2) Stationary equilibrium, where short-period expectations may be disappointed, but this disappointment has no effect on long-period expectations.

(3) Shifting equilibrium, where disappointment of short-period expectations may encourage revision of long-period expectations.

The first version provided the simplest theoretical structure which can be expressed in logical time (i.e. with no explicit reference to time), for the purposes of posing counter-arguments to that part of the neo-classical orthodoxy expressed in terms of logical time. But the third version is the closest to historical 'reality' (although it is still notional, abstracting from reality).

Expectations in turn are formed with reference to expectational equilibrium in that decision-makers may be guided by what they perceive to be the 'normal' values of variables. The perception of normalcy, like a shifting equilibrium, can change over time, but at any one time provides an anchor for decision-making. The need for elements of stability in market behaviour explains the significance of institutions in Post Keynesian theory, which in general equilibrium theory are viewed as impediments to reaching equilibrium (cf. Richardson, 1960). One example is a customary structure of wage differentials, while another would be the tenacity to a particular form of money in spite of its erosion by inflation (Kregel, 1980b). Again we have a parallel between the theorist's attempt to use concepts which make some sense of the complexities of the real world, and their modelling of attempts by economic agents to construct a rational basis for decision-making.

Post Keynesians further argue that the equilibrium concept should not rule out of consideration of those factors which they regard as the most important in the working of the economy (see, in particular, Shapiro, 1978). Like neo-Austrians (but for different reasons), they consider a position of general equilibrium (as the outcome of given technology and preferences) to contradict the essential nature of a market economy. First, if the motive of investors is to accumulate wealth, then a state of rest in the economy is in no sense optimal; the driving force is to increase asset values. Since these values are exchange values, rather than use values, they cannot be predicted with any certainty. As Keynes pointed out:

> The whole object of the accumulation of wealth is to produce results, or potential results, at a comparatively distant, and sometimes at an indefinitely distant date. Thus the fact that our knowledge of the future is fluctuating, vague and uncertain, renders wealth a peculiarly unsuitable subject for the methods of [neo-]classical economic theory. (Keynes, 1937, p.213)

Further, accumulation is undertaken independent of any future expenditure plans (note the 'indefinitely' in the quotation above), so that there is no corresponding demand for future goods; accumulation today does not constitute demand tomorrow.

The goal of accumulation is served by technological change, by the creation of product demand, and by speculative increases in the value of financial assets. None of these developments is compatible with general equilibrium. The first implies that there is an endogenous impetus for changes in production conditions, one of the 'givens' of general equilibrium. The second implies that consumer-production processes which most favour accumulation determine the type of standard commodities which are available. The third requires analysis of the type of uncertainty which cannot be captured in probability distributions, and thus of money, which, in Hahn's (1983) admission, has no role in general equilibrium theory. Finally, general equilibrium theory precludes analysis of the institutions by which production, distribution and exchange function. Post Keynesian theory holds that these institutions are products of economic history itself.

This expression of the Post Keynesian position seems to be an argument for endogenizing ever more variables, which would, if applied to a logical time analysis, severely limit the explanatory power of theory. Rather, the argument against general equilibrium theory is that it encapsulates all endogenous variables by deterministic relationships within one system, producing a timeless solution which carries no explanation except with respect to any variables held back as exogenous. The concept of equilibrium in historical time can, however, isolate particular parts of the economic system for study in partial equilibrium analysis; explanation is sought by isolating what are judged in particular contexts to be the most important variables. This partiality can mean 'macroeconomic', i.e. isolating the behaviour of macroeconomic variables from specific micro-foundations. The central difference from the abstraction involved in general equilibrium analysis is that 'everything else' (which might include institutional structure, long-term expectations, technology, etc.) is assumed to be given, although always admissible as variables; it is not excluded by the universality of the axiomatic logic of the equilibrium concept itself. Further, since equilibrium is a point to which variables notionally gravitate over time, and since Post Keynesian theory is not tied to optimality conditions, the emphasis of analysis can be as much on a process over time as on the notional end point.

Misunderstanding about the distinction between the notional concept of equilibrium in historical time and the general equilibrium, mechanical-time concept has dogged the interpretation of Keynesian analysis. The neo-classical synthesis could only be achieved by reinterpreting Keynes's theory in terms of the same general equilibrium framework as neo-classical theory. Since it is important to understand the distinction, we now consider two examples of general equilibrium interpretation of Keynesian ideas; the first concerns Harrod's (1939) growth theory, and the second Tobin's (1958) portfolio theory. More detailed discussions of each may be found in Kregel (1980a) and Chick (1983, pp.213–88).

Harrod's growth theory is conventionally classified as 'Keynesian', because he considers the implications of effective demand deficiency for the long run (Samuelson, 1948, pp.748–51). Keynes's short-period analysis had avoided consideration of the effects of investment on production capacity. But by considering the investment required to sustain given levels of output, and the saving required to finance that investment, Harrod devised the concept of a warranted rate of growth, where these requirements are met. He showed that, if the actual growth rate were different from the warranted rate, then it would move progressively away from it. If actual growth were greater than the warranted rate, planned investment would exceed planned saving, the only solution being a rise in income to increase planned saving, but which would also induce an increase in planned investment, and so on. In the reverse case, where growth started off below the warranted rate, the adjustment process would instigate a downward income spiral. The warranted rate of growth is thus an unstable dynamic equilibrium.

From the correspondence between Harrod and Keynes (Keynes, 1973b and 1973c) it becomes apparent that Keynes did not understand that Harrod had been employing a mechanical-time usage of equilibrium. Keynes found implausible his own, historical-time, interpretation of Harrod's argument that, if the actual growth rate should happen not to coincide with the warranted rate, then secular expansion or stagnation was the inevitable outcome. Now, in fact, that was not what Harrod's theory states. It states that, at a point in mechanical time, if the actual and warranted rates happen to differ, then there is a force for divergence. Now, at the next 'snapshot' in mechanical time, this force will have endogenously changed the saving rate and the capital–output ratio, so that the warranted rate itself will have changed. Eventually the warranted rate will change sufficiently to 'cross over' the actual rate, and reverse the income trend; in other words, the theory is really one of cyclical fluctuations.

Since neither made his notion of equilibrium sufficiently explicit in the exchange for him to understand the other, Keynes continued to interpret what Harrod said in terms of historical time, and eventually the correspondence broke down when Keynes rejected the warranted rate as a concept of no practical importance since it was so unlikely to obtain in reality, i.e. having argued that Harrod's theory did not correspond to processes in historical time. Keynes pointed out that the warranted rate was a purely notional concept, and thus of limited practical relevance. But, since orthodox economists have generally failed to understand Keynes's use of equilibrium when it pertains to historical time, they presume that Harrod's theory is a long-run version of Keynes's short-run theory.

The second example, Tobin's portfolio theory, was explicitly put forward as an attempt to translate Keynes's theory of liquidity preference for the general equilibrium framework (see Tobin, 1958, section 2.6). Nevertheless, because of the widespread misunderstanding of the significance of Keynes's alternative methodology, Tobin's theory is generally regarded among the orthodoxy as a Keynesian theory. Certainly it provides a theory of demand for money as an asset, as a function of the interest rate, but there the similarity ends. Financial investors choose portfolios on the basis of a balancing of the expected return, and variance of return, from the range of available assets, including money, subject to their individual preferences as regards risk. But each set of portfolio choices is depicted as occurring in a discrete period of mechanical time. Expectations are formed for that period, and decisions made accordingly. If the probability distribution of returns has changed in the next period of time, the equilibrium portfolio is changed accordingly.

The process is perfectly reversible. In general equilibrium, however, there is no uncertainty (other than perhaps stochastic variations from equilibrium values, or information gaps which can in principle be filled) so that it is always possible to identify assets with a higher expected return than money with no risk of capital loss; there is in fact no rationale for holding money as an asset in general equilibrium. (This conclusion has been reached by general equilibrium theorists of varying degrees of strictness, see for example, Gordon, 1978, p.432; Hahn, 1983, p.l.)

This contrasts with analysis set in historical time, where trading is not confined to discrete intervals, and where successful accumulation requires designing portfolios so as to provide capacity to enter or leave markets at exactly the right time, i.e. at turning points. Historical time further precludes expectations being held with certainty in the form of probability distributions. There may be a notional equilibrium position, reflected in an expectation as to normal returns on assets, but that is irrelevant to speculative activity, which revolves around turning-points, not averages. While a stable interest rate in general equilibrium models arises from the uniform expectation that that is the equilibrium rate, it arises in a Keynesian model from a difference of opinion between borrowers and lenders, i.e. between those who expect interest rates to rise and those who expect them to fall.

6.5   Marxian Theory

In the Classical tradition, Marxians also adopt the historical-time concept of equilibrium, as a notional concept. An equilibrium thus refers to the outcome of historical tendencies. The meaning of equilibrium is a state of rest which results from a balancing of opposing forces, rather than the convergence of complementary forces. And indeed, most Marxian theory is constructed on the basis of opposing forces: of class struggle, and of contradictions within the working of capitalism. But Marx was more concerned with an absence of balance between forces, with the periodic eruption of crises, culminating eventually in the demise of capitalism. Thus, for example, Shaikh (1992, p.77) points out that '[t]here is never any state of equilibrium in which market prices "converge" to prices of production. Thus prices of production never exist as such.'

Nevertheless, it can be argued that the notion of equilibrium is used as a benchmark, against which this imbalance may be studied, and it is used within a range of time-periods. Modern interpretations of Marx vary in the degree to which the equilibrium concept is employed. First, equilibrium can be used to apply to market exchange; an equilibrium price is established from the equality of demand and supply. In this sense, equilibrium actually obtains in the real world in particular markets; it is thus a partial equilibrium concept. But equilibrium in this sense is not regarded as being very important in non-crisis conditions; then, supply always equals demand, since both are determined by the conditions of production. It is these conditions of production which are regarded as the important object of study. But in crisis (or disequilibrium) conditions, expected demand falls short of supply, both in individual markets and in aggregate, and a downward spiral ensues.

The eventual outcome of crisis is a return to equilibrium in the sense that sufficient numbers of workers have been added to the reserve army of the unemployed to tame workers' power, and defuse the struggle between workers and capitalists, and that sufficient capital value has been destroyed to allow greater concentration of industry and thus a return to acceptable rates of profit. But because the contradictions which brought about the crisis in the first place re-emerge eventually, the equilibrium as such is not important relative to the forces promoting instability.

A further use of the equilibrium concept is in determining the conditions for reproduction, i.e. the conditions for a sustained and balanced expansion of both the capital goods sector ('Department 1') and the consumption goods sector ('Department 2'), given the consumption requirements of the labour force and the physical input requirements of the two sectors, under given technological conditions. This part of Marxian analysis seems to abstract from the dynamic analysis of the push for accumulation, with technology continually changing (in the direction of increasing capital intensity). Harvey (1982, p.171) suggests, however, that Marx was simply making explicit the contradiction between the conditions for harmonious reproduction and inevitably changing technology – quite the reverse of positing an actual balance of forces allowing continuous reproduction.

Finally, the equilibrium concept is applied to the very long run in the sense of a prediction of the features of capitalism in its final form. It is more a statement about tendencies than about steady states: the tendency for unemployment to rise, for industry to become more concentrated, for the profit rate to fall, and so on.

Although the theoretical content differs in many respects, the uses of the equilibrium concept by Marxians and Post Keynesians have important similarities. The starting point of Marxian theory is that the important features of market economies relate to instability and change, rather than steady states, because of the motive of accumulation, and the power structure which allows this motive full expression. Equilibrium is of most use as a benchmark by which causal forces are identified in logical time, and against which to measure actual instability in historical time, i.e. as a centre of gravitation. Further, a much wider range of variables (including political and sociological variables) is regarded as endogenous to actual economic processes than is admitted to general equilibrium analysis. But, rather than relying on a mammoth simultaneous equation system, their theories focus on different aspects of the system separately, by means of partial equilibrium analysis, in the same way as Post Keynesian theory.

A major difference, however, is that Marxian theory has a notional equilibrium position to describe the later stages of capitalism. The *a priori* basis of Marxian theory is one which applies over long periods of history, allowing long-run equilibria to span much longer runs than Post Keynesian analysis. In addition, there are some who have attempted recently to reformulate Marxian theory in general equilibrium terms, i.e. in terms of mechanical time, on the basis of class-determined behaviour in place of individualistic optimizing behaviour (Roemer, 1981). There is a precedent for this in the work, for example, of Lange and Taylor (1964), designed for planners within a post-capitalist state (work to which Hayek took such great exception). It is ironic that the model designed to prove the capacity for co-ordination within a decentralized market economy should be used to analyse the interactions within a centralized planned economy; in such an economy, the accumulation motive and the contradictions of capitalism are absent, which were thought to make the general equilibrium framework unsuitable for analysis of capitalism. Those who now express Marxian theory in general equilibrium form are acting in the tradition of the deterministic aspect of Marxian theory, abstracting from the peculiar historical features of a particular economy's esperience. But, as long as it is used simply as a useful method for deriving the logical consequences of particular assumptions, rather than as an exclusive representation of Marxian theory, then Marxian general equilibrium analysis can be complementary to non-mathematical analysis of social relations (Harvey, 1982, p.44).

6.6   Conclusion

The way in which equilibrium is used in macroeconomic theory is of fundamental importance in determining the scope as much as the method of enquiry. By avoiding explicit use of the equilibrium concept, most neo-Austrians limit the generality of their theoretical statements. By concentrating on market process, their analysis is focused on the operations of particular markets at particular historical points in time. The scope for general statements comes from a faith in the beneficence of market forces which cannot be supported by any equilibrium analysis within the neo-Austrian framework. The accusations of nihilism tend to be reserved for those with a similar methodological position who do not share that faith (see, for example, Coddington's, 1982, position on Shackle). As Carvalho (1983–84) argues, neo-Austrian theorists using subjectivist expectational time equilibrium without a separate historical-time equilibrium analysis cannot make general statements about market co-ordination.

The general equilibrium framework of mainstream theory was designed to provide theoretical back-up for faith in market forces, or at least to specify the conditions which would justify that faith. The general equilibrium method is, however, hidebound by the conditions for good scientific analysis by Cartesian/ Euclidean criteria. A logical mathematical structure built on a set of axioms as to individual behaviour generates 'solutions' rather than causal statements about economic process. Within the model equilibrium is the normal state of affairs, and for consistency, individual behaviour must reflect that fact. There is no scope, therefore, for analysing disequilibrium behaviour, and thereby the process by which equilibrium is reached. The method allows conclusions to be reached about the effects on equilibrium of changes in exogenous variables. Scope for explanation is limited by the reliance on the exogeneity/endogeneity distinction combined with the purpose of endogenizing as many variables as possible. Without any direct correspondence between mechanical and historical time, the only logical criterion for accepting or rejecting the model as applicable to real-world situations is the instrumentalist one of the success of its predictions.

Much of the confusion about the significance of Keynes's work stems from a refusal among the orthodoxy to contemplate an alternative use of the equilibrium concept. This confusion was fuelled by Hicks's (1937) early attempt to express Keynes's departure from the orthodoxy using a logical time, general equilibrium framework, rather than the partial equilibrium use of logical time (which in any case formed only part of Keynes's method). That Keynes could not countenance this use of the equilibrium concept is made clear by the absence of effective communication between Keynes and Harrod on the subject of equilibrium in growth theory. The alternatives, being the partial equilibrium use of logical time and equilibrium defined as a centre of gravitation in historical time, place the *onus* of Post Keynesian analysis on causal forces and the process of gravitation respectively, rather than the state of rest. This is consistent with a view of market economies as being governed by the motive (among those with the economic power to exercise it) of accumulation, in the interests of which the economy is kept in perpetual motion. (The main likelihood of lack of motion is a stagnant state of unemployment equilibrium, where the forces for accumulation are incapable of instigating an upturn.) Equilibrium is used (both in logical and historical time) in a partial sense, isolating particular relationships from other influences. This practice is necessary if all influences are in fact viewed as endogenous over some period of time, including the tastes, technology and market institutions which are the givens of general equilibrium theory. The practical necessity of partial equilibrium analysis is reflected in the use by economic agents of concepts of 'normalcy' to provide an anchor (potentially mistaken) for behaviour in expectational time.

Insofar as Marxian theory can be interpreted in terms of equilibrium, the Marxian use of equilibrium is also a partial concept in logical time, or a notional concept situated in historical time. But it is in this case even more important as a benchmark for lack of equilibrium. Marxian analysis focuses on the contradictions inherent in capitalism; the resulting opposing forces periodically erupt in crisis. Crises are necessary to create the conditions for a subsequent period of unstable equilibrium. History in Marxian theory means something more than the passage of time, however; it is the vehicle for a dialectical process which eventually replaces capitalism with socialism. For those concentrating on the deterministic aspect of Marxian theory, mechanical time general equilibrium analysis has proved to be an appealing tool to use. But its application to particular historical situations is limited by the diversity of paths which capitalism has in fact taken in different countries. General equilibrium Marxian analysis is thus limited in its application to answering theoretical questions as to the eventual outcome given particular assumptions. In general terms, general equilibrium analysis is antipathetic to analysis of social relations as such.

The discussion of equilibrium remains incomplete, however. We have only alluded to the role of expectations so far, but they are of vital importance in providing the connection between the present and the unknown future in historical time. We turn now, in the next chapter, to see how the formation of expectations is modelled within each school of thought; we shall see here a powerful illustration of the significance of the distinction between mechanical, historical and expectational time.

7   Expectations

7.1   Introduction

In the last chapter it was shown that the meaning of equilibrium (as a state of rest) depends on the way in which time is incorporated into the theoretical framework. Once time is incorporated as a temporal concept (i.e. not as logical time, which specifies causal sequence rather than temporal sequence), questions arise as to how behaviour (in aggregate or individually) deals with time. In particular, since all actions are taken with respect to the future, expectations of that future will play an important role in governing behaviour from one period to the next.

Shackle's notion of expectional time deals most explicitly with expectations formation at the individual level; it is the discontinuous, subjective framework within which individuals order their expectations. But to derive macroeconomic conclusions, a more aggregative use of time is required within which the environment of individual expectations formation can be analysed. The two general categories of non-expectational time which have been used are historical time and mechanical time. The main distinction between the two is that the former is not reversible, while the latter is. As a corollary, expectations in one state with respect to a future state will in the former case not be symmetrical with expectations formed in that future state. In the latter case, comparative static analysis can compare a move from state A to state B with a reversal of that move, with expectations in state A with respect to state B influencing the first dynamic adjustment path, and expectations in state B with respect to state A influencing the reverse adjustment path. If the equilibrium solutions of state B and state A, respectively, are to be determinate, then so must the formation of expectations.

Analysis of individuals' capacity to formulate expectations has close parallels to economists' capacity to make predictions. The problem of induction necessarily limits the degree of certainty with which any expectation may be held. How far an individual can be sure of lack of knowledge depends on the scope given for creative behaviour. Boland (1982, Chapter 4) argues that we can be no more sure of a lack of knowledge than of knowledge. But if we allow for creative behaviour, generating new knowledge in the future with respect to new products and processes, then it follows that full knowledge of the future is logically impossible. The problem for the economist then is how to model behaviour based on incomplete knowledge. In fact the determinacy with which expectations are modelled depends significantly on whether scope is given for new information, rather than gradual acquisition of existing information.

A related determining factor in modelling expectations is the presumption, or otherwise, of market stability. If the theoretical framework is built on the premiss that parameters have values which ensure dynamic stability, it is natural to model individual behaviour as being based on the same presumption. But without the presumption of stability, i.e. if the theoretical framework allows for indeterminacy of outcomes, it is natural to model individual behaviour as reacting to that indeterminacy. Within a stable general equilibrium system, the nature of a new equilibrium state can be known from existing information combined with information about the exogenous shock which displaced the economy from its original equilibrium state. Thus individuals who acquire this information can in principle know what the equilibrium values of variables are. If, however, existing information is insufficient to determine the outcome of a shock to the system, because behaviour is creative, because there is no shared perception as to the stability of the system or its likely resting-place following the shock, or because expectations formation itself is indeterminate, then the actual outcome of the shock cannot be predicted deterministically.

These general considerations involved in incorporating expectations formation into macroeconomic theory leave scope for different ways of modelling expectations within the broad categories touched on so far. But these differences are still overwhelmed by the significance of the different views of time, and the consequent meaning and theoretical role of equilibrium.

7.2   Neo-Austrian Theory

Again, it seems natural to start with the neo-Austrians, since their theory emphasizes individuals' decision-making under conditions of uncertainty. In fact, however, it is only relatively recently that expectations have been given widespread attention within this school of thought. Lachmann (1976b) suggests that expectations were not previously a focus of analysis because of the influence of Hayek's early adherence to general equilibrium theory. While Hayek highlighted expectations as an important feature of decision-making, he presumed that they would converge, contributing to the fulfilment of the equilibrium conditions.

In fact, Hayek (1948) signalled his move away from general equilibrium analysis with his discussion of the role of expectations in the conditions for equilibrium. He specified 'correct anticipations' as a condition for equilibrium;

but he then proceeded to discuss 'anticipations' in the wider context of the acquisition of knowledge. The knowledge on which anticipations are based is necessarily incomplete (although individuals will generally attempt to acquire the knowledge most relevant to their actions). Thus Hayek did not draw a strict distinction between known facts about the past and unknown facts about the future. Rather, since all knowledge is subjective, incomplete knowledge about the future is in a similar dimension to incomplete knowledge about the past (see also Lachmann, 1943). It is thus likely that an additional reason why most neo-Austrians have only recently discussed expectations explicitly is because expectations had been subsumed in the general analysis of knowledge acquisition.

According to Littlechild (1978, p.21), neo-Austrians, since Mises, have shared the view that it is the purpose of economics to study the unintended consequences of actions, beyond those perceived by the actors. Here is the presumption that economists have access to a special kind of *a priori* knowledge which extends beyond that of individual economic agents, and allows more complete predictions to be made. It is the perception that actions in general have consequences which are either unintended by the actors themselves or unforeseen by other actors, which requires perpetual adjustment somewhere in the economic system. In Hayek's words: 'The point which we must constantly bear in mind is that economic adjustment is made necessary by unforeseen changes' (Hayek, 1972, p.107). Indeed, Hayek proceeds to point out that the stability of macroeconomic aggregates disguises the underlying continual adjustment of individual behaviour to changes in relative prices.

The emergence of a theory of expectations within the neo-Austrian school in the 1970s, as distinct from the general theory of knowledge, can be traced to two main causes. First, the rational expectations revolution was built initially on Austrian building blocks. The basic premiss is that rational individuals use all available information to generate expectations. More important, however, was the second cause, which was the recognition of the importance of Shackle's work on behaviour under conditions of uncertainty. While Shackle himself is not strictly neo-Austrian, he had been a student of Hayek's at the London School of Economics, and had absorbed an interest in neo-Austrian concerns. In turn, his work now constitutes the main inspiration for neo-Austrian thinking on expectations (Lachmann, 1976c).

First, Shackle's views are based on his conceptualization of the world as being 'kaleidic' (Shackle, 1972). A kaleidoscope is a pattern-creating device whereby movement will create a totally new pattern of coloured pieces, by means of mirrors. In the same way, Shackle sees the economy as being perceived as a series of patterns, each new pattern confounding expectations. The discontinuity of this kaleidic process corresponds to the discontinuous notion of expectational time.

Shackle then focuses on the question of how individuals form predictions on which to base decisions, within such a kaleidic world. As Keynes (1973a) had done in his work on probability, Shackle points out the severe limitations to numerical probability analysis as a basis for predictions. In particular, many 'experiments' are what he calls 'crucial' in the sense that conducting the experiment for the first time changes the environment for any further experiment, and thus prevents the derivation of a frequency distribution. An entrepreneur, for example, would regard the opening of a new plant as a crucial experiment. The availability of capital to finance future new plants, for a start, would be affected by the success or failure of the first experiment. Bank managers cannot be expected to extend finance indefinitely on equal terms to a large enough number of experimental investments to allow the entrepreneur to work out the probability of success of any one such investment. Indeed, the scope for the experiment itself to change the environment for future experiments is compounded by the scope for changes in the environment due to other causes. The entrepreneur must thus make a decision on the new plant independently of any probability distribution of the return on the investment.

Entrepreneurial decisions, in the absence of probability information, are made on the basis of the creative use of such knowledge as is available. New projects appear profitable which have not been attempted before because the necessary information was not available, or available information had not been combined in such a way as to point to the new project. The combination of information proceeds according to a theory, subjectively held by the entrepreneur, as to how the investment return is to be generated.

While probability of loss or gain cannot be used in decision-making, the possibility of gain or loss is clearly of importance. Shackle thus replaces the concept of probability with the concept of 'potential surprise'. Instead of saying that an outcome had 'low probability' Shackle would posit that the outcome would be 'very surprising', while a high probability outcome is replaced by an 'unsurprising' one. The concepts of probability and surprise are logically quite different. He illustrates his meaning with the example of a hat-box, of normal size. If the box were found to contain a bowler hat, or a top hat, or a panama, this would not be in the least surprising. If a picture hat were pulled out, however, this would be surprising, because it challenges the conventional notion of the size of hat kept in a normal hat-box. While any number of small hats would be unsurprising, they cannot each be assigned a probability of a hundred per cent; nor can they be assigned probabilities which sum to a hundred per cent, since that precludes any surprising outcome. Applying this argument to an entrepreneur, it may transpire that an outcome arises that had not originally been anticipated from a particular investment. There is no reason to change the original estimate of the degree of surprise which the original range of outcomes would have generated. But the surprise provides no reason to change behaviour, or the theory on which it is based (Shackle, 1955).

The notion of surprise is a purely subjective one. What would be surprising to one individual may be unsurprising to another; further the willingness to take actions whose consequences are potentially surprising (in a favourable or unfavourable direction) will differ from one individual to another. But it is the emergence of surprising outcomes which puts psychological pressure on individuals to change their belief system about the way in which the economy works. It is the incidence of surprise which forces the periodic adjustment of behaviour (while Hayek had regarded behavioural adjustment as being continuous). The stock market, for example, operates on the basis of diverse expectations, co-ordinating 'bulls' who buy with 'bears' who sell; the periodic revision of expectations which results from surprises (which are inevitable given diverse expectations) makes the market restless.

Where Shackle diverges from the neo-Austrian tradition is in his conclusion that market processes are not necessarily orderly. 'External events' which conflict with anticipated events, in Hayek's view, immediately produce a reaction on the part of individuals in the direction of efficient resource allocation, given the new circumstances. In Shackle's world, individuals only react to events which are surprising, relative to a subjective evaluation of potential surprise. This implies both a sluggishness and discontinuity of response to new information. Further, if expectations of the degree of surprise which would arise from the range of possible outcomes influence all decision-making, it cannot be maintained that decisions are made only on the basis of relative prices which have arisen in the past. The restlessness of markets where divergent expectations are the norm – financial markets, for example – cannot be guaranteed to generate that adjustment of individual behaviour which would ensure the most efficient allocation of resources. Within a general equilibrium framework, diversity of information can be shown to be consistent with optimal outcomes (reflecting optimal decisions with respect to information costs) (Grossman and Stiglitz, 1980). But, while neo-Austrians have traditionally expressed faith in the beneficence of market forces with or without a general equilibrium concept in the background, Shackle raises questions about that faith.

Lachmann (1956) addresses the problem of potentially divergent expectations and concludes that market institutions have developed in such a way as to promote convergence. Consistently mistaken expectations on the part of any individual, for example, will cause their removal from the market if the outcome is less favourable than the expectation. Further, futures markets emerge to ensure convergence through the price system. Thus Lachmann expresses his faith in markets at a deeper level; it is a faith that institutions react to divergent expectations by eliminating their scope. Again, Shackle would not necessarily share this faith.

Nevertheless, Shackle is repeatedly mentioned by neo-Austrians as a descendent of the original Austrians (Littlechild, 1978, p.16) or as a current influence (Lachmann, 1976c). While his radical subjectivity has most in common with the neo-Austrians, we shall see that many of Shackle's concepts (if not the full force of his analysis) contribute also to the Post Keynesian theory of expectations formation at the micro level. But, just as the early adherence to general equilibrium analysis coloured neo-Austrian thinking on expectations, we consider next how expectations have fared in the mainstream general equilibrium framework as it was developed to encompass macroeconomic analysis.

7.3   Mainstream Theory

The first method employed for modelling expectations formation within the mainstream framework was adaptive expectations. The essence of this method is that there is a lagged adjustment in expectations formation to the emergence of new information. The extreme case is the cobweb model, where producers (particularly of agricultural products) assume that the next period's price will be the same as the current price. If the system starts in disequilibrium, with demand not equal to supply, then this assumption generates conditions which change the price level in the next period. If the cobweb is stable, then the oscillation in the price level gets progressively smaller, and eventually settles at the market-clearing level; otherwise, the oscillations get progressively larger and the market 'explodes'.

The more sophisticated version of this model, which was developed in macroeconomic analysis in the 1950s and 1960s, took a form which was used in a wide range of applications in addition to expectations formation. The expected value of a variable was modelled by a distributed lag function applied to past values of that variable. In other words, the price level expected in the next period is a fixed proportion of the price level in the current period, plus a smaller fixed proportion of the previous period's price level, and so on for a number of periods. In the same way Friedman (1957) defined permanent income as a distributed lag of income levels over a range of periods past, and Jorgenson (1963) measured investment demand as a distributed lag of past income levels.

The rationale was that expectations adapted only gradually to new information. If we define $_tP^e_{t-1}$ as the price level expected, in period t, to hold in period $(t-1)$, P_t as the actual price level in period t, and λ as a fixed positive fraction, then expectations are formed as follows:

$$_tP^e_{t+1} - {}_{t-1}P^e_t = \lambda \, (P_t - {}_{t-1}P^e_t) \quad 0<\lambda<1. \tag{7.1}$$

If, for example, the actual price level at time t, P_t, was 100, but had been expected in the previous period $(_{t-1}P^e_t)$ to be 96, then the price level expected for period $(t-1)$, $_tP^e_{t+1}$, would be some fraction, λ of four greater than $_{t-1}P_t$; if λ was one-half, then the price level expected for the next period would be 98, even though the actual price level had already reached 100.

If we take $_{t-1}P^e_t$ across to the right-hand side of the equation, then $_tP^e_{t-1}$ is jointly determined by the price level in the current period and the price level expected for that period, together with the coefficient of adaptation, λ. But then the price level expected for period t could also be expressed as a function of the actual and expected price levels for the previous period. Indeed, since every expectational variable is determined by past actual and expected values of variables, then they can also be expressed as functions of past actual levels of variables alone, i.e. by a distributed lag structure. From equation (7.1) we can thus derive the following:

$$_tP^e_{t+1} = \lambda P_t + \lambda (1-\lambda) P_{t-1} + \lambda (1-\lambda)^2 P_{t-2} + ... 0<\lambda<1. \tag{7.2}$$

This method was first used for price level expectations by Cagan (1956), and became the standard expectations-formation model until the growing popularity of rational expectations in the 1970s. It provided the means for dealing with situations where the price level was changing sufficiently fast for the divergence between actual and expected values to be significant. It provided also a systematic treatment of expectations formation within mechanical time, incorporating behaviour in response to expectational errors. The adaptive expectations method was used, and developed, primarily in econometric work; before the concern with micro-foundations developed in the 1960s and 1970s, econometric macro models were the main focus of theory development. The primary criterion was the instrumentalist one, and adaptive expectations had significant predictive success.

The popularization of rational expectations theory grew out of the concern that adaptive expectations could not be explained by the axioms for rational individual behaviour. Why should individuals not immediately use to the full whatever information was available? The systematic errors postulated by the adaptive expectations method suggested that individuals were not maximizing utility by making maximum use of available information. But in spite of this critique, adaptive expectations continued to be used by many mainstream theorists, primarily those using disequilibrium models. Before turning to rational expectations, therefore, we consider further the case to be made for adaptive expectations.

First, the environment in which they were first introduced was one of mild cycles around a steady growth path; both the price level and the rate of unemployment were relatively stable in the 1950s and 1960s. In that type of situation, it is more reasonable for behaviour to be governed by the trend than by minor fluctuations, than if the cyclical pattern is more violent. Indeed, if expectations did not adapt fully to each fluctuation, that could in itself help to dampen the fluctuation. For example, if entrepreneurs responded to an unexpected rise in income with only a moderate rise in investment, then the upturn would be more damped than if investment demand adapted fully to the income rise. Indeed, even when cycles are more marked, there is confusion about whether changes are transitory (cyclical) or 'permanent'; on average, expectations will only partially respond to a variable change (Laidler, 1981).

It must be remembered, however, that a distributed lag does not necessarily measure expectations adaptation; it is simply lagged values of the variable with declining weights ($\lambda, \lambda(\lambda-1), \lambda(\lambda-1)^2 \dots$). The empirical success of the model might be due to the correlation of variables with their past values for reasons other than expectations formation. It is a general problem within economics that it is impossible categorically to identify causal relationships. But it is a particularly serious problem in this case where the distributed lag function is so successful econometrically, whether as a proxy for expectations or not.

But additional reasons have been adduced to justify applying adaptive expectations particularly to labour market analysis, in such a way as not to counter the axioms of rational behaviour. First, there are practical considerations to take into account when considering the institution of wage settlements. These are generally established for a contract period of at least a year. During a period of inflation only those workers whose contracts are up for renewal can act to protect their real wage. But at any one time, most workers will be tied to a contract which may have underestimated inflation. The lag observed in labour's response to mistaken expectations may then be purely the result of the institutional lag before they can act on the new information. Such wage contracts can be viewed as being rational according to the axioms for rational economic behaviour if they are voluntarily entered into by both sides as a means of sharing risk (where there is a perception of risk of inflation being overestimated as well as underestimated).

Second, there is the possibility of money illusion among workers, i.e. they perceive a fall in the price level only after a lag. This is the crucial assumption in the monetarist account of Phillips curve analysis. An expansion of output can be undertaken following an increase in the money supply only if additional labour is forthcoming. Firms can attract more labour at higher money wages, when even higher price increases are underway, only if labour fails to perceive that the real wage has not risen, i.e. only if they suffer from money illusion. After a lag, the erosion of the real wage is correctly perceived, the supply of labour contracts again, and employment and output return to their earlier levels. Cyclical employment and output can thus be explained by the slowness of labour to adjust to new information about the general price level.

The assumption of money illusion is regarded by rational expectations theorists as irrational, constituting an *ad hoc* adjustment to macro models, insufficiently backed up with micro-foundations. But slow responses can still be justified on the grounds of imperfect information (Laidler, 1981). Employers, for example, have control over, as well as current information on, their product prices; these are the prices relevant to their price level expectations for the purposes of calculating the real wage. Workers on the other hand are interested in the general price level, over which they have no control and only partial information *ex post*. This difference alone would account for their different degree of adjustment to the changing conditions of the cycle. More generally, inadequate information could account for general behaviour along adaptive expectations lines, where expectations are formed by habit and convention, and new information is assimilated with caution.

This argument sounds rather Keynesian, and indeed adaptive expectations have been employed primarily in disequilibrium, neo-classical synthesis macro models which are labelled 'Keynesian'. But, while there are some elements in common with Keynes's theory of expectations, these elements take on a different character when incorporated in a mechanical time, general equilibrium framework. Most important, expectations are passive rather than active in this setting. They are only important in response to an exogenous shock to the system; they cannot by themselves instigate a change in direction for the economy. It follows that, once expectations are explained endogenously, they can only influence the path returning to equilibrium, following an exogenous shock.

Now it is understandable why it should be regarded as important within this axiomatic framework to endogenize expectations. If some elements of expectations are not explained by the economic variables in the model, then it is tantamount to admitting that they cannot be said to be derived from the rationality axioms. Coddington (1982) has taken this argument to its logical conclusion. If we insist on keeping some element of expectations exogenous, he argues, then we are admitting to some non-rational behaviour. If economic agents are non-rational in this respect, then there can be no assurance that they are rational in any other respects; economists could form no conclusions at all as to individual behaviour.

The alternative to this nihilism, within the general equilibrium framework, is to explain all expectations within the model (except, perhaps, for a stochastic element). Expectations' only role in that case is to govern the way in which individuals adjust their behaviour in a disequilibrium state caused by some other, exogenous, factor. Not only must expectations formation be fully determined within the model, but they are constrained also by the stability requirements of the model. Even those attempting to explain persistent unemployment do not envisage a perpetual downward, or upward spiral. Given the observed relative stability of capitalist economies, or, at worst, their sluggishness, it is conventional to model expectations in such a way as to ensure a return to equilibrium. In general, models do not have the coefficient of adaptation taking a value of unity (the cobweb theorem case) with elasticity conditions such as to generate an exploding system. By imposing stability conditions, adaptive expectations theorists provide a means of modelling behaviour which takes account of mistaken expectations, and does not conflict with the presumption that market forces return the system to equilibrium.

Rational expectations theorists reacted to adaptive expectations in the same way as 'pure' general equilibrium theorists reacted to disequilibrium analysis in general. Just as wage rigidity was dismissed as an *ad hoc* way of explaining unemployment, adaptive expectations was dismissed as an *ad hoc* way of explaining relative rigidity of wages. The movement away from adaptive expectations was part and parcel of the move to express macroeconomics in terms of a full general equilibrium system, grounded explicitly in neo-classical micro-foundations. It was certainly the case that, if adaptive expectations theorists insisted on the rationality of the behaviour they were modelling at the macro level, then a similar notion of rationality should have pervaded their microeconomics also. Now in fact, since adaptive expectations simply define the path of adjustment from one equilibrium to another, the effect of specifying that path in microeconomics also would not have brought about a fundamental change in microeconomic analysis; it would simply have to be accepted that markets would take several periods of mechanical time before clearing. The case of adaptive expectations was weakened, however, by the unwillingness to press it to its logical conclusion at the microeconomic level.

But, in any case, rational expectations theorists consider adaptive expectations to be irrational, and therefore not sustainable at either the macro or micro level. If individuals are rational, then they make optimal use of available information equating the marginal cost of acquiring information to the marginal benefit it provides, and avoiding systematic errors. Optimizing individuals taking full advantage of all trading opportunities are in equilibrium (otherwise there would be unexploited opportunities). Thus their expectations are fulfilled; in contrast, adaptive expectations are unfulfilled until the final equilibrium position is reached. Rational expectations is thus the natural method of modelling expectations which deals with temporary equilibrium positions, between which there is change of which expectations are relevant, but which ensures that expectations at each temporary equilibrium are fulfilled.

Laidler (1981) describes rational expectations theory as 'neo-Austrian', and indeed the original influence was from that quarter (as was the general concern over micro-foundations) although the general equilibrium framework has profoundly affected the expression of that neo-Austrian influence (see also Kantor, 1979). The originator of the rational expectations concept within general equilibrium analysis was Muth (1961), who had worked on an inventories study with Herbert Simon, employing behavioural analysis. Simon's views of managerial behaviour started with the limitations on information, which constrained the degree to which behaviour could be rational in the sense of the neo-classical concept of rational economic man. Instead, Simon (1955) suggested that behaviour is determined by 'bounded rationality', i.e. it is rational given the limits on available information. He later (Simon, 1976) further developed this notion to distinguish between substantive rationality, the pursuit of goals subject to constraints, and procedural rationality, referring to the reasoned processing of information. Individuals make full use of information, but what is available is limited for any one individual, and differs as between individuals.

Muth absorbed the significance of information processing for expectations formation, and modelled it in such a way as to incorporate it into the 'substantive rationality' context of constrained maximization analysis set in mechanical time. The notion that individuals make full use of available information (which contrasts with adaptive expectations) is a description of 'reasonable' behaviour to which neo-Austrians and Post Keynesians also subscribe. But the nature of reasonable behaviour is severely constrained if disappointment of expectations is limited to stochastic deviation. By definition, expectations must be correct, given available information, in the sense of being distributed normally around the 'correct' prediction. Expectations need not be correct in the sense that the outcome in the next period must be what was expected in the first period; as long as the available information is incomplete, any equilibrium will be only temporary. But within any one period of mechanical time, individual actions based on rational expectations must produce an outcome in that period which accords with those expectations. In the long run, the only information which is not available must take the form of random shocks; systematic shocks, like a government announcement of monetary target, will be absorbed into individuals' expectations, allowing swift movement through a series of temporary equilibria to the new equilibrium. Only random changes in the money supply can avoid being incorporated into expectations, and thus continually disturb the economy away from long-run equilibrium. This has strong policy implications (to be explored in chapter nine) since money supply changes can only alter the level of output and employment to the extent that they can move the economy persistently away from long-run equilibrium (Lucas, 1977).

If expectations are (on average, i.e. aside from stochastic deviation) to be satisfied given available information, then they must conform to the same probability distribution as the predictions of an economic model using the same range of information. The weak rational expectations hypothesis states that expectations are equal to the unbiased forecasts of any macroeconomic model; the strong hypothesis limits expectations to the forecasts of only one 'correct' model of the economy. The model on which expectations are based is thus crucial to the analysis.

The rational expectations depiction of human behaviour is not intended to be realistic (Lucas, 1980). Indeed the approach is instrumental, resting its case on the success of its empirical findings (Lucas and Sargent, 1981). Since individuals are modelled as making unbiased forecasts, i.e. as avoiding systematic error, then so must the model on which their forecasts are based. No econometric model ever achieves completeness in the sense of explaining all variation in the value of a variable other than stochastic variation. It is well known that an econometrician cannot capture the full complexity of an economic system in a model, certainly prospectively, but also retrospectively. In other words, probabilistic predictions, by definition, cannot be expected to be completely satisfactory. The value of econometrics lies in its capacity to enhance our knowledge of economic relationships, but no serious econometrician would pretend to the ability to make consistently unbiased predictions. And indeed, rational expectations econometricians have not been noticeably more successful than any others in avoiding systematic error.

Testing the validity of any theory is prone to difficulties (see Desai, 1981, and Pesaran, 1982, for discussions of the difficulties in this particular case). But the empirical success of the rational expectations hypothesis is methodologically crucial because it is that model itself which is said to generate individuals' predictions. Once the analysis is limited to econometric analysis, there is no scope for the weak rational expectations hypothesis, since any model can only allow for itself being the correct model, so all hinges on the success of the rational espectations model's predictions. If, as is often the case, the model itself makes systematic errors, then it fails by its own criteria.

Adaptive expectations theorists further point out the difficulties involved in specifying the time period over which expectations are rational (see, for example, Laidler, 1981). No period of calendar time is made explicit in the model, implying that there may be an intermediate period during which expectations are not 'rational' in the sense of the hypothesis, as long as expectations are rational by the end of the period. This is a general problem associated with testing a theory in historical time when the theory has been formulated in mechanical time; the two are not logically compatible. Of course, the implication drawn by adaptive expectations theorists is that rational expectations only refer to full equilibrium, while intermediate positions are disequilibrium positions. Rational expectations theorists have, however, in fact expressed the policy implications of their hypothesis in terms of calendar time, implying that their hypothesis itself refers to calendar time and that expectations are always formed 'as if' according to the rational expectations hypothesis.

While the hypothesis is intended to stand or fall on the basis of its predictive success, it has so far proved difficult to establish that success. It remains, then, to consider the hypothesis in terms of its internal logic. Certainly, it completes the picture of general equilibrium micro-foundations for macroeconomics which accord closely with the axioms for rational behaviour. Maximizing behaviour certainly must extend to the acquisition and use of information. Further, if only equilibrium positions are admissible, given this maximizing behaviour, then all expectations must be fulfilled, i.e. be proved correct (allowing for stochastic deviation). Expectations are thus if anything more passive than in the adaptive expectations framework. The only scope for shocking the system is given to those exogenous variables which do not impinge systematically on individual experience, while expectations have been endogenized. Unless the system is unstable, rational expectations serve only to propel the system towards full equilibrium. A variable only deviates from its equilibrium value due to some exogenous shock. If all individuals believe the economy to be stable, their actions will ensure that stability. For example, if a share price rises due to an exogenous shock, and people believe the market in that share to be stable, they will sell the share at its high price, expecting it to fall, and so it will.

Suppose, however, the economic system is dynamically unstable; there is nothing inherent in the rational expectations hypothesis to rule out instability. Then rational expectations will anticipate this instability – an inflationary spiral, for example. Workers would not supply labour unless money wages kept up with anticipated inflation, and so the inflationary spiral would indeed occur. But there is no longer the coincidence between individual and collective rationality that is implicit in rational expectations analysis. In this case, collective rationality would justify government intervention, in the form of a prices and incomes policy possibly to produce the socially-desirable outcome of stopping the inflationary spiral of which individual rational activity is incapable. Thus, the strong results of the hypothesis stem from the initial position that the economy is dynamically stable, with collective and individual rationality coinciding (see Evans, 1984, and other contributions in Frydman and Phelps, 1984). In other words, the strong policy results associated with the rational expectations hypothesis depend on the world conforming to a stable general equilibrium model.

In turn, a stable general equilibrium model requires stringent conditions to be placed on expectations formation. At an early date, Hahn (1952) demonstrated that the equilibrium framework required some mechanism for expectations to converge; otherwise, disparate and divergent expectations would induce actions which could not be counted on to ensure the efficient allocation of resources. Thus, equilibrium analysis could only be employed if there were some way of creating a market in future trades, whose price could perform the same market-clearing function as in the Walrasian process of clearing a market in current goods. Thus, general equilibrium analysis could only be applied to goods with futures market, i.e. only to a limited range of goods.

These considerations limit the scope of the expectations analysis, rather than question its logic. And indeed Hahn has chosen to forego general equilibrium macroeconomics rather than pay the price of accepting rational expectations (Hahn, 1977, 1983). There is, however, one important logical conundrum associated with the hypothesis of maximizing behaviour as applied to information gathering. Individuals are depicted as equating the marginal cost of acquiring information with the marginal benefit to be derived from the information itself. But how can anyone possibly know the marginal benefit to be derived from information until she knows what it is? In the world of rational expectations hypothesis, the purpose of positing maximizing information-gathering behaviour can only be to provide a reason for expectations not to be based on complete information – the marginal cost of learning is too great. But if the marginal benefit from information is known, that information can only take a limited range of forms. It can only refer to the values of particular variables, not to anything outside the range of variables employed in a rational expectations model for example. Again, we have reinforcement of the view that it is the rational expectations model itself which is being presented as a 'correct' account of economic relationships; it is only logically consistent with a stable general equilibrium system where relative prices are the only variables relevant to economic agents.

The rational expectations hypothesis is, as its proponents claim, the apotheosis of the general equilibrium framework in the sense that it allows macroeconomic results to be generated from the axioms of rational behaviour. The individual information-gathering and predicting behaviour, as modelled, is totally consistent with the theorist's view of her own behaviour in gathering data and making predictions. If the relevant information for making predictions is that employed in a closed deterministic model, data which are published, then it is only rational for non-economists to acquire the same information (unless the marginal cost of acquiring data is too high). While the view of rational individual behaviour has similar roots to the neo-Austrian view, once that behaviour is couched in general equilibrium terms, there is no possibility for individuals to exercise imagination, or even different degrees of alertness; all they can do with respect to the future is to act passively in response to exogenous shocks. Muth (1961) described individuals as 'purposeful', but pursuit of their purposes is laid down by the maximization calculus as applied to the 'correct' model of the economy.

There has certainly been a rational expectations revolution in the sense that it is now the dominant model of expectations formation; even most New Keynesian models use rational expectations; the rational expectations method has more general application than that employed by the New Classicists (see Begg, 1982; Frydman and Phelps, 1984, for example). Indeed it adds a new range of interesting challenges to the general equilibrium school of thought, one which satisfies Johnson's (1971) criteria for a paradigm change: the appearance of the overthrow of an orthodoxy, difficult techniques which allow younger members of the profession to excel relative to their elders trained for different methods, and so on. But there has been no paradigm change in fact, since the rational expectations hypothesis has simply taken the prevailing orthodoxy as applied to macroeconomics to its logical conclusion.

Consistent also with the Cartesian/Euclidean mode of thought, rational expectations theorists stress the continuity of economics as a science, presenting the rational expectations hypothesis as another step towards the ideal economic model. Thus Lucas (1980) and Begg (1982) see rational expectations as having superseded Keynes's theory of expectations formation. Rational expectations have made that theory 'operational' by endogenizing the process of expectations formation. Most of the effective critiques of the rational expectations hypothesis have, however, come from the Post Keynesian school, which suggests that they do not share Lucas's and Begg's view. We now explore the Post Keynesian position on expectations.

7.4   Post Keynesian Theory

Set in a context of historical time, Post Keynesian expectations have a different role to play from expectations in the mainstream framework. Actual economic behaviour, in historical time, cannot be guided by the periodic settlements of account which occur at the conclusion of each period of mechanical time in the general equilibrium framework. The function of expectations in the latter framework is to determine the adjustment path from one period of mechanical time to the next, until full general equilibrium is reached. In the Post Keynesian framework, they determine behaviour in a context of perpetual absence of equilibrium. The problem is not simply the Clower problem whereby employers determine the level of current output on the basis of their *perceptions* of the level of demand. Corporations must determine their investment plans on the basis of expectations of demand for their products, for which there may not yet be a market, and for which the current level of output and employment can offer no useful guide. Yet it is the level of investment which is regarded as the most important determinant of the current level of output and employment. Expectations are not something to be added into the Post Keynesian model, but rather an inherent feature (even when expectations are 'given').

While Keynes did not share the radical subjectivism of the Austrians, nor did he share the objectivism of mainstream theorists. Avoiding dualism, Keynes accepted the existence of objective facts, but also the subjectivity with which they are observed, or absorbed into arguments; knowledge is then neither objective nor subjective. Thus, for example, a corporation's sales figures for the previous year are objective facts (not necessarily totally accurate), but the interpretation of these facts and their use in predictions of sales figures for next year necessarily involve judgement. While any individual's argument is thus subjective in this sense, Keynes still maintained that it is always susceptible to rational discussion; the more weighty a counter-argument, the more likely the individual is to reject her initial argument. Indeed Keynes's (1973a) work on probability led him to consider probability in a sense other than a numerical property of frequency distributions. For practical purposes, individuals form a qualitative view as to the probability of a particular outcome, given the available, limited, state of knowledge. Probability in this sense has more to do with the process of persuasion and argument than with mechanistic experimentation (Carabelli, 1985).

Keynes stressed the limitations on numerical probabilistic statements, because of the general lack of experimental data. At the same time, he was conscious of the significance of changing structure; even if numerical probabilistic statements could be made, how would it be possible to translate these into predictions within a context which had changed from that of the experiments? It was this concern which underlay much of Keynes's reservations about econometric methods (Lawson, 1985a; Pesaran and Smith, 1985). Keynes therefore turned the issue on its head. Starting from the premiss that the economic environment is continually changing in a way which cannot be captured by deterministic models, a prediction carries more weight the more successful it is in spite of this changing environment. Keynes's method was thus to accept that the changing structure of the economy was too complex to model, and to look for regularities which transcended these changes. The consumption function was one such regularity (which he still qualified with a listing of factors which could disturb that regularity). It is this search for regularities which motivates much of the long-period Post Keynesian analysis. It is also the explanation which Keynes provides for individuals' behaviour in attempting to form expectations in an uncertain world.

The Post Keynesian use of the term 'uncertain' is different from the general equilibrium usage. When Tobin, for example, talks of uncertainty, he means that the future value of a variable is unknown, although its probability distribution is known. Post Keynesian uncertainty means that the numerical probability distribution is not known either; without the relevant frequency distribution on which to base a numerical probability estimate probability is assessed on the basis of whatever knowledge is available. Risk refers to the expected standard deviation around the expected mean value, where numerical frequency distributions are available. But in the Keynesian case, if the expectation of either mean or variance is subject to uncertainty, or lack of confidence, so is the estimate of risk itself. (See Keynes, 1937, for his clearest statement on uncertainty. See Lawson, 1985, for an analysis of the connection between Keynes's theories of probaaility and expectations.)

Confidence in a prediction depends on a judgemental weighing up of relevant evidence in relation to perceived ignorance, and thus is non-deterministic (Dow, 1995). Changes in mood can thus alter expectations fundamentally, with widespread consequences for economic activity. Keynes (1936, Chapter 12) emphasised this point with respect to the 'animal spirits' of entrepreneurs, which ultimately governed their decisions to invest. Coddington (1982) argues, in terms of a dualistic model of thought, that if 'irrational' subjective elements governed one set of expectations, then they must also influence other expectations. If entrepreneurial expectations are to be treated as exogenous, then so must consumer and government expectations, by which time economists would be unable to say anything definitive at all about individual behaviour. Post Keynesian methodology, however, does not force sharp, and uniform, choices between duals. Instead, expectations can be treated differently in different contexts.

First, since group as well as individual behaviour is an acceptable unit of study, it is possible that expectations formation can be studied separately on a group basis. Thus, for example, consumer behaviour is governed by different sets of group *mores* than investment behaviour (see Runde, 1991). Consumption is largely socially determined, with consumers also subject to common external influences through advertising, reinforcing peer pressure. Widespread fear of redundancy, for example, can make reduced consumption of particular items socially acceptable, which would not be regarded as acceptable in a generally buoyant labour market. Entrepreneurs, corporate managers and financial investors also each have group *mores*, as well as common channels of information and communication on which to base their expectations. Financial markets are particularly susceptible to group expectations, since it is the actions of the majority which determine the actual outcome. This is not to rule out individualistic behaviour – attempts to beat the market – but to stress the powerful role of the group in generating expectations for the individual. It is thus legitimate to consider separately the expectations formation of each of these groups.

Second, the type of uncertainty which each group faces is different. Entrepreneurs considering a project using a new production process or new product face an extreme form of uncertainty; the relevant time horizon over which the project will actually start generating output could be a number of years, during which new and different processes or products could be introduced. Also, such events would seriously affect the value of the assets purchased by the firm already committed to its new project. In contrast, current consumption is much less exposed to surprise. Not only is the scope for the introduction of new products limited in the time between purchase and consumption, but the consequence of a (retrospective) consumer mistake is limited by the consumer's spending capacity, and is likely to be relatively minor. The expectation of a consumer about the attributes of a consumer good involves subjectivity, as does the entrepreneur's expectation of return on the investment, but the former is much less open to violent shifts, on an individual or group basis. The role of expectations is thus not as major for consumer behaviour as for investor behaviour for the purposes of macroeconomics. (This argument refers purely to current consumption; consumer durables expenditure is better classified as investment, being, apart from anything else, subject to greater uncertainty than current consumption expenditure.)

Third, the variables for which expectations are relevant to different groups of decision-makers may be conducive to different forms of modelling, particularly for empirical purposes. For example, the general price level is an important variable for workers in collective bargaining. Past rates of inflation (possibly combined with information on current cost and demand conditions) provide considerable guidance in predicting future rates of inflation; except in hyperinflationary conditions, the range of possible inflation rates is fairly limited. Further, the consequences of disappointed expectations are a shortfall of real income by the degree of the forecast error. It is not at all coincidental that the attempts to systematize expectations formation in the neo-classical synthesis should have concentrated on price level expectations; they lend themselves most easily to extrapolation from past experience (which is the only information available to work with).

Investors' 'animal spirits' cannot be satisfactorily analysed in this way, and the macroeconomic consequences of capturing only the stable element in animal spirits are serious. The accelerator model has been used to systematize as much of investors' decision-making as possible (Hicks, 1980–81, p.140). But the essence of animal spirits is the necessarily large component of judgement in long-term forecasts of returns to real assets. Animal spirits can only be forecast with the aid of observations on the 'mood' of entrepreneurs. They may be stable for some time, expectations themselves being generated by past experience; but if past experience does not prepare entrepreneurs for surprises, then these surprises will cause a shift in expectations and thus in investment plans. For the purposes of stabilisation policy, it is important for these shifts to be picked up quickly by economic analysts, because the consequences are so major for the level of output and employment. For the entrepreneur, the 'surprise' can consist of huge capital losses and the threat of bankruptcy. This is more significant for the macro economy (though less significant at a human level) than an unexpected fall in real income of workers by a few percentage points. For these reasons, it is legitimate to employ different techniques for modelling expectations formation with respect to different variables.

Keynes (1936, Chapter 12) focused on two major categories of expectations: long-run and short-run expectations. The former are relevant to the purchase of relatively illiquid assets, intended for holding for periods of years, while the latter are relevant to the purchase of assets held with a view to sale for capital gain (or of inputs to current production). The scope for the latter type of purchase is greater the greater the degree of sophistication of financial markets. Within a developed monetary economy, long-run and short-run expectations come together in the choice of entrepreneurs between purchasing new or existing capital goods, or to postpone investment by purchasing financial assets, and the choices of financial investors as to the provision of finance for entrepreneurs or for other financial investors (or not at all). It is the outcome of all these choices, which depend on the prevailing sets of long-run and short-run expectations, and the confidence held in them, which determines the willingness and financial capacity to purchase new capital goods, and thereby determines the level of output and employment.

To the extent that shareholders are the owners of the means of production, the existence of active stock markets ensures that it is short-run expectations which are relevant to those seeking capital gain. Long-run expectations as to the yield on assets over their lifetime are the main preserve of entrepreneurs, or business managers. Most plant and machinery is sufficiently illiquid that it will normally not be purchased with a view to capital gain on resale. A new investment will be undertaken if the expected yield is favourable. The expected yield of an addition to the capital stock is the marginal efficiency of investment, which differs from the neo-classical marginal physical product of capital by being a judgemental, nominal value. The marginal efficiency of investment (i.e. of a change in the stock of capital) is lower the larger the capital stock to the extent that supply constraints in the capital-goods sector will eventually cause the supply price of capital goods to rise. In addition, as long as output markets are not competitive, output prices may fall as output increases to the new capacity. (The neo-classical marginal physical product in contrast falls as the stock of capital rises due to the law of diminishing marginal returns to a factor.) But the position of the marginal efficiency of capital curve, which influences the position of the marginal efficiency of investment curve, is determined by the state of long-run expectations, which is essentially a judgemental evaluation of future events which cannot be captured by numerical probability analysis.

The marginal efficiency of investment (MEI) is favourable if it is high relative to other returns, particularly the rate of interest on bonds. The comparison with the rate of interest may arise from its role as the cost of borrowed funds, or because it represents the opportunity cost of employing money to finance new investment in capital goods. This comparison of rates of return has caused some unease among Post Keynesians who want to get away from anything similar to the marginal decision-making in the neo-classical model, which has endogenised the investment decision. Minsky (1975) succeeds in de-emphasizing the MEI/ interest rate comparison by expressing the expected return on a capital good purchase in capitalized form, which generates the demand price which entrepreneurs would be willing to pay for new capital goods. As long as this exceeds the supply price of capital goods, the investment plan will proceed. The capitalization factor could of course be the going rate of interest, but it could alternatively incorporate the subjective liquidity preference of the entrepreneur.

But the investment decision is still exogenous in that it depends ultimately on animal spirits, a shift in which will alter investment plans irrespective of the interest rate. The long-run expectations which govern the MEI calculation for a particular investment would normally be stable once formed, in the sense that, even if they were to prove mistaken, the investment would already be in place; i.e. they would be stable over the relevant period for aggregate investment demand. Nevertheless, widespread mistakes would prompt a reassessment of future investment strategies, and could thus generate sharp changes in investment plans. Shackle's theory of individuals' retention of a stratagem for behaviour until confronted by a 'surprise', provides a useful framework for analysing long-run expectations. Information on the incidence of bankruptcies, or of abnormally high rates of profit, for example, would be signals for shifts in long-term expectations. But investment behaviour is not independent of short-run expectations, which govern both the rate of interest and the returns on other assets, as well as the market's current valuation of the shares of investing companies. Keynes's best-known examples of uncertainty referred to long-run outcomes: the price of copper twenty years hence, for example. But uncertainty, in the sense of lack of confidence in one's predictions, is equally applicable to short-run expectations where it is crucial to predict turning-points. Stock prices, for example, can fairly safely be predicted to be within a given range on any one day. (Ease of purchase and resale make the long-run price irrelevant to the majority of traders in the stock market.) For a trader, it is the point at which a price stops falling and starts rising that buying action must be taken, while sales should be made when prices stop rising and start falling, if capital gains are to be maximized and losses minimized. Expectations as to the exact day on which the market turns, just as expectations as to the price of copper twenty years hence, are things that 'we simply do not know' (Keynes, 1937, p.214).

In a general equilibrium world, where traders recognize that the world is so, share prices only rise because of an unanticipated exogenous shock. The turning-point occurs when traders' expectations adjust and the return to equilibrium can commence. Without a general equilibrium framework, there is no rational basis for the turning-point to occur at any particular time or at any particular price. All depends on the judgemental evaluations of individual traders, and their perceptions of each other's evaluations. Yet it is the prices determined in stock markets which determine the cost of buying title to existing plant and machinery as an alternative to buying new plant and machinery.

This line of argument can be applied to any financial market. Since each participant has only limited access to objective knowledge which is relevant to asset prices in the future, asset price expectations must of necessity be largely judgemental. Markets are not totally unruly since there are group habits and conventions which govern behaviour; also, facts held with a high degree of certainty enter into the process of expectations formation. Nevertheless, this group behaviour can be destabilizing, since it serves to reinforce any market discontinuity which is generally agreed to be a turning point.

As we shall discuss in more detail in Chapter 8, the role of money is essential to such market conditions. The greater the uncertainty attached to any prediction, the greater the unwillingness to commit resources where the outcome is very unsure. Money is the asset whose return is known, in money terms, and which allows postponement of decisions with respect to other assets. The rate of interest, the price of money, is thus also a judgemental variable, since it includes the premium attached to liquidity. In short, if economists and economic agents alike do not view the world as a general equilibrium system, then expectations are conditioned by the uncertainty with which they are held. While past events influence these expectations, the past is a poor guide to the future in many instances. Where expectations can reasonably be based on past experience, and where actions are conditioned by habits and conventions, expectations do not take an active role in the Keynesian framework. But in asset markets, where speculation about future asset values is central, uncertainty about these values can make expectations unstable in the face of incontrovertible mistakes. The capacity to hold money when confidence in predictions is particularly low allows investors not to commit themselves for indefinite periods, with important consequences for the level of output and employment.

Again, many long-period Post Keynesians reject the significance of expectations along with the significance of micro-foundations. Garegnani (1979) argues that Keynesian expectations fluctuate around some normal level, and it is on that normal level which we should concentrate our attention. (A parallel is evident with the fluctuation of output around a normal trend in the rational expectations framework.) But we have seen that whatever constitutes the 'normal' level for any variable at any one time is based on past experience which is subject to surprises. The entrepreneur's response to surprise is analogous to a scientist facing a Kuhnian crisis – should the current paradigm be shored up, or replaced with another (see Earl, 1984, Chapter 5)? In other words, the prevailing entrepreneurial paradigm, and thus the perception of normality, is itself judgemental. It is grounded in actual past values, but held on the basis of a theory as to how the future relates to the past.

The notion of normalcy is essential for the formation of any expectations, and for the making of contracts. Thus, wage contracts denominated in money wages can be seen as a contributor to the decision-making of both employer and employee, injecting one variable whose value is known throughout a given period into an otherwise uncertain future. But there is no necessity for that normalcy to mean 'long-term average value'. Because the future is unknowable, expectations as to normalcy cannot continually be proved correct. Otherwise, we are in a general equilibrium world. It is the outcome of the combination of animal spirits and short-run expectations in financial markets which determine the level of investment, and thus effective demand. It is thus these expectations which determine whether or not perceptions of 'normalcy' are justified, and which generate the 'normal' values of variables in the future.

7.5   Marxian Theory

The role of expectations in Marxian theory is not as explicit as in Keynes's theory, or indeed as in mainstream theory. Where the atemporal logical-time framework is not employed, Marxian theory is set in historical time, so the connection between one period of historical time and the next is important. But it is the class imperative rather than expectations of the value of particular variables which most clearly govern individual actions. Yet Marx did specify the actions of capitalists in terms of expected values of variables, as is required within historical time.

At one level, Marxist theory is designed itself to improve the long-run expectations formation of the working class. False consciousness promotes the view that current social conditions, and the current organization of production, are immutable. Historical analysis, however, demonstrates that a dialectical process is at work whereby capitalism will give way to the next mode of production, socialism. If workers understood the consequences of acquiescence, or lack of acquiescence, in the current system, then they would act in such a way as to speed up the arrival of socialism. (This sounds uncannily like the implicit goal of rational expectations economists, to educate economic agents – particularly government – so as to speed up the return to long-run equilibrium. Why else go to the trouble of specifying a model, when private individuals already act as if it were true?)

As in Keynes's model, the scope for workers' expectations to have significant macroeconomic impact is regarded as limited relative to the expectations of industrial capitalists or financial capitalists (the equivalent of Keynes's entrepreneurs and speculators). It is expectations about the future prices of financial assets which determine the supply of and demand for credit, and thus the interest rate which industrial capitalists must pay the financial capitalists. Since interest must be paid out of gross profit, that rate determines the effective floor to the gross profit rate. In turn, it is the comparison between the expected price of output and unit variable cost (including interest payments) which determines the level of output. If that comparison is unfavourable, then a general overproduction crisis ensues, as the manifestation of the rate of profit falling below some minimal acceptable level.

Marx is not explicit about the way in which expectations are generated. There is in fact a partial parallel between Marx's treatment of expectations and the traditional Austrian treatment. In both, the key expectations are those of capitalists; they are key because they are active rather than passive. The competitive environment requires innovative behaviour of capitalists, i.e. the capacity to seize or create opportunities ahead of competitors. The relevant expectations, therefore, are those of the areas of production most likely to yield the highest surplus value. It is the nature of such creative behaviour that it cannot be modelled explicitly.

Where Marxists diverge from the Austrians is in focusing theoretical attention on that aspect of expectations formation which can be analysed on a class, or group, basis, i.e. on that aspect of expectations formation which can be analysed systematically. This systematic behaviour derives from the inherent tendencies of capitalism to generate crises, i.e. from the absence of equilibrating tendencies. Because there is an inherent tendency for the rate of profit to fall as the organic composition of capital increases, the perception of the tendency towards overproduction will eventually be realized by all capitalists. It is, therefore, of limited importance how this tendency is first perceived. What is important is the cumulative effect of the reactions of those capitalists who first perceive the trend; by reducing output, they exacerbate the inadequacy of effective demand, encouraging other capitalists to perceive the emerging trend. Similarly, the reaction to crisis, by both labour and capital, will be class-based rather than atomistic (Harvey, 1982, pp.326–7).

Thus Marx shows how a crisis stemming from production conditions (the falling rate of profit) manifests itself in exchange conditions (through falling expected price of output relative to unit costs). He also gave exchange conditions an independent role in generating crises, or in exacerbating production-based crises. The credit system is a necessary feature of capitalism, allowing the search for surplus value to proceed in the face of the falling rate of profit. The capital represented by credit is 'fictitious capital', formed on the expectation of commodity production; its value is fictitious. It is the supply of and demand for credit, whose value depends on the expectations of borrowers and lenders, which determine the rate of interest. Even without an overproduction crisis, speculation among lenders can encourage them to hoard money, rather than lend it to producers, causing a financial crisis and a collapse in fictitious value. This financial crisis can promulgate a production crisis if the increasing rate of interest or lack of availability of credit reduces the expected rate of profit below the acceptable minimum, or if producers share finance capitalists' expectations and they also choose to hoard money rather than expand capacity and output.

Overall, then, expectations in Marxian theory are only important in the sense that they are a necessary feature of a model set in historical time. To the extent that the theory postulates a determinate historical tendency for the rate of profit to fall, with consequent periodic crises, then expectations do not play an independently active role. The faster expectations pick up the beginnings of a crisis, the more quickly will the crisis be fuelled. But as long as the crisis is inevitable, there is no scope for expectations to change anything fundamentally.

Just as the deterministic world of general equilibrium does not allow for active expectations, so the deterministic world of Marxist disequilibrium does not allow them either. (Expectations are active in the sense of determining the particular competitive behaviour of capitalists, but not the basic dialectical process.)

But not all of Marx's theory fits into this deterministic framework. While Marx's own work on money and credit is not straightforward to interpret, much of the subsequent developments in Marxist analysis are devoted to exploring financial crisis, and its relationship with production crisis (de Brunhoff, 1973; Harvey, 1982, Chapters 9,10; Panico, 1983; Lavoie, 1983.) In financial markets, the scope for speculation, and thus the importance of expectations, is much greater than in goods markets. Here, too, expectations can play an active role, precipitating a financial crisis independently of production conditions.

7.6   Conclusion

As long as macroeconomic analysis allows for change, then it must address the question of how behaviour (in aggregate, or individually) reacts to the possibility of change. We have seen that the way in which expectations formation is treated by each school of thought parallels the way in which members of each school themselves react to the possibility of change in the economy which they study.

Neo-Austrians traditionally consider the formation of opinions as to the future in the same subjectivist light as the formation of opinions as to the past. Although avoiding general equilibrium as a framework of analysis, they nevertheless share the position that market behaviour, responding to relative prices, promotes the efficient allocation of resources. Although the economy never reaches equilibrium, behaviour is always equilibrating. There is no scope for expectations to be other than in the correct direction even if not correct) on the basis of available information. More recently, neo-Austrians have taken as their inspiration Shackle's work on expectations, which analyses how expectations are formed in the absence of full, or even probabilistic, information. Shackle emphasizes the creative, imaginative aspect of expectations.

Mainstream theorists have more explicitly incorporated expectations behaviour into their models of equilibrating behaviour. Disequilibrium, neo-classical theorists predominantly employed the adaptive expectations model, whereby individuals react with caution to new information. Expectations are purely reactive, since they must be endogenous if rational. But now most mainstream theorists employ rational expectations on the grounds that it is the only possible representation of rational behaviour. Here too, expectations are purely passive, being equal (aside from stochastic deviation) to the predictions of the rational expectations model (in the case of the strong rational expectations hypothesis). All hangs on the capacity of the model itself to generate unbiased predictions.

Keynesian expectations involve both active and passive, both objective and subjective elements (i.e. they are judgemental, with more or less knowledge), and are modelled differently for different economic groups. Most important are the long-run expectations of entrepreneurs and the short-run expectations of speculators in financial markets. The former base their investment plans on the expected return on investments over a period of years, taking account of the expected prices of alternative assets. The price and availability of borrowed funds depend on perceptions of borrowers' and lenders' risk and liquidity preference, while the price of existing capital goods depends on the trading behaviour in the stock market, geared to turning points. While expectations may be stable for long periods, the potential for instability is always present, since there is no mechanism by which expectations can successfully adjust continuously to new information about the past.

Marxian expectations theory is only implicit in the analysis of capitalists' accumulative behaviour. In that part of the theory which is analysed deterministically, instability in the form of crises is inevitable, not cause for uncertainty as in the Post Keynesian framework. Even expectations consistently mistaken in direction could not avert the crisis. And indeed, expectations are implicitly presumed gradually to adjust so as correctly to perceive the onset of crisis. In the analysis of financial markets, however, there is more scope for expectations to take an active role, in much the same way as in Post Keynesian monetary theory. It is perhaps the historical experience of lack of determinacy (which Marx, if not orthodox Marxists, would have predicted) which has encouraged the recent attention among Marxists to financial speculation, and thus to expectations formation in financial markets. Once indeterminacy, even only in the short run, is allowed for, then expectations are no longer constrained to a particular inevitable outcome, and can affect behaviour in indeterminate ways.

It has been difficult to keep money out of this discussion. Once indeterminate outcomes are allowed in some schools of thought, and the consequences considered for decision-makers, and thus for the level of output and employment, the role of money looms large as the receptacle for uncertainty. The next chapter is devoted to considering how each school of thought incorporates money in their analysis.

8 Money

8.1 Introduction

So far, we have explored the different treatments, within each school of thought, of three concepts which have considerable bearing on the type of theories which each school has developed. In each case, the choice of conceptual framework reflects a view on how abstraction from reality should proceed. That choice cannot be judged conclusively on the basis of observations. One choice may be more 'realistic' than another. Time, for example, is irreversible in reality. But theory inevitably involves abstraction from reality and there is no ultimate criterion acceptable to all schools of thought which can arbitrate in favour of one abstraction over another. Even instrumentalism does not allow an identification of which particular aspect of a conceptual framework accounts for inaccuracy in prediction.

The conceptualization of money has proved to be particularly contentious. Certainly money has a direct counterpart in reality, in a sense which equilibrium, for example, need not. Of course, the presence of a phenomenon in reality does not require that it be included in a conceptual framework; and indeed much of macroeconomic theory has excluded explicit treatment of money. Where money is included in the framework, there has been a major difference between its inclusion as a separable variable on the one hand, and as a pervasive feature of all economic activity on the other.

The bulk of modern mainstream monetary theory has treated money as a separable variable. On that basis, most effort has been directed to specifying the demand for money function, and the transmission mechanism whereby a change in supply affects other macroeconomic variables. Within this framework, debates on these issues are of major importance, and are the subject of an extensive literature. Here, however, we concentrate on the conceptual framework adopted by each school of thought, and discussion of differences within each school of thought will concentrate on conceptual differences. In order to provide a focus for such a large subject, we will compare the different treatments of money in terms of its role in business cycle analysis. The conceptual treatment of money will be shown to be interdependent with the conceptual treatment of micro-foundations, equilibrium and expectations.

From Hume (1752) up to the turn of the century, monetary theory was dominated by the Quantity Theory of Money, based on the tautology that the value of transactions over a particular time period (PT) is equal to the stock of money multiplied by its rate of turnover (the velocity of circulation) during that period (MV). According to Fisher (1911), the velocity of circulation is determined primarily by the institutional arrangements of the banking and payments system; although these arrangements can change from time to time, they are sufficiently stable for velocity to be treated as a constant at any one point in time. There is then a one-to-one correspondence between the changes in money supply (M) and the changes in the value of transactions (PT).

Now, the *volume* of transactions (T) is determined by production conditions in relation to consumer preferences; the relative values, or prices, of different goods are determined by these 'real' givens. And indeed the rate of interest, the cost of borrowing money, is determined by its equality with the marginal physical product of capital, given this level and composition of production. (The relevant rate of interest is the real rate as distinguished from the nominal rate by Fisher, 1930.) All these 'real' factors were viewed as being determined independently of the stock of money; there was in consequence a dichotomy between real and monetary variables, between value theory and monetary theory. As a result, since the volume of transactions was determined independently of monetary variables, the relationship between the stock of money and the value of transactions must refer to the general price level alone; thus the Quantity Theory stated that money supply changes could only affect the general price level.

The neutrality of money was, however, a long-run equilibrium result. Debates within monetary theory focused on the interaction between real and monetary variables in the short term. But the 'short term' has different meanings depending on what is meant by long-run equilibrium, whether it is an actual position attained within logical time, or a notional position which is never attained, in historical time. The greater polarization of schools of thought on this issue within modern macroeconomics has forged more distinctive treatments of money than were evident even when Keynes was developing his monetary theory.

At one level, the issues at stake can be expressed in terms of the Quantity Theory: whether (as a reflection of reality or as a reasonable abstraction) the supply of money, the volume of transactions and the general price level are independent or not (see Schumpeter, 1954, p.703). If not, then the Quantity Theory equation provides no causal explanation of the general price level in terms of the money supply. These questions may be posed with respect to the short term and the long term. If there is interdependence in the short term, then further discussion is required of whether non-neutrality in the short term is compatible with neutrality in the long term. Even Hume allowed for monetary growth to stimulate economic growth in the long term, i.e. for some interdependence between M and T (Rotwein, 1973).

At another level, the issues relate to the origins and nature of money itself. Why economies became monetary economies, and what performs the role of money is determined by institutional factors which in turn reflect past economic and financial history. If in reality the money supply, transactions and the price level are interdependent, their interrelationship may then be of a profound nature; institutional change resulting from this interdependence may affect what constitutes money itself. A choice of abstraction which treats money as a separable, independent variable would then face particular difficulties in drawing conclusions to be applied in reality.

At a third level, money's role will be analysed differently in the context of production than in the context of exchange; the former would require more emphasis on the passage of historical time and money's function as a store of wealth, denominator of contracts and measure of wealth, while the latter would suggest more emphasis on simultaneous transactions within mechanical time and money's function as a means of payment, as well as denominator of contracts. We turn now to consider how each school of thought is represented in terms of these issues.

8.2   Neo-Austrian Theory

Modern neo-Austrian monetary theory has its origins in the work of Bohm-Bawerk (1889) and Mises (1912), and was given its fullest expression by Hayek (1931a, 1933); see also Rothbard (1976b). The Quantity Theory is accepted as a valid argument applied to general equilibrium; in a comparative static comparison between states with two hypothetical money supply levels, where the financial structure (and thus the velocity of circulation) remain unchanged, as do the physical conditions of production and where (given complete certainty) money is held only for transactions purposes, it follows logically that only the general price level will differ as between the two positions. Agreement over this equilibrium outcome stems from the congruence between the neo-classical and Austrian perceptions of the functioning of a market economy, in so far as it is represented in a general equilibrium framework.

But the neo-Austrian rejection of the Quantity Theory arises from their methodological objection to focusing on macroeconomic variables, and on comparative static exercises, on the grounds that they distract attention from the processes underlying actual economic events out of equilibrium (see Mises, 1912, section 2.8). First, the money supply and the general price level as such do not have any operative meaning since they do not enter into the decision-making of individuals. The money supply is made up of all the means of exchange held by individuals. The aggregate significance of this stock depends on its distribution, and the relative preferences of individuals holding more or less money. It also depends on the structure of financial institutions, and the subjective judgements of individuals as to which assets they consider as usable in exchange; a cheque for example may be acceptable in exchange between individuals who know and trust each other, but not otherwise, without additional security. The 'true' money supply is thus subjective, and not identifiable or measurable. In turn, the general price level is not the value of money; money's value is determined by the money price of each and every commodity. The individual's decision as to how much money to hold is determined by the expected price of the particular purchases for which the money is intended, not by the prices of all commodities indexed in some aggregative way.

Menger (1871, 1883) analysed the emergence of a monetary economy as the unintended consequence of purposeful individual actions, to develop roundabout methods of exchange and to meet the need for a liquid asset, given the uncertainty attached to expectations. This analysis (emphasizing the first of these motives for developing money) is now being applied to radical re-examinations of monetary arrangements (Dowd, 1993 and Cowen and Kroszner, 1994). Originally, what was used as money was a commodity which itself had use value; as it became more commonly used in exchange, more commodities would have exchange value expressed in terms of this money commodity. As financial systems developed, the connection with use value was limited to a backing of paper money by a form of money which had had use value, like gold. Over time, the connection became progressively more tenuous, but could still be traced. The Modern Free Banking School and the New Monetary Economists see monetary problems arising from the role of the state which is seen as intervening in the Mengerian process by manipulating the supply of the standard of value and allowing the undisciplined expansion first of fiat money, then of credit money. Both approaches advocate reliance on market discipline to restore monetary stability (Dow and Smithin, 1995). Given the lack of attention to Menger's second motive for developing money, equivalent to Keynes's precautionary motive responding to uncertainty (Loasby, 1991), it is not surprising that the neo-Austrian theory of money in relation to aggregate activity is the Quantity Theory of Money.

Hayek developed his monetary theory specifically to address the problem of explaining the business cycle, a task later taken up by Garrison (1989). The normal state of the economy is a perpetual state of flux, as entrepreneurs expand production in new fields, and as consumers change their subjective evaluation of different products. Along with this process goes a continual rearrangement of relative prices, which in turn act as signals for future actions, and a continual change in income distribution as new technology, products and preferences benefit some groups at the expense of others. Aggregated in some way, the money supply and the general price level may be rising or falling, together or in opposite directions. There is no necessity for them to move together, and indeed it would be extremely unlikely with all these relative changes occurring. The interest rate may fluctuate in line with fluctuations in savers' time preference; but if it is the pure outcome of market forces it is the 'natural' rate.

Suppose, however, that there is a systematic easing of credit conditions, initiated by the monetary authorities rather than savers, so that the interest rate falls below the natural rate. The reduced cost of borrowing makes more attractive the prospect of 'waiting' for future profits represented by undertaking new capital investment projects, i.e. more 'roundabout' methods of production. The result is an across-the-board increase in capital expenditure, increasing the relative price of capital goods, and encouraging an expansion of output and employment in that sector. This expansion cannot be sustained, however, since it is not based on an increased rate of time preference among savers; increased income will thus be expended at pre-expansion rates on consumption, i.e. voluntary saving will not increase. (Indeed, it would decrease if it were influenced by the lower interest rate.) Meanwhile, the diversion of resources away from the consumption-goods sector, combined with rising demand for consumption goods from the workers newly employed at higher wages in the capital-goods sector, pushes up consumer-good prices. It is the resulting fall in real incomes of those employed in the consumption-goods sector which constitutes the 'forced saving' which ultimately finances the new investment.

Scarcity in the consumption-goods sector attracts activity back from the capital-goods sector. But the process cannot easily be reversed, since physical resources have now been tied up in capital goods and intermediate goods for the capital-goods sector, so that there is a capital shortage for the consumption-goods sector. (Capital is thus viewed as being non-malleable, i.e. it cannot be converted easily to alternative uses.) In addition the labour released now by the capital-goods sector cannot be absorbed easily into production of consumer goods since the necessary capital is not available. The ensuing contraction of output and employment is thus one of excess consumer demand and capital shortage. This reactive cycle proceeds until all 'mistaken' capital expenditure has fully depreciated, and the capital stock accords with the natural rate of interest.

Hayek's theory of the business cycle is thus a monetary one, in the sense that it is started by the actions of the monetary authorities, causing a deviation of the interest rate from its natural rate. The cycle itself, however, is constituted of real phenomena, as Machlup (1974, p.504) points out. Its length is determined by the time it takes to unwind the new investment which was mistakenly undertaken on the basis of the 'false' interest rate signal. As a corollary, monetary factors within the private sector cannot cause cycles, since by definition they maintain the rate of interest at its natural rate. The problem lies with public sector influence on financial institutions. It is thus not surprising that Hayek (1978) should argue in favour of privatizing the entire banking system in order to remove that influence; this is one of the primary inspirations for the Modern Free Banking school.

Indeed, the role of money in neo-Austrian economics is almost exclusively concerned with the public sector responsibility for managing the financial system. Not only are manipulations of credit availability regarded as a major cause of business cycles, but attempts to reduce unemployment by government spending financed by increased growth of the money supply are regarded as a major cause of stagflation. The problem lies in the neo-Austrian perception that an economy's natural state involves contraction of some sectors as others expand; a theory about equilibrating market forces precludes the possibility of persistent unemployment. If the contracting sectors are kept going by government spending (or regulation) then their product prices are prevented from falling. If the correct relative prices are to be maintained, then all other prices must rise accordingly. Persistence in this policy not only means rising inflation to maintain price differentials, but also money financing keeps the interest rate perpetually below its natural rate, diverting excessive resources into roundabout methods of production, and away from the sectors in which they are in fact most needed.

The acceptance of the Quantity Theory of Money as appropriate when applied to the long run means that a connection is perceived between the money supply and the general level of prices. Nevertheless, the focus on dynamic processes within institutions in the neo-Austrian theory of money, as of other variables, introduces the possibility of institutional change as part of the outcome of inflation. In other words, while neo-Austrians accept the argument that a given rate of increase in the money supply leads to an equal rate of inflation in long-run equilibrium in mechanical time, the outcome in historical time will reflect institutional change in response to inflation.

Mises (1912, Chapter 2) suggests, for example, that the demand for real money balances may fluctuate under inflationary conditions (see also Rothbard, 1976b). First, Mises suggests that particularly rapid money supply increases and inflation arise initially from unusual circumstances: a money-financed war, for example. A return to normal circumstances is widely expected to bring inflation down again, so that idle money balances are accumulated until that time. This abstention from spending allows inflation to fall again. If the government is then tempted to continue the high rate of money creation to finance expenditure at war-time levels, the sectors in which this expenditure is made have their prices held artificially high, so that other sectors must also increase prices to maintain relative price ratios, and inflation resumes. Consumers, their expectations of falling inflation disappointed, run down their money stocks, so that inflation now proceeds at a faster rate than money supply increases. But the rapidly eroding value of money reduces public confidence in the financial system. On the one hand, a flight from currency fuels runaway inflation. On the other hand, a financial crisis occurs, with alternative forms of money being sought, and new financial arrangements being required.

The process then, over the long run, is of inflation first at the same rate as the money supply increase, then lower, then higher. Before the system can settle into long-run equilibrium, the effect of inflation on the confidence held in the financial system may induce a liquidity crisis and changes in the financial structure which include changes in what is subjectively regarded as the means of exchange itself. This divergence from the Quantity Theory result shows how important it is, whether the historical or mechanical notion of time is being used, and thus whether dynamic institutional responses to initial causes are taken into account.

Within the neo-Austrian framework, money as such does not play an active (or causal) role other than because it is administered by the public sector. Financial institutions and transactions habits develop in response to individual utility-maximizing behaviour. Barring public sector activism, the interest rate is a natural rate, consistent with the appropriate rate of growth of the capital stock. There is thus no need to elaborate on the demand for money at a macro level and indeed the capacity to do so (demand being subjective) is lacking.

8.3   Mainstream Theory

Mainstream monetary theory also has roots both in the Quantity Theory and in the marginalist revolution. But by retaining the general equilibrium framework, mainstream monetary theorists were able to retain the Quantity Theory as a long-run theory within the same framework as their short-run disequilibrium analysis. The orthodox theoretical background against which Keynes introduced his *General Theory* (and of which his *Treatise on Money* was a part) consisted of theories of money's non-neutrality in the disequilibrium short-run, superimposed on the Quantity Theory which posited long-run neutrality. The resulting monetary theory, while having much in common with Austrian theory, took its distinctiveness from the general equilibrium framework in which it was expressed. Thus Wicksell (1934–35,Volume II), for example, discussed economic fluctuations as being caused by changing credit conditions which caused deviations of the money rate of interest from its natural rate. But, while Hayek's natural rate of interest was whatever the private sector alone would throw up, and was thus potentially variable, Wicksell's natural rate was the real return on capital in long-run, full-employment equilibrium.

Contemporary general equilibrium monetary theory is the product of two important post-war developments. First, the Quantity Theory was given a new lease of life by Friedman's (1956) restatement of the theory, in terms of the underlying demand for money function, and Patinkin's (1956) exploration of the (real balance) mechanism which allowed short-run disequilibrium positions to be analysed in terms of the adjustment from one long-run equilibrium position (defined by the Quantity Theory) to another. The relevance of the Quantity Theory was further reinforced by Friedman and Schwartz's (1963a) historical study of United States data which showed a close correlation over long periods between the money stock and nominal income; later work, backed up by Phillips curve analysis, emphasized the more specific correlation between monetary growth and the rate of inflation over long periods. The conclusion that money is neutral in equilibrium encouraged the habit among general equilibrium theorists who were not monetary theorists to conduct analysis in real terms, without reference to money. Monetary theory then seemed to be relevant only to disequilibrium analysis.

The second major development was the move within general equilibrium theory toward neo-Austrian principles, whereby attention is focused on micro-foundations and the optimizing behaviour of individuals; the outcome remained distinct from neo-Austrian economics, however, because of the continued retention of the general equilibrium framework. This second development was also spurred on by Patinkin's (1956) work which included explicit discussion of micro-foundations. Some, defining each position of analysis as an equilibrium position, retained the habit of excluding explicit consideration of money on the grounds that it was neutral. Others, however, sought an explanation for the demand for money and its market function in terms of the axioms of individual rationality; this required a more thorough investigation of the nature of money. We now explore the significance of these two developments in some detail, touching on the main issues which have exercised mainstream monetary theorists, and considering particularly the accounts given of money's role in the business cycle.

First, let us consider the conjunction of the Quantity Theory and Walras' Law on which much of general equilibrium theory was grounded. That Law states that, of n markets, if $(n-1)$ are in equilibrium, then the nth must also be in equilibrium. If the nth market is the money market, then its equilibrium state is implicit in that of all other markets and need not be treated explicitly. This argument is subject to a *reductio ad absurdum*; it can be applied successively to the $(n-1)$th market, and then the $(n-2)$th and so on until explicit analysis of only one market is necessary. Put another way, for the system as a whole to be in equilibrium, each and every component must be in equilibrium. It is a matter of judgement where the cut-off point is set: which market's equilibrium is to be studied explicitly, and which can be left implicit by Walras' Law.

It was the Quantity Theory which suggested a cut-off point which left the money market implicit. The Quantity Theory states that the general price level is proportionate to the stock of money in long-run equilibrium. Changes in the money stock do not influence the long-run level of output and thus output demand is independent of the money stock and the absolute level of general prices. This is the 'homogeneity postulate': product demand is homogeneous of degree zero with respect to the absolute price level. As a corollary, product market equilibrium can be studied independently of the money stock and the absolute price level, and purely in terms of relative prices. Thus equilibrium analysis could be conducted in real terms.

One of Patinkin's major contributions was to demonstrate that not all of the Quantity Theory, Walras' Law and the homogeneity postulate could hold in disequilibrium. If the money stock were changed, then, in the process of adjustment to the new price level, he argued that product demand would be influenced by the temporary change in real balances, i.e. the homogeneity postulate would be violated and money would be non-neutral in disequilibrium. (Archibald and Lipsey, 1958, argued rather that it was Walras' Law which was violated in disequilibrium, i.e. that the money market alone was in disequilibrium during the adjustment period and that, in any case, each of the Quantity Theory, homogeneity postulate and Walras' Law all held in long-run equilibrium. This proposition was debated in a symposium in the *Review of Economic Studies,* October, 1960.) Changes in real balances are an inevitable feature of disequilibrium, where changes in the money stock and prices are disproportionate. Whether these changes affect product demand, violating the homogeneity postulate, seemed to hinge on the question of whether or not they constitute net wealth (see Pesek and Saving, 1967; Ahmad, 1970).

An alternative expression of the adjustment mechanism emphasized the effect of the change in interest rates which occurred along with the initial money supply change (Metzler, 1951). Indeed, the interest rate is a monetary rate in disequilibrium, i.e. it is influenced by factors additional to the real propensity to save and to invest. Thus the loanable funds theory allows for a supply of funds from new credit, in addition to savings, and a demand for funds for hoarding, in addition to demand for investment finance, in disequilibrium. Equilibrium is envisaged as a state where the money supply is stable and there is no wish to hoard. Since the value of financial assets varies inversely with interest rates, a money supply increase is associated with an increase in wealth quite independent of the real balance effect. The rise in expenditure encouraged by the rise in wealth sets in train the upward pressure on prices which is required to restore long-run equilibrium.

Once this argument was extended to apply to rates of change in the money stock and in the general price level, i.e. inflation, the question of expectations arose. Did the homogeneity postulate, which expressed product demand in real terms, refer to 'real' in the sense of the actual price level or its expected rate of change? Was the demand for real balances formulated in terms of actual or expected prices? Friedman's (1956) incorporation of the expected rate of inflation in his demand for money function was extended later to apply to other markets, particularly the labour market (Friedman, 1975). This allowed the formulation of the short-run Phillips curve as a disequilibrium adjustment path from one position on the long-run Phillips curve to another. Since the disequilibrium is initiated by money supply changes, money is non-neutral in the short run, during which expectations adjust to the actual rate of inflation, but neutral in the long run with a return to the natural rate of unemployment on the long-run Phillips curve, with inflation at a level commensurate with the new rate of growth of the money stock. Neutrality in the face of continued inflation, rather than a steady price level, is called 'super neutrality'.

Once we consider the long run in terms of a steady rate of inflation rather than a steady price level, new questions arise as to whether the homogeneity postulate can still be maintained; might there not be some tendency for continued inflation to alter the demand for real balances? Cagan (1956) argued that this could only be so in disequilibrium, when inflationary expectations still differed from actual inflation (see also Levhari and Patinkin, 1968). But Tobin (1965) maintained that money would lose its efficiency under continued inflation, transactors would economize on money balances, and the efficiency of the economy would fall, lowering the long-run rate of growth. Money would then not be superneutral.

The method of analysis employed throughout these discussions of money's role in disequilibrium and in long-run equilibrium is profoundly ahistorical. Comparative static analysis is used, in effect, to see what happens to the equilibrium values of real variables when money is explicitly introduced to the model, compared to when it is excluded. A classic case in point was the debate over the implications of the development of non-bank financial intermediaries between Brunner and Meltzer (1963) and Tobin and Brainard (1963). The debate was couched in terms of a barter economy into which are introduced, successively, banks and non-bank financial intermediaries. The method presumes that the structure of the underlying model into which these new variables are introduced remains constant throughout. The problems involved did not go unrecognized (by Patinkin, 1956, for example). But the tradition of barter economy–monetary economy comparisons remained standard in mainstream monetary theory (see, for example, Fisher, 1978, Appendix A).

These comparisons highlight the micro-foundations question of why money is used at all. The efficiency argument for conducting transactions with money rather than other goods provides a sufficient reason for money to be held, and held in proportion to the value of transactions, PT. But empirical evidence suggests that money holdings do not vary in strict proportion to the value of transactions (or their proxy, income) so that other variables (particularly the interest rate) have some role in the short run. A more complex demand for money theory is required. Friedman (1956) in fact expressed his restatement of the Quantity Theory as a theory of the demand for money as an asset, an asset which is unique as a means of exchange. Money is thus portrayed as an asset which can act as a store of value at the same time as providing exchange facilities.

As long as the asset demand for money is stable as a function of the interest rate, then the traditional result of long-run non-neutrality of money still holds. Even an infinitely interest-elastic demand for money need not impede the attainment of full employment equilibrium as long as the real balance effect is in operation. Laidler (1981) makes the case that, although shifts in the demand for money are not always accurately predicted, there is a general consensus that the function is reasonably stable. These empirical observations are backed up by theoretical justifications for the demand for money to vary with the interest rate, stemming from Tobin (1958) and Baumol (1952). Subsequent work incorporated the influence also of price level expectations, both as regards the expected real purchasing power of transactions balances and as regards the relative rates of return on alternative assets. The typical monetary theory textbook (Fisher, 1978, for example) devotes much of its space to the specification of the demand for money function; within the neo-classical synthesis, indeed, the Monetarist–Keynesian debate was a debate about the interest elasticity of the demand for money, i.e. about the slope of the LM curve.

Yet this inventory-theoretic approach to the demand for money can only refer to situations of disequilibrium. In the abstract situation of general equilibrium, all known mutually-advantageous trades in spot and futures markets have taken place. There is no rationale for holding money since no further transactions are anticipated. In the case of temporary equilibrium, although transactions are anticipated and futures markets are not available in all products, other interest-bearing assets are available. Put another way, the marginal utility of money equals its marginal cost in equilibrium (which is negligible), as long as no interest is paid on money. Yet, if money is held, its utility must be positive. Given the importance of money within mainstream theory, the difficulty experienced in rationalizing money's role in the economy and its existence in equilibrium is a serious one. Gale (1982, p.182) is correct in arguing that it is not essential for monetary theory to explain the origins of money. Yet the inability to integrate money into general equilibrium analysis in a satisfactory way demonstrates the problems of an ahistoric method; the problem stems from the comparative static approach whereby analysis starts with a real exchange economy into which money is introduced as a separable variable.

The primary emphasis in mainstream theory has always been on the transactions demand for money, where money is held in one period for transactions in the next. Hahn concludes that money transactions can only be explained as a transactions technology for which money is an input. Why any particular asset should perform this function can only be explained, circularly, by the fact that it performs the function; according to Hicks (1979b) it stems from a mutual trust on the part of transactors; according to Tobin (1980a) it is like a language which is useful to the extent that most people use it; according to Hahn (1981, pp.21–2) use of money is consistent with a Nash equilibrium where, if there is a rule that money be used in transactions, then it is to everyone's advantage so to use it. Further rationalization is possible by explaining trust and conventions of payment in terms of economizing on information gathering on transactors, but this is difficult to model in a world of representative individuals whose trustworthiness is uniform (Gale, 1982).

Hahn (1981) identifies uncertainty as the key to explaining money's role; it is uncertainty about future values which encourages contractual money payments and receipts as well as the demand for money as an asset with a certain rate of return. This idea has been developed in the form of the buffer stock theory of the demand for money as precautionary demand (Gale, 1982, 1983; Laidler, 1983). But what is meant by uncertainty is in fact quantifiable risk, i.e. uncertainty about the position of a value within a known probability distribution. As long as all returns are known within a probability distribution, it is rational to prefer assets with mean returns above zero to money whose mean return is zero. There is still no scope for an asset demand for money (see Hahn, 1981, pp.17–8; also Chick, 1983, pp.213–8). (The same argument applies to the portrayal of money in temporary equilibrium as to full general equilibrium.) Only capital market imperfections, which impede the substitutability between money and other assets, can rescue the demand for money in an equilibrium framework.

This argument has been taken furthest by the New Monetary Economics theorists (Cowen and Kroszner, 1994). Their argument makes the logical extension to mainstream theory, that it is not justifiable to consider money as different in kind from any other asset. This theoretical conclusion is combined with the empirical observation of financial market innovation, which has allowed increasing use of non-money assets in transactions. This trend has been extrapolated to allow the conclusion that all transactions could be performed with assets whose value varied with the value of the issuers' portfolios, i.e. without money as we currently understand it. The general price level would be determined in relation to a standard of value (a commodity-bundle for example), but this standard of value would not itself perform money functions. That this outcome has not yet emerged is regarded as the result of state interference in the operation of financial markets. The New Monetary approach relies heavily on the feasibility of capital market perfection in the absence of state interference.

New Keynesian economics is the main area for focus on market imperfections. But, curiously, the emphasis has been placed on imperfections with respect to the asset side of the banks' balance sheet, rather than on bank deposits. Credit creation is seen as having the causal power, with the supply of bank deposits simply seen as a by-product. New Keynesians see the importance of banks in terms of the supply of credit, where capital market imperfections prevent alternative sources of finance from being perfect substitutes. Small firms in particular are limited in their access to bond and equity markets, and may therefore be constrained in their activities if banks limit the supply of credit. Credit-rationing in turn is analysed as the consequence of differential access to information on borrowers' credit-worthiness as between borrower and lender. Credit rationing is thus an equilibrium outcome of profit-maximizing behaviour by banks, where profits are a function not only of interest earnings but also of defaults (Stiglitz and Weiss, 1981). Choice-theoretic foundations, applied in an equilibrium setting, are thus preserved while giving money, or rather credit, an active role.

For New Classical theorists, it is the supply of money, rather than credit, which plays the key theoretical role; it is the government's role as determining the supply of money by the banks which is crucial. (Demand for money remains passive, as a technical input to exchange.) But, since the money supply can only affect relative prices in the short run if they are unanticipated, monetary policy can only alter real variables if money supply changes are random. The strength of this result stems from the way in which expectations formation is modelled; individuals are presumed to know the set of equilibrium prices which would obtain under different money supply assumptions. Thus, although money is necessary as an explanation of fluctuations, there is no scope for money to play a role in conveying information, or indeed in preventing information from being conveyed.

The presumed exogeneity of the money supply gave it a key causal role, providing the explanation for business cycles in monetarist theory as well as in New Classical theory. Friedman and Schwartz's (1963b) classic statement of the role of money in the business cycle is derived instrumentally from studying correlations between data series over the cycle, but it is explained conventionally in terms of an orthodox transmission mechanism (see, also, further developments in Friedman, 1971, 1975). The initial mechanism is similar to that in the neo-Austrian theory; a money supply increase lowers interest rates, encouraging additional expenditure. This process is, however, helped along by the real balance effect, as excess money balances are run down. The price rises which follow increased product demand encourage increased output and employment. But as workers' expectations adjust to the erosion of the real wage, and as the value of real balances is eroded, employment begins to contract again, and expenditure falls back as attempts are made to restore real money balances to their desired level. Other things being equal, this cycle would persist with ever-decreasing amplitude until price expectations accorded with the long-term equilibrium position. The 'overshooting' which causes a cyclical pattern even in a shift to a new equilibrium is exacerbated by such financial factors as the money multiplier exaggerating initial high-powered money changes, causing inflation to overshoot, and thus the demand for real balances to fall temporarily below the new equilibrium level.

The generalized use of the rational expectations approach now limits the scope for the money-supply explanation of the business cycle. Rational expectations theorists cannot rely on slowly adjusting expectations to explain the amplitude of the cycle; rather they adopt the neo-Austrian explanation that it takes time to unwind the real effects of mistaken investment undertaken when interest rates first fall. Further, persistent cycles as a result of government action are only feasible to the extent that that action is unanticipated. But evidence on cycles over the last decade has not lent much support for the monetary-surprise explanation for the impetus for cycles, particularly when governments have implemented New Classical theory by announcing their money supply strategy. Attention has thus been turning away from the money supply as a key causal variable to other exogenous variables, notably technological change. The resulting real business cycle theory in fact takes the money supply to be endogenous, passively expanding in response to demand. This endogeneity can be understood as an absorption of the perception of actual endogeneity from the applied literature (see for example Goodhart, 1994). Or it can be understood as an expression of the habits of real analysis in mainstream theory; it has always been the case that the real (as opposed to nominal) money supply was determined in the private sector.

Money is thus in decline as a variable of importance to mainstream theory; the focus is now limited to the scope for monetary surprise by central banks, and the related question of the credibility of information disseminated on monetary policy. Money is still seen as the determinant of the general price level. But, while there may be some scope for mistaken expectations (for a variety of reasons) to allow fluctuations in the nominal money supply (and thus prices), the real money supply remains the product of choice-theoretic behaviour in the private sector.

8.4   Post Keynesian Theory

The Post Keynesian view of money derives from the Post Keynesian view of the nature of a monetary economy. Thus, far from posing questions in terms of whether 'introducing' money into a model of the economy affects real variables, money as such is regarded as an integral feature of a monetary economy. Since the emphasis is on production rather than exchange, money's significance is seen more in terms of its influence on investment than in the act of exchange; money is seen more as a link between the past and the future than as a mode of instantaneous exchange. The emphasis on money as an inherent feature of the institutional fabric, entering into the (exchange or production) process in historical time has much in common with the neo-Austrian approach. But neo-Austrians view private sector financial activity as generating a natural rate of interest, which encourages some kind of optimal investment pattern (given available information). Post Keynesians, in contrast, see the rate of interest as a monetary variable and private sector financial activity as thereby impeding the attainment of optimal levels and patterns of investment. Finally, the historical process of financial development is explained at a social rather than individual level; it would thus be misleading to search for micro-foundations at the level of individuals.

It is these methodological features which account for the distinctiveness of Keynes's own monetary theory in relation to the orthodoxy of that time. (See Davidson, 1972, for a full account of Keynes's monetary theory along these lines.) The categorization of the demand for money according to transactions, precautionary and speculative motives had already appeared in the work of Marshall (1923) and Hawtrey (1919), while Wicksell (1936) and Robertson (1928, 1940) had discussed the rate of interest as a monetary phenomenon in the short run (although not in the long-run). But Keynes (1982) had explored the history of monetary economies in order to understand the role of monetary institutions within a capitalist economy. It was this fundamentalist approach which led him to develop a different method of analysis: to undergo his 'long struggle to escape from habitual modes of thought and expression' (Keynes, 1936, p.viii). It was this methodological shift which accounted for the discontinuity between Keynes's monetary theory and that of his orthodox predecessors and contemporaries.

In the *General Theory*, Keynes set out to invalidate Say's Law, by showing that planned saving need not be brought into equality with planned investment at the full employment level of output. It was the level of output (or income) itself which equalized planned saving and investment. In the orthodox model, it was the rate of interest which performed that function; the equilibrium rate was that which equated the mariginal product of capital and the rate of time preference of savers at the margin. An important feature of Keynes's counter-argument was therefore to point out the significance of the rate of interest being a monetary, rather than a real, variable. Financial markets could be shown to have an influence on output and employment, quite apart from the behaviour of the monetary authorities, and an influence which could extend into the long run.

This active role for money stems from the theoretical framework employed, where equilibrium is used as a historical-time concept, and where there is scope for uncertainty, in the sense of an absence of quantitative probabilistic forecasts. Considered historically, indeed, the very existence of money assets is associated with uncertainty. In a barter economy, goods which are exchanged, other than for immediate consumption, are of uncertain value. Similarly, payment in kind leaves uncertain the value of profits as well as the value of wages. Use of money as a transactions intermediary, as well as making exchange more efficient, reduces (or at least redistributes) the uncertainty attached to exchange and to the value of stocks of wealth. An analogous situation is the use in international trade and in international reserves of a stable third currency (the United States dollar, say) instead of either of the traders' own unstable currencies. When an asset ceases to be a commodity, and becomes a 'money', can be said to be determined by the conscious attribution of a rate of interest, which is the subjective measure of the liquidity foregone in lending that asset, or acquired by borrowing it (see Heinsohn and Steiger, 1984).

The particular asset which becomes accepted as money must, according to Keynes (1936, Chapter 17) satisfy three requirements (see also Davidson, 1972, chapter 9; Chick, 1983, Chapter 17):

(1) *There must be a low degree of substitutability between the money asset and other assets.* This means that the measure of money should include all assets which act as a means of payment or as a store of value and which are readily substitutable for a means of payment. Since acceptability in payment is a matter of convention, depending to a considerable degree on the confidence held in the issuer of the money asset, the relevant range of assets can be expected to change over time. For practical purposes, in times of financial stability, a given measure will serve over long periods. The significance of the low substitutability requirement is, however, that economists should be alert to changes in payment conventions during periods of instability. Further, there must be alertness to changing degrees of substitutability between means of payment and alternative stores of value.

(2) *Carrying costs must be low relative to liquidity.* Liquidity is the ease with which an asset can be exchanged for other assets where 'ease' refers both to institutional arrangements and to perceived risk of capital loss; money is the most liquid asset. (Kaldor, 1960, expresses this liquidity premium alternatively as a negative marginal risk premium which is zero only for money.) Liquidity, like carrying costs, is partly determined by institutional arrangements. But it is also partly a matter of judgement in that it relates to perceived risk in exchange. This judgemental element is exacerbated by the fact that perceived risk and thus liquidity depend on market conditions, both in terms of level of activity and in terms of perceived trends. Thus, for example, real assets in relatively fixed supply like property and old masters trade easily in active markets during speculative booms. The carrying costs associated with holding them until a sale is required are high, however, preventing them from being used in payment, except in extreme circumstances. Only highly liquid assets with relatively low carrying costs are thus used as a means of payment.

(3) *The supply elasticity of money must be low.* If money is to be held between payments, for unpredictable periods, then it must be able to retain its value relative to goods. If the money asset were in elastic supply, then its value would be eroded if an increase in demand always called forth an increase in supply. In fact, because an institutional structure is built up over the years around a particular type of money asset, there is marked reluctance to give up using it even when supply elasticity increases. But eventually,

an alternative money asset may emerge which is expected to retain its value better than the old one. (Keynes initially expressed this condition in terms of 'elasticity of production', where production involves a labour input. Although this notion is distinct from elasticity of supply as a result of innovation among private sector financial institutions, Keynes proceeded to use the concepts of production and supply interchangeably.) Keynes saw the money supply as determined by the (public and private sector) banking system (see Dow, forthcoming, c). Even the money supply, then, is influenced by judgemental factors, insofar as they influence bank credit creation. For any set of expectations and monetary policy stance, however, Keynes treated the money supply as given.

The significance of institutional and judgemental factors in the first two attributes of money (in a model not tied to general equilibrium) is their propensity to promote instability. Since both the demand for any money asset and the supply of credit (and thus money) are influenced by these factors, the interest rate is not determinate. Robertson (1940) noted this departure within Keynes's monetary theory, which in turn was played down by Keynesian monetary theorists within the neo-classical synthesis. But it was perhaps the third factor on which Keynesian theorists have differed most amongst themselves. This third condition indicates clearly that Keynes assumed that, whatever was used as money, its supply would be constrained in some way. But subsequent Keynesian theorists have often taken the money supply to be endogenous, in the sense of being determined by demand on the part of the non-bank public, rather than by the monetary authorities' active constraint of supply in conjunction with the banks. This endogeneity resulted either from the perceived passive behaviour of the monetary authorities (following Keynes's own prescription of interest rate stability) and from the responsiveness of financial institutions to the demand for credit (Kaldor, 1983). In consequence, much Keynesian analysis, particularly within the neo-classical synthesis has been conducted in real terms; if the demand for money was always met, then money could play no independent part in the macro process. (Thus Johnson, 1971, could present the monetarist counter-revolution as restoring money to macro theory following its abandonment by Keynesians.)

It is important to address this issue of money supply endogeneity, since it has been taken to contradict the centrality of liquidity preference to Keynes's theory (see Kaldor, 1982; Moore, 1988). Cottrell (1994) too focuses on this issue in his survey of the Post Keynesian monetary theory literature. In fact money supply endogeneity and liquidity preference need not be contradictory – indeed they have been shown to reinforce each other, with banks' willingness to create credit being a function partly of their liquidity preference (see Dow and Dow, 1989; Wray, 1990).

The Post Keynesian notion of money supply endogeneity was influenced considerably by the Radcliffe Report (1959). Endogeneity refers to the capacity for institutions to create new money instruments, or for new financial institutions to emerge, to satisfy excess demand for money. It is certainly widely recognized that attempts by the monetary authorities to control the supply of money by one definition tend to be thwarted by such institutional responses. Indeed, this phenomenon is consistent with portfolio theory, which suggests that financial assets can be increased in supply only in so far as there is demand for them; Tobin (1963) first put forward this argument to prove that financial institutions cannot increase their liabilities, and thus their profits, indefinitely. And indeed, it can be argued that it is the very capacity of the financial system to expand in the face of rising demand for financial instruments which justifies confidence in the money assets on which the system is built – unless the system expands excessively, i.e. to the point of financial crisis, in which case the reverse is true. The interdependence of the demand for and supply of money within Post Keynesian theory mirrors the interdependence of demand and supply within all other markets. Endogeneity of supply need not be incompatible with Keynes's low elasticity of supply criterion. The nature of that endogeneity is discussed below in terms of the business cycle. But first we pursue the issue more generally in terms of the nature and role of money in the Post Keynesian framework.

The consequences of money supply endogeneity for the role of money in the macro economy depend very much on the methodological framework employed. We saw, in the case of mainstream, general equilibrium analysis, that endogeneity robs any variable of explanatory power; the entire focus is on the exogenous variables and the equilibrium solution, rather than what has happened to the endogenous variables to bring about that solution. Within Post Keynesian methodology, it can be argued that nothing, short of acts of God, is exogenous to the entire framework, although some variables will be exogenous to some partial analysis within that framework. (Thus, for example, the OPEC oil price is endogenous to a discussion of collusive bargaining behaviour in the oil sector, while the price of oil is exogenous to the behaviour of small manufacturers.)

In terms of the reality about which theories are constructed, the only logically autonomous element is the past, i.e. the only givens are events which have happened in the past. In a historical-time model, this notion can be captured in a way that it cannot in reversible mechanical time. In terms of monetary theory, the low elasticity of supply of a particular money asset in the past generates confidence in it for the future which is thus exogenous. If a financial crisis should occur which destroys confidence in that money asset, that will constitute an exogenous fact for the future, requiring action to repair confidence, or to provide an alternative money asset. As a corollary, there is only a limited sense in which money is 'intrinsically worthless', as Hahn (1980, p.1) puts it, namely that production costs are negligible. As neo-Austrians argue, money has worth in the sense that it is held with confidence on the basis of its history; although few currencies are still backed by gold, which has use value, there is confidence in the capacity of governments to maintain the exchange value of currency in the same way as when it was backed by gold. The 'trust' inherent in the financial system which seems so unsatisfactory in the general equilibrium framework sits comfortably in a framework which studies institutions as being the product of history. Herein lies the Post Keynesian case for a continued regulation of financial markets (see Dow, forthcoming, a).

Given this historical perspective, it is impossible to consider analysing an economy as if it were a barter economy, and then, maintaining the same structure, assess the effect of introducing money. Keynes made clear that he regarded his monetary theory as part of an entirely new framework designed specifically to analyse a monetary economy:

> [I]t is my belief that the far-reaching and in some respects fundamental differences between the conclusions of a monetary economy and those of the more simplified real-exchange economy have been greatly underestimated by the exponents of the traditional economics. ...The idea that it is comparatively easy to adapt the hypothetical conclusions of a real wage economics is a mistake. Accordingly I believe that the next task is to work out in some detail a monetary theory of production. (Keynes, 1973b, pp.410–11)

Indeed Keynes took his original inspiration for this monetary theory from Marx's notion of the monetary circuit within a capitalist economy, where money is not simply the means by which goods are exchanged for each other, but is itself the object of production (Rotheim, 1981).

We saw in Chapter 7 that Keynes at times assumed expectations to be constant, but the theory was always constructed in such a way that expectations were recognised to play a part. So he constructed his theory to incorporate the monetary features of a monetary economy, even when they were not given an active part in the analysis. The role of money in Post Keynesian analysis is determined by the context of historical time and uncertainty in which it is placed, just as analysis of money requires that attention be paid to historical time and uncertainty. Conversely, it is the absence of these features in mainstream theory which makes it so difficult to incorporate money and explain its presence. (See Davidson, 1977, for a full exposition of this argument.)

Within the context of historical time and uncertainty, money not only acts as a means of payment, but also as a store of value, and a unit of account. The latter function is not unimportant. If the governing motive of behaviour is accumulation, then, it is important how accumulation is measured. Money allows a measure of value which can be used to standardize the value of heterogeneous assets. This function is particularly important with respect to capital goods which have no identifiable 'real' value independent of their monetary value. This prevalence of money as a reference point in accumulation puts emphasis on money more than any other financial asset, and indeed the money value of an asset is that amount of money which could be received in exchange for the asset. In the same way, contracts are denominated predominately in money, as the most stable value reference point. (See Davidson, 1972, for a full discussion of the implications of the prevalence of money contracts.)

Inherent in the acceptability of a money-asset for the purposes of payment and unit of account is the presumption that the asset maintains its value relative to key variables in a more stable way than alternative assets. (Once a money asset is used as a unit of account, and indeed as a means of payment, comparison between alternative assets with respect to their stability relative to other variables other than in terms of money becomes difficult.) This feature also makes it suitable as a store of value. The need for a liquid asset as a store of value arises from the existence of uncertainty about the future of values of alternative assets. We saw that Tobin's depiction of portfolio choice within mechanical time, with no true uncertainty, left no room for money. But first, in historical time, there is continual scope for speculative trading, and the greatest capital gains and the smallest losses are made by those who trade at precisely the right time. But buying at the right time requires having money ready for when that time should transpire, which cannot be predicted accurately. For a firm considering buying a capital good, the purchase may be delayed until the price is at its most favourable. In the meantime the funds may be kept in liquid securities rather than money, but as long as the funds are used for buying existing financial assets rather than new physical assets, the effect on output and employment is in the same direction as if money itself were held. Put another way, Keynes's theory of liquidity preference can be interpreted in terms of decisions about moves along the liquidity spectrum of assets, rather than decisions about moves into or out of money itself, with very similar results (see Keynes, 1936, p.167; Townshend, 1937; also Dow and Earl, 1982, Chapter 8; Wells, 1983).

Second, uncertainty about the expected returns on alternative assets prevents individual investors from taking the decisive steps which Tobin portrays. At any one time, therefore, money will be held by some investors as they form expectations: in the absence of firm expectations as to the capital value of alternative assets, it is irrational to rush into buying such assets rather than more liquid assets. Uncertainty thus provides an additional rationale for the holding of money to the transactions motive. This is captured by the precautionary motive (Runde, 1994). The speculative motive relies on a presumption of certainty (whether warranted or not): that the prices of alternative assets will fall.

Systematic elements in liquidity preference arise from the Post Keynesian view that uncertainty (in Keynes's sense) does not lead to random behaviour. (Indeed the reverse may be the case; it is possible in some instances that the greater the uncertainty, the greater the reliance on conventions, and the more systematic the behaviour; see Heiner, 1983.) Keynes (1937) outlined the conventions which influence expectations: reliance on group expectations, extrapolation from the past, and so on. But such expectations are vulnerable to disappointment which, if severe enough, causes a collapse of confidence in current expectations, and the emergence of new conventional expectations. Thus it is not only the expectation of capital loss from holding securities which causes a rush for liquidity, but also a collapse of confidence in whatever expectations are currently held. Whatever is acceptable as money in such a situation provides a relatively safe haven until a new set of expectations is held with some confidence. If these new expectations are of falling asset prices, then money or other assets with fixed nominal value, will continue to act as a haven.

There is no scope for a natural rate of interest, since any stability is vulnerable to change. But a normal rate of interest will be held as a convention, as an anchor for decision-making, although the convention itself is vulnerable to surprises. The actual rate of interest is the outcome of the demand for and supply of liquidity in the light of the prevailing conventional view of what the normal interest rate would be. The actual rate of interest is thus determined by the state of expectations about asset prices, and the confidence with which they are held on the one hand, and the willingness and capacity of financial institutions to supply credit on the other, all in the light of conventional interpretations of past history. The importance of these variables for output and employment stems from the consequences for the purchase of new capital assets. A rush for liquidity is associated on the one hand with an unwillingness on the part of entrepreneurs to tie up borrowed capital in illiquid assets like capital goods, when there are doubts about their future value, and on the other with the unwillingness on the part of financial investors and financial institutions to retain assets in the illiquid form required by entrepreneurial borrowers. The interest rate is thus not the variable which equates planned investment and planned saving, but that which equates the demand for and supply of liquidity, where these are interdependent.

The systematic pattern in financial behaviour and its effect on output and employment can best be understood with reference to the business cycle (see Keynes, 1936, Chapter 22; also Keller and Carson, 1982; Dow, 1986–87). This framework also serves to illustrate the endogenous and exogenous features of the supply of money under different economic conditions. The major contribution on the interdependence of financial and production cycles has been made by Minsky (1975, 1982); see also Dow and Earl (1982, Chapters 2–5, 11).

Consistent with the historical equilibrium framework, there is no static equilibrium starting point to the cycle; we simply start by considering an economy in an expansionary phase. The expansion is fuelled by optimistic expectations about returns on new investment, which are self-fulfilling as effective demand increases. Confident expectations about increases in asset prices in general encourage minimal holding of idle money balances. At the same time, the same expectations held by financial institutions allow credit expansion to proceed apace. Eventually activity is diverted into markets for assets in relatively limited supply (real estate, etc.) where a high return in the form of capital gain is anticipated, and away from production where expected returns are more modest. The employment and output peak is thus determined by confidence in expected returns in speculative markets. Depending on the regulatory structure of the financial sector, and the degree of euphoria in speculative markets, it is possible for the financial expansion to continue until crisis point is reached. Generally, before that stage is reached, euphoria is dampened by more minor setbacks, like the failure of a market price to rise as much as expected or by capital losses due to mistaken decisions made in the heat of euphoria. As soon as confidence falters, the ripple effects of a cut-back in speculative buying extend through the financial system, with multiple effects resulting from the high gearing ratios associated with low liquidity preference. Financial institutions and other investors engage in a rush for liquidity; supply of credit contracts just as demand for it rises. In the meantime, physical investment has already peaked and the accelerator is putting production on a downward spiral, increasing the credit needs of employers and unemployed alike. Only when expectations are held with some confidence that new investment projects can earn a reasonable return will the turnaround occur; what is reasonable will depend partly on returns on existing assets, which in turn depend partly on the prevailing state of confidence in financial markets.

In summary, there is a systematic and interdependent pattern to the demand for and supply of money over the cycle. The endogeneity of the money supply can be seen to be accommodating in the upturn, but frustrating in the downturn. Further, the more accommodating it is in the upturn, the greater the danger of an irreversible financial crisis; the more frustrating it is in the downturn, the more prolonged the period before the next upturn. The pattern and level of production and employment over the cycle is interdependent with this cycle in liquidity preference and availability of liquidity.

Finally, it was pointed out earlier that some Post Keynesians have chosen not to analyse money explicitly on the grounds that its supply was endogenous (either due to policy action, or elastic institutional response). Others who focus on Keynes's theory of effective demand as the key issue have argued against analysing money on the theoretical grounds that it is only relevant to analysis of exchange, not of production (Eatwell, 1979; Eatwell and Milgate, 1983; Milgate, 1983; Magnani, 1983). While analysis of exchange can contribute to an understanding of short-run cycles, they argue that it detracts from an understanding of long-term trends.

As we have seen, however, the financial aspect of cycles is inextricably tied up with the 'real' production cycle. The choice to invest in new capital goods is a choice to borrow money, or not to lend it. The turning points in production cycles are determined by activity in financial markets and speculative markets;

full employment may never be reached at the cycle's peak. The average level of output and employment is thus influenced significantly by financial markets. Further, financial crises have irreversible consequences for production; not only are healthy financial markets required for efficient exchange, but they are necessary for the successful promotion of accumulation. Indeed, the view that production is a means to the end of accumulation means that activity in production and in financial speculation should not be separated, and these cannot be separated from money. Thus, even in the long run the rate of interest is a monetary phenomenon.

This difference of opinion has methodological origins. The position couched in terms of long-run analysis stems from the view that theory should constitute an exclusive complete system. It is pointed out correctly (e.g. by Eatwell, 1979) that Keynes did not always include money explicitly in his arguments. But, then, Keynes's method allowed for different chains of argument to be employed for different purposes. Indeed, few Post Keynesians would reject the notion that long-run models without money served a useful purpose – as long as they sit alongside models which do focus on money explicitly. Thus, for example, while Garegnani (1978, 1979) makes the case for long-run analysis of effective demand, he retains the Keynesian notion of the rate of interest as a monetary variable even in the long run (following Sraffa, 1960, p.33).

This debate is echoed within Marxian theory, to which we now turn, although it is the traditional Marxian position to regard monetary theory as peripheral, and more of a radical innovation (in the sense of reinterpreting Marx) to construct theory around monetary variables.

8.5 Marxian Theory

Marxian theory, like Post Keynesian, is a theory of production in a monetary economy; while monetary factors are not often explicit, it is not because they are assumed to be absent, simply assumed constant. Indeed, the fact that *Capital* starts with a theoretical analysis of money is an indication of its importance in Marx's theoretical structure (see de Brunhoff, 1973, Introduction). Methodologically, the approach is similar to that later adopted by Keynes and was subject to similar misinterpretation. While the monetary nature of a capitalist economy was regarded by Marx as fundamental, the fact that monetary variables did not feature explicitly in all aspects of his analysis has traditionally been interpreted as signifying that money is not in fact important. There has, however, been a recent revival of interest in Marxian monetary theory, led particularly by de Brunhoff. The modern Marxian analysis of financial crisis bears strong similarities to Post Keynesian theory of business cycles, not least because Marx's own theory of credit was not fully developed. In addition, Panico's (1980, 1983) development of Marxian theory of the long-run determination of the rate of interest suggests a satisfactory solution to the apparent lack of a monetary theory of the rate of interest in Marx's work.

Marx's monetary theory is historical, in the sense that the nature and role of money are analysed in terms of the historical development of economic structure. Like Keynes, Marx saw the functions of money as means of exchange, unit of account and store of value as being intimately connected (see Lavoie, 1983, pp.61-2). In pre-capitalist economies, money is used as a means of payment, a means of exchanging a commodity produced by a person's own labour for another commodity. This is described by the circuit C-M-C', where C and C' are different commodities, and M is money. One commodity, C, can be sold for money, M, with which the second commodity C' may be bought. There is scope for trade credit, so that purchase of C' is possible before C has been produced; but this is only possible if the seller of C' has acquired money which has not yet been converted into commodities. In other words, there is a fixed stock of money corresponding to production; credit simply consists of a redistribution of the means of exchange.

In a capitalist economy, the aim of capitalists is to make profits, to accumulate, to amass value. Money is employed to finance capitalist production, where workers are employed in order for surplus labour value to be extracted. This is described by the circuit M-C-M', where now labour (or labour value in the form of capital goods) is acquired with an initial stock of money, M, in order for that labour to yield surplus value, amounting to (M'-M), by producing the commodity C which is sold at a profit for M'. The exchange of C for M' is the realization of the increased value; money is the general commodity by which the value of all other commodities is measured, the general equivalent. But the realization of value is made difficult in a capitalist economy by the fact that money is no longer a given stock of commodity money whose value is stable, but a combination of money and credit determined by the behaviour of the banking system. Credit in such a system is a vehicle for expanding the stock of money available for financial capital expenditure, on the basis of the stock of commodity money (as bank reserves). The realization problem stems from the contradiction between the capacity of banks to expand credit, and the consequent reduction in the exchange value of money; ultimately, credit expansion can bring about a financial crisis; such a crisis, involving a resumed preference for commodity money at the expense of credit money, serves to reaffirm confidence in the commodity-money system on which the financial (credit) system is built. Marx thus retains an objective basis for the monetary system in commodity money, which reflects more easily the context in which he was writing than the present arrangement of financial institutions.

This connection between the quantity of money and value does not mean, however, that Marx accepted the Quantity Theory of Money in the traditional form, where the supply of money is exogenous and velocity of circulation is stable (Lapavitsas, 1994). Rather Marx saw causation running from production to money; credit was created to finance circulation, but it did not cause circulation. The supply of credit was endogenous to the production process. Indeed, money circulating as a result of credit creation could be hoarded (thereby reducing the velocity of circulation). While increasing liquidity preference in Keynes's theory is regarded as an impediment to the proper working of the economy, hoarding in Marxian theory is regarded as a positive contribution to the monetary system; it allows the value of money to be preserved when the supply of credit is increased excessively.

Marx did not have a theory of business cycles as such, but his theory of financial crisis is readily adaptable to a theory of more regular, cyclical phenomena (Lapavitsas, 1994). But there is dispute as to whether financial crisis can occur independently of production crisis, or whether it is simply one manifestation of overproduction. The theory of accumulation and crisis is one of the significant areas of fragmentation in modern Marxian theory (Norton, 1992). The predominant elements of Cartesian/Euclidean thought in Marxian analysis promote an 'either/or' approach to the question of crisis causation: either it has its origins in financial crisis or in production crisis. The difficulties this poses for analysis are apparent in statements such as the following:

> Such speculative crises have substantial effects; they can put a strain upon surplus value production and disrupt the course of accumulation. It then appears that the sole origin of crises lies in financial manipulations ... But Marx demonstrates that (speculative fevers) are surface froth upon much deeper currents making for disequilibrium. ... The difficulty here is to disentangle the pure surface froth of perpetual speculation from the deeper rhythms of crisis formation in production. (Harvey, 1982, p.325)

There appears to be a contradiction between the capacity for financial crisis to affect production on the one hand and the denials on the other hand of the importance for the 'deeper rhythms' of the capitalist process of financial crises which occur independently of production crises. No contradiction is necessary if producers' investment decisions are seen to be governed by both the financial and production aspects of accumulation in a speculative environment. There need then be no sharp dichotomy between a 'surface froth' and 'deeper rhythms'; such a dichotomy arises from the conventional deductivist interpretation of Marx's method, where causal chains must be common to all analysis, long-term and short-term. Overproduction crisis may be the more frequent cause of financial crisis, but there is no inherent reason to rule out a feedback from financial crisis, independently caused, to production.

Let us consider first a financial crisis caused by overproduction, i.e. by 'real' factors. Financial crisis is the upshot of demand and supply conditions in the credit and money markets. Credit expands with producers' requirements for financing production activity. When it transpires that producers' expectations have been unrealistically optimistic, i.e. when overproduction becomes apparent in some product markets, loans cannot be repaid and further credit is required as working capital. Bankers in turn retrench on their credit policies as the risk attached to loans increases, so that the supply of credit contracts as demand for it increases, raising interest rates. The multiplied effects of contracting effective demand for goods further increases the demand for credit in other industries, while financial institutions attempt to draw in the pyramid of credit before multiple failures occur. It is this hoarding behaviour of bankers which preserves the confidence held in money, as opposed to credit, and allows for the regeneration of the credit system after the crisis.

But a crisis can also start in financial markets. The initial over-expansion of credit can have been to finance speculative activity in markets for existing assets. Increasing borrowers' and lenders' risk, when it becomes apparent that expectations about asset prices were unrealistically high, encourage a rush for liquidity by borrowers, as well as by bankers, again with multiple contractionary effects on credit and rising interest rates. This purely speculative financial cycle can impinge on production by influencing investment plans. Expectations of returns on existing assets rising relative to those on new capital goods encourages a postponement of investment plans; accumulation on the part of corporations can be served equally by capital gains on existing assets as by surplus value extracted in production. In turn, the contraction of credit which follows a speculative bubble impedes the financing of new investment projects. As in the Post Keynesian theory of cyclical behaviour, the interest rate in Marxian crisis theory is determined by competition in financial markets. It is both the symptom of past production and financial conditions, as well as a factor in plans for the future. The major 'real' effect in the Marxian model, however, where the changing structure of capitalism is of more concern than levels of output, employment and capacity, is that a financial crisis (however caused) allows the destruction of value which in turn allows the greater concentration of ownership of the means of production.

While competition in financial markets determines the rate of interest in the short run, the question remains as to whether there is any long-run tendency in the rate of interest, as with the rate of profit. The answer lies in distinguishing between the class of money capitalists and that of industrial capitalists (see Panico, 1980, 1983). The former are the owners of money-capital or its creators (banks), on whom industrial capitalists depend for financing new investment. Both classes have accumulation as their goal. The money circuit can be amended to take this into account, adding the circulation of money, M, from money capitalists (including banks) to industrial capitalists to finance production of commodities, C, generating surplus value, which is realized on the sale of the commodities for a larger amount of money, M'o; the original capital, M, is then repaid with interest, together totalling M'. The expanded circuit is thus of the form: M - M - C - M' - M", where M' is the original value M plus surplus value, and M" is the original value plus interest. (Bankers enter into each of the sets of transactions, while money capitalists in general enter only into the first and last.)

Surplus value is thus shared between the industrial capitalist and the money capitalist as profit and interest, respectively. In this sense, the rate of interest must act as a floor to the expected rate of profit, influencing the decision to invest. This conclusion conflicts with the Ricardian notion of the rate of profit determined by the given wage rate to which Marx elsewhere adhered; this remained an unresolved contradiction in Marx's analysis.

The share of surplus between profit and interest is determined by class struggle between bankers and industrialists. For long periods there will be a historically-determined convention as to the normal rate of interest, the level depending on the relative power of bankers during the relevant period. In turn, industrial capitalists can protect their profits by their price-setting behaviour. Thus, an increase in interest rates unaccompanied by a relative increase in the power of bankers need not eat into profits if product prices are increased accordingly. Indeed, Marx (1894, Part V, Chapter 34) did at one point adopt a cost-push theory of inflation, with the rate of interest a major influence in prices.

This view of the long-term rate of interest contrasts sharply with that of Ricardo, as well as of contemporary mainstream theorists, where the rate of interest and the rate of profit are equal and uniform as a result of competition; here the rate of interest, even in the long-run, is a monetary phenomenon. Also, while Ricardo (and, elsewhere, Marx) had treated the real wage as given, leaving the rate of profit (equal to the rate of interest) as the residual, Marx's monetary theory has the price level, and thus the real wage, endogenous to the struggle between money and industrial capitalists. Attempts by money capitalists to increase their return by raising interest rates provoke an increase in product prices on the part of industrial capitalists, and thereby an erosion of the real wage. Further, the long-run rate of profit net of interest is as much the outcome of the relative power of industrial capitalists as of the physical capacity to attract surplus with an increasing organic composition of capital.

This class explanation of the rate of interest can still be translated into a monetary theory of the rate of interest. The relative power of the two capitalist classes can be represented by the need for liquidity of each, and by their capacity and willingness to supply it. Both classes can, under different economic conditions be borrowers and lenders with respect to the other. Such an expression of class power would bring Marxian monetary theory closer to Post Keynesian monetary theory. Otherwise, the dependence of the rate of interest on class drives a wedge between the two approaches.

There is, further, debate about the extent to which money capitalists and industrial capitalists are protagonists, and how far the two groups overlap. In many countries, the coincidence of the money-capitalist and industrial-capitalist classes coincide. This also raises the question of the significance of the monetary authorities in their influence on interest rates, an issue which we explore in the next chapter, which deals with policy issues.

Marxian monetary theory as presented here is in a state of evolution which in some sense mirrors that of general equilibrium monetary theory, in that attempts are being made to convert a traditional 'real economy' analysis into a monetary economy analysis. The process is aided by the germs of an integrated monetary theory put forward by Marx himself.

8.6   Conclusion

The respective treatments of money by each of our four schools of thought, and differences within those schools, illustrate the significance of their treatments of micro-foundations, expectations and equilibrium, and ultimately of the underlying modes of thought.

Neo-Austrians analyse money in terms of its significance for individual decision-makers; its only significance at the macro level is that the financial system is regulated and manipulated by the monetary authorities. The price of money, the interest rate, is the key monetary variable, since it enters into decisions of entrepreneurs as to whether to borrow in order to engage in more roundabout methods of production. All decision-making is speculative, and expectations about relative rates of return are subject to unsystematic error. While the decision to hold more or less money, therefore, is also speculative, there is no role for speculative demand for money in the Keynesian sense. This is the result of the absence of any basis for systematic trends of uncertainty, particularly trends started by crowd behaviour. But the prevalence of uncertainty in actual economic decision-making is the justification for employing equilibrium as a historical concept. While the Quantity Theory is accepted as a tautology, given the assumptions of stability of velocity, and so on, the tendency for the structure of the financial system to adapt to changing conditions limits the applicability of the theory. Money's importance is that of a variable entering into investment decisions which happens to be under the influence of the public sector.

Mainstream analysis on the other hand is limited in the extent to which money can be incorporated at all. The attempt to develop micro-foundations for general equilibrium macroeconomics, based on the axioms of rational individual behaviour, has failed to come up with an adequate rationale for holding money in equilibrium. The mainstream framework limits the type of uncertainty which is consistent with equilibrium, and the capacity of economies to reach it; similarly, expectations formation is constrained to follow a deterministic pattern which ensures return to long-run equilibrium. Nevertheless, while the demand for money is endogenous to the system (no matter how tenuous its rationale), the exogeneity of the money supply is of considerable importance, constituting, until the growth of real business cycle theory, the major source of explanation of business cycle fluctuations. But then, any exogenous variable which was a technical input to production or exchange could provide such an explanation. Money's peculiarity, then, is not a result of its peculiarity as a commodity (which cannot be explained within the mainstream framework) but a result of its control by the monetary authorities. This, combined with the Quantity Theory, which implies that inflation is caused by increases in the money supply by the authorities, is why money is of such importance in policy applications of mainstream theory.

Post Keynesian theory, like neo-Austrian theory, takes as its starting point the institutional features of a monetary economy, and the speculative nature of decision-making. But, since systematic behaviour under uncertainty is suggested by the social (rather than individual) analysis of financial institutions and behaviour, the role of money as a receptacle of uncertainty takes on major significance. In particular, the systematic features of the business cycle include as an important element the low liquidity preference of the upturn phase, as maximum capital gains are sought on margin, and the rush for liquidity as confidence in the prospect of capital gains collapses. The cycle also provides a framework for analysing the endogenous nature of the money supply. The path of this endogeneity mirrors, and is interdependent with, that of liquidity preference, accommodating demand for credit in the upturn, but frustrating it in the downturn. The inherently speculative nature of markets in which activity is concentrated during the peak of the boom phase ensures that the interest rate is then governed by purely monetary phenomena. Investment decisions made in this 'short-run' environment, together with the damaging consequences for the financial system of a financial crisis if credit expansion in the boom phase is excessive, ensure that monetary factors influence the long run also.

The common features between Post Keynesian and Marxian analysis ensure that there are several features in common in their monetary theory. Money in Marxian theory is also studied as an institution which is conditioned by its history. With the development of financial institutions to meet the needs of expanding production, there developed also a range of markets in financial assets which offer scope for speculation. The analysis of the role of money in the crisis phase bears a strong resemblance to the Post Keynesian theory of business cycles. But in Marxian theory, the crisis is a necessary feature of capitalism and hoarding is regarded in a positive light as the means by which the crisis is brought about; the crisis cleanses the system, while restoring confidence in money, creating the conditions for a return to normal full-capacity output. In the short run, the rate of interest is a monetary variable. It is also a monetary variable in the long run, representing the share of money capitalists of surplus value. The distribution of that value between industrial capitalists, as profit, and money capitalists, as interest, is determined by the relative power of the two classes. The outcome of their struggle, if each tries to increase its share, is for product prices to rise, real wages to fall, and thus the share of labour in the total value of output to fall. There is, however, a major difference of opinion between traditional Marxians and those currently working in monetary theory about the active or passive role of money and finance in the capitalist process.

We are already on the brink of establishing the policy stances which follow naturally from these stances on theory. It is the task of the next chapter to explore these policy implications, not least in terms of the leap that is required from statements in terms of an abstract theory to policy recommendations in particular economic contests.

9 Methodology and Macroeconomic Policy

9.1 Introduction

We have considered macroeconomics at three levels so far: mode of thought, methodology and theory. In this chapter we extend the discussion to a fourth level: policy applications. By policy is meant government measures taken to influence the economy. It is a commonly held view among applied economists that study of methodology is a luxury for economists, perhaps better left to philosophers. But we have already seen how the methodological stance of each school of thought has determined the type of theory regarded as admissible. It also influences the policy applications of theory in a variety of ways.

First, a school's methodological stance includes a view as to the purpose of theory, particularly in relation to policy questions: is theory first and foremost an intellectual exercise or a means toward the end of guiding policy (or need these be mutually exclusive as primary goals)? Second, there is the all-important question of how theory corresponds to reality and thus how far it is capable of guiding policy. Third, the theoretical structure required by a particular methodological stance determines the types of question which theory can answer; these questions may or may not correspond to questions of importance to policy-makers.

Having said that, it is still possible for different schools of thought to come up with similar policy recommendations. But, to be most effective, any particular macroeconomic policy measure should be part of a coherent overall macroeconomic strategy. It is usually important for the success of any policy that it be employed cohesively as part of a package, not only to ensure consistency, but also to ensure that there is the grounding for flexible response to changing conditions. Accordingly, it is helpful to consider the reasoning behind particular policy proposals and the range of policy measures of which each is envisaged as a part.

We will now proceed to consider the policy stances which arise from each school of thought's methodological position and resulting theoretical structure.

In each case, we consider first their methodological position on the relation between theory and policy. Then particular policy proposals are discussed in the areas of inflation and unemployment policy, and the related areas of the conduct of monetary policy and of international economic policy.

9.2   Neo-Austrian Policy

Relation between theory and policy

Modern neo-Austrian theory takes as one of its main purposes to make the workings of the economy more intelligible, on the basis of an understanding of human action. Further, the context in which theory is most frequently presented is one of economic policy. Indeed, Hayek's work in particular combines economics and politics in questions about the role of the state. Implicit in neo-Austrian theory, then, is the view that one purpose of economic theory is to guide policy. But economic theory is presented as only one aspect of the 'science of human action'; the broader purpose of neo-Austrian economic theory is to analyse the role of government economic policy.

The clearest statement of the role of neo-Austrian theory in relation to policy issues is found in Hayek's critique of socialist planning: 'it is not necessary, for the working of this [market] system, that anybody should understand it. But people are not likely to let it work if they do not understand it' (Hayek, 1949, p.124). Hayek goes on to argue that the growing acceptance of a planning role for government was the outcome on the one hand of analytical economists being 'far too much concerned with the reconstructing of the purely abstract foundations of economic science to exert a noticeable influence on opinion regarding policy' and on the other of the historical school of economists limiting their task to description (Hayek, 1949, p.125). Hayek thus advocates policy-oriented analytical economic theory which explains the actual workings of economies, and thereby provides a theoretical basis on which to assess the relative merits of government intervention.

There is thus a claim that neo-Austrian theory bears a direct relation to reality. Indeed, it is the relationship between theory and reality which forms a significant part of the theory of human action. The only significant known fact is known through introspection of the purposefulness of human action. Other facts, particularly product prices, *may* be observed objectively, but are of limited importance since they are the outcome of the subjective estimates of opportunity cost on the part of sellers and utility on the part of buyers (Buchanan and Thirlby, 1973). It is the formulation of these subjective estimates which is of particular interest to the theorist. It is of interest also to the individual trader-as-theorist; future market prices are the outcome of subjective evaluations of currently available information, which includes the motivation and judgement of other traders. Without knowing intimately the mental processes and information access of each individual, it is impossible to predict accurately day-to-day outcomes. But given theory built on the assumption of purposeful action and an understanding of the institutions prevailing in any particular context (which ultimately can be explained in terms of purposeful action) these market outcomes can be explained.

The significant aspects of the reality which neo-Austrian theory can explain, therefore, are not observable in a manner which allows quantification. In spite of Hayek's (1937) espousal of the principle of falsification, therefore, the scope for empirical work in the normal sense is extremely limited; it is only feasible at the level of individual or organizational behaviour, certainly not at the macroeconomic level. Neo-Austrians reject general equilibrium theorizing because purposeful action is seen as continually changing the structure within which actions are taken; this in itself precludes econometric work where the structure of the model is given for observations over several periods. In addition, action is regarded as inherently unpredictable, so that no systematic modelling of behaviour is possible. The alternative of macro-modelling where macroeconomic variables are not derivable from microeconomic theory lacks appeal because it has broken the tie with the linchpin of purposeful action. Certainly, a variable like the general price level is calculable from the objective facts of product prices. But it has no meaning for individual action, which only takes account of prices of products in which trades are being considered. Prediction of the future level of prices in general is therefore not useful. As we shall see below, however, macroeconomic concepts such as unemployment and inflation, which must be measured centrally to be known, form an important part of neo-Austrian theory on the role of macroeconomic policy.

This wedding of theory to individual behaviour determines the range of policy issues to which neo-Austrian theory lends itself. In the area of macroeconomic policy, which we discuss in the next section, the question of whether or not governments should attempt to stabilize the economy can be addressed, but not how much, or in what way. Where particular macroeconomic policies are discussed, the neo-Austrian critique is always couched in microeconomic terms (Hayek, 1972). And indeed, the major proportion of discussion of policy issues (except in Hayek's case) is of microeconomic policies: industry regulation, monopoly legislation, policy to deal with externalities from particular activities, etc. (Littlechild, 1978, 1981).

A major area of policy analysis precluded by neo-Austrian methodological individualism is the promotion of economic growth, other than as a microeconomic problem (Lachmann, 1976b). Lachmann (1977, pp.323–37) considers the role of planning in the form of central information generation as a means of promoting growth. Having acknowledged the potential benefits of such information, however, he concludes that the market will generate institutions to provide this information where it is judged to be necessary. While capital theory (influenced by Böhm-Bawerk) has traditionally been a distinguishing feature of neo-Austrian thought, modern neo-Austrians reject the application of capital theory at the macroeconomic level of Böhm-Bawerk, on the grounds that capital is heterogeneous:

> In my view this controversy about a fictitious macroeconomic magnitude [capital] is a symptom of the arid mathematical formalism that afflicts both schools. For in a market economy a uniform rate of return on all capital invested does not exist. (Lachmann, 1976a, p.147).

Inflation and unemployment policy

While inflation and unemployment data have no significance at the level of individual behaviour, they do reflect the prevalence of rising prices of individual products (on average) and of individuals without employment. And indeed they have significance as the data on which policy-makers base their judgements. Hayek has consistently, since his early debates with Keynes (Hayek, 1941), identified persistent inflation and/or unemployment as evidence of misguided attempts by governments to influence the macroeconomy. (Hayek's critique of Keynes's policy prescriptions is of Keynes as a descendant of classical theory, which also relied on aggregative concepts.) That the co-existence of inflation and unemployment in the 1970s is interpreted as an outcome of frustrated governmental attempts to reduce unemployment is encapsulated in the title of the volume devoted to Hayek's (1972) critique of Keynesian economics: *A Tiger by the Tail: The Keynesian Legacy of Inflation*.

Unemployment can arise through the decline of some sectors, where adjustment of workers' expectations, search behaviour and retraining all contribute to a transitional period of frictional unemployment. Since the normal working of the economy involves a continuous process of changing relative positions of firms and industries, such unemployment is inevitable. The extent of frictional unemployment, however, can be worsened if there is downward rigidity of money wages; successful adjustment requires an adjustment of relative rewards in different industries to reflect the relative strength of product demand. Successful adjustment, with wage floors set by trades unions, therefore requires upward wage adjustment in growing industries. The net effect on costs, and thus prices, is always in the upward direction, rather than some balance between increases and decreases. Union power can thus account for the co-existence of inflation and unemployment, with the former accelerating if the wage floor increases with inflation. The effects of union power are reinforced by the price-setting behaviour of firms in uncompetitive markets (Lachmann, 1977, pp. 295–6).

One possible policy implication, then, is for government action to be taken to weaken trade-union power. Most Western governments, however, at least in the 1950s and 1960s, employed demand management policies to reduce unemployment. These included measures to prevent the decline in demand in particular industries, and thus the decline in the relative price of their products which free market forces would have brought about. Again, the price level was underpinned, requiring price increases in the expanding industries to maintain the appropriate relative price configurations. Rigidities in the price structure were also reinforced by government regulation of private industries, as well as price-setting in the nationalized industries.

These measures were accompanied by monetary growth which, according to Hayek's (1933) theory of the trade cycle, increases output and employment in the capital goods sector above their natural levels, putting upward pressure on the prices of both consumer and capital goods. Continual monetary expansion maintains the upward pressure on prices. While Hayek supports the monetarist policy stance of reduced monetary growth as a means of reducing inflation, he does not regard it as the full solution, as long as there are rigidities in the price mechanism itself:

> If we want to preserve the market economy our aim must be to restore the effectiveness of the price mechanism. The chief obstacle to its functioning is trade union monopoly. It does not come from the side of money, and an exaggerated expectation of what can be achieved by monetary policy has diverted our attention from the chief causes. Though money may be one of them if it is mismanaged, monetary policy can do no more than prevent disturbances by *monetary* causes: it cannot remove those which come from other sources. (Hayek, 1972, p. 119)

Thus, Hayek's macroeconomic policy stance is derived from neo-Austrian methodological individualism; macroeconomic solutions are to be found at the microeconomic level. Hayek's macroeconomic policy is that governments should not engage in macroeconomic policy. Nevertheless, he recognizes that the transition to an absence of policy, as well as to increased competitiveness of labour markets, requires significant structural change. He thus makes positive policy proposals to ease the transition, such as worker profit-sharing schemes (Hayek, 1972, pp. 117-8).

Implicitly, in making such proposals, Hayek is accepting the notion that governments, and their advisers, may have information which is not available to the individuals concerned in a policy issue. As soon as neo-Austrians go beyond arguments for individualism rather than government intervention, and make policy proposals at the macro level, they are implying that economists have superior knowledge of the unintended consequences of human action; this poses a conflict with the limited goal of making the economy intelligible, given the informational limitations of those not actively involved in trading in particular markets. This conflict is implicit in the type of statement made elsewhere by Hayek, for example:

> If man is not to do more harm than good in his efforts to improve the social order, he will have to learn that ... where essential complexity of an organised kind prevails, *he cannot acquire the full knowledge which would make mastery of the events possible.* He will therefore have to use what knowledge he can achieve, not to shape the results as a craftsman shapes his handiwork, but rather to cultivate a growth by providing the appropriate environment, as the gardener does for his plants. (Hayek, 1975, p. 42).

Yet, neo-Austrian theory states that the institutional environment itself is the outcome of purposeful action. Thus policy prescriptions for institutional change also seem to be excluded by methodological individualism. Proposals for change in public-sector, rather than private-sector, institutions require a further justification which differentiates these institutions from freely formed, non-coercive private-sector institutions. Among neo-Austrians, this complex area has been explored in depth only by Hayek (1960). But it is central to the justification of any policy proposals from a methodological individualistic perspective.

The conduct of monetary policy

Given the present institutional structure of the banking system, with bank reserves supplied by the monetary authorities, Hayek shared the monetarist view that inflation can be reduced by reducing the rate of growth of the money supply. Further, he argued (Hayek, 1975) that the reduction should be made as quickly as possible. The problem with excessive monetary growth is only partly due to inflation as such, which diverts activity to heavily indebted firms whose capital gains as a result of inflation 'artificially' increase their rate of return on equity (Lachmann, 1977, p. 300). But, in addition, as long as the interest rate is held below the natural rate, mistaken investment will occur; as a corollary, the sooner interest rates emit the 'correct' signals, the more appropriate will be the level and composition of investment.

But then, what ensures that money supply growth will be maintained at such a rate that the natural rate of interest will prevail? First, the notion of the money supply as a quantifiable stock is alien to the neo-Austrian view of money as being whatever is subjectively perceived as money. But, in any case, Hayek perceived monetary authorities as pursuing the aims of a few interest groups, which are not necessarily the aims of money-users in general. In fact, as long as the economy is in a constant state of flux, with some industries expanding and others contracting, money requirements cannot be predicted accurately. (The total stock of money could rise or fall and the general price level fall or rise, without the real natural rate of interest being affected.) The system must be sufficiently elastic to meet needs which are warranted by market forces. There is a particular reluctance to impose strict limits on monetary growth because of the dangers they would pose of financial crisis once the limits were reached (Hayek, 1978, p. 77). (There is a contradiction here with the policy proposal to curtail any monetary growth at a stroke in order to restore the interest rate to its natural rate.)

Indeed Hayek (1978) opted for the logical extension of neo-Austrian theory in advocating that money creation be taken out of the public sector altogether. Under a free banking system, competition between banks, whose own notes would then be money, would ensure the appropriate elasticity of supply. There would be no need for commodity backing of the banking system, since competitive forces would discipline any excessive issue of notes by any one bank. (Followers of Hayek have proposed a variety of schemes for providing a standard of value; see for example Dowd, 1993.) Hayek advocates that this reform be carried out as soon as possible to avert inflationary pressures; the public thus are to be persuaded of the greater truth of the neo-Austrian version of economic processes than the predominant view, which Hayek alleges, supports Keynesian policies:

> There is thus an immense educational task ahead before we can hope to free ourselves from the gravest threat to social peace and continued prosperity inherent in existing monetary institutions. (Hayek, 1978, p. 130)

International economic policy

Neo-Austrian policy for international economic relationships is a logical extension of domestic policy. Its aim is to promote the activity of free market forces as the best way of allocating resources: an important feature, then, is the promotion of relative price flexibility. Thus Hayek (1978, pp. 109–13) in fact argues against flexible exchange rates, since they allow relative price changes at the economy level, *en bloc*, impeding relative price changes at the micro level. Rather, he argues that national currencies should be fixed irrevocably against each other to allow relative price changes to occur without offsetting exchange rate changes. Thus declining industries could not be protected by an exchange devaluation (which would at the same time lower all other prices of domestic goods in international markets).

The international economy is treated as a natural extension of the domestic economy. The domestic economy is characterized by goods, tastes, expectations, etc. which are heterogeneous because of the heterogeneity of individuals' subjectivity, but also because of the spatial dispersal of individuals. The international economy simply extends that heterogeneity over more individuals and a larger spatial area. The neo-Austrian objections to discussing macroeconomic aggregates extend to discussions of international economic relations in terms of the macroeconomic variables of each country. On the one hand, the domestic policy stance of promoting competition is extended internationally. On the other, international economic relations add to domestic market forces; for example, an excessive issue of notes by all banks within one country (with a free banking system) would be discouraged by a flight into sounder foreign money. Indeed, Hayek (1978, p. 129) advocates free banking in terms of a 'Free Money Movement comparable to the Free Trade Movement of the 19th century'; free trade of course is a major feature of neo-Austrian international policy.

9.3   Mainstream Policy

Relation between theory and policy

Unlike neo-Austrian theory, mainstream theory is presented explicitly as an abstraction from reality rather than as a representation of reality. It is this which allows scope for analysis in terms of macroeconomic aggregates, and representative individuals and firms, in spite of the atomistic nature of the basic axioms. Theory is expressed as a metaphor for reality. While the use of theoretical abstraction allows considerable range for policy statements, it introduces the problem of how to translate an argument expressed in terms of a metaphor into a policy prescription for application in the real world. This problem is common to all theories, which involve abstraction from reality. But the formulation of general equilibrium theory gives a particular character to the problem. Further, the methodological differences within the broad category of general equilibrium theory have important implications for the form which the problem of policy application of theory takes.

It is not at all straightforward to glean from much of the policy literature the view taken of how to deal with the transition from theory to policy prescription. Within the neo-classical synthesis, the transition appeared to have been taken care of by econometric models of the macroeconomy (Cuthbertson, 1979). The criteria for good econometric models were primarily instrumentalist, but also included conventions as to what constituted a reasonable configuration of explanatory variables. Within this framework, policy questions took the form: 'What would be the outcome of a ten per cent increase in government expenditure?' The econometric model, which had already established a connection between theory and observation, would generate a simulation analysis result, which could be compared with the simulation of an alternative policy measure, to allow a decision to be taken.

The rational expectations critique of the neo-classical synthesis was explicitly methodological, suggesting that an inadequate theoretical foundation for this econometric work rendered it inevitably incapable of predictive success. This critique raised consciousness of the whole issue of the specific methodological questions associated with translating theory into policy prescription. It is one thing to capture regularities in economic relationships in the past with an econometric model; that is certainly an important means of checking the applicability of the theoretical metaphor to reality. It is another matter to extend that metaphor to predict the outcome of a change in the activities of government, which performs a very special rôle in the economy. The particular feature of government on which rational expectations theory focused was the degree to which its activities could be anticipated correctly by individual economic agents. This raised two related issues: To what extent is government behaviour systematic in pursuing its own goals, and to what extent does this allow individuals to anticipate government activity?

While the neo-classical synthesis had treated government behaviour as exogenous, a decision-variable for policy-makers, the rational expectations approach was to endogenize government behaviour, and to include expectations as to that behaviour in the decision-making of individuals. This was all done explicitly in conformity with the axioms of rational behaviour. This leads to the strong policy result that only unanticipated action by government can throw individual behaviour off its equilibrium path; i.e. have a real impact on the economy (Sargent and Wallace, 1975). To be successfully unanticipated, government action must deliberately conform to a random pattern; as a corollary, systematic policy action will be fully anticipated, and discounted in individual behaviour. Thus deliberate randomness is the only surviving exogenous variable, aside from those events outside the purview of individual decision-making (natural disasters, etc.), and random private-sector behaviour.

However, by endogenizing all behaviour in this way, rational expectations theorists have backed themselves into a corner reminiscent of neo-Austrian economics. If governments already act optimally with respect to their goals, according to the rational expectations formulation, and if individual decision-makers are represented as already taking account of all existing information concerning future influences on government policy (which is all that is available to the modeller), there is no apparent logical basis for deriving policy conclusions which would lead to advice to the government to do other than it would have done anyway (Sargent, 1984). Policy advice is only justified if existing behaviour, conditioned by expectations based on available information, is not optimal.

The attention drawn by rational expectations theory to the *process* of government decision-making, and to the reactions of the private sector to anticipate government behaviour, has added some realism to the mechanical policy discussion of the neo-classical synthesis. Yet the structure of the model itself still determines the nature and scope of policy discussion. The following passage from a macroeconomic text book is very revealing. It is an analogy designed to explain the monetarist rationale for policy by rules, rather than being open to the discretion of policy-makers in response to emerging situations; it is equally applicable to rational expectations advocacy of a non-intervention rule, given the shared view of how the economy works.

> Imagine that you are listening to an FM radio station in a crowded part of the wave band. The signals are repeatedly and randomly drifting, so that, from time to time, your station drifts out of hearing, and a neighbouring station in which you have no interest comes through loud and clear. What should you do to get a stronger and more persistent signal from the station you want to hear?
>
> The Keynesian says, 'Hand on to the tuning knob and whenever the signal begins to fade, fiddle with the knob, attempting, as best you can, to stay with the signal.'
>
> The Monetarist says, 'Get yourself a good quality AFC (automatic frequency control) tuner; set it on the station you wish to hear; sit back; relax; and enjoy the music. Do not fiddle with the tuner knob; your reception will not be perfect, but on average you will not be able to do any better than the AFC.' (Parkin and Bade, 1982, p. 9)

Note that the entire analogy rests on the assumption that what required correction is *random*. This view is inherent in the mainstream theoretical framework, which is built on the presumption of the equilibrating tendencies of market economies.

Outside the rational expectations approach, government behaviour is still treated as exogenous, and thus open to advice; the formulation of that advice is discussed in terms determined by the mainstream framework. Thus governments are portrayed as pursuing a clearly defined set of goals, subject to a set of constraints. The choice of goals is a normative matter which can be distinguished from the positive matter of pursuing them. Policy instruments are then selected for an optimal strategy to meet targets required to achieve these goals, and their optimal values established (Theil, 1961; Tinbergen, 1952, 1965). Attention is paid to what is called the uncertainty attached to the government's capacity to establish the optimal values for the targets (to achieve the desired rate of growth of the money supply to meet the inflation goal, for example). But uncertainty, consistent with its treatment elsewhere in the mainstream framework, is defined as random deviations from a known mean; variables can then be ascribed 'certainty equivalents'; the only relevance of this form of uncertainty (which is in fact risk) is that some instruments and targets may be subject to less variance around the mean than others, introducing an additional factor into the choice among the range of possible instrument and targets (Brainard, 1967; Poole, 1970).

In practice, much policy advice arising from the broad mainstream framework is much more pragmatic, taking account of the particular context in which the advice is to be employed. But the above is more representative of the *professed* view of the policy process, as represented in textbooks, for example. Curiously, the most *consciously* pragmatic policy prescriptions come from an unexpected quarter: pure general equilibrium theory. This component of the broad mainstream school of thought has traditionally eschewed policy discussions. However, Hahn (1973b) has been notable in addressing the questions of the applicability of general equilibrium theory to policy questions. Unlike rational expectations theorists who equate observations with positions of equilibrium, Hahn rather takes the view that the conditions required for a stable market equilibrium are so restrictive as to demonstrate the general inapplicability of the theory to practical questions. As a result he has sometimes stepped outside this framework in order to discuss policy questions (see Hahn, 1983, p. ix).

Perhaps the most difficult stumbling block in applying mainstream theory is the pervasive use of mechanical time. The question of historical time is central to many policy discussions within the framework, yet most of the theory is couched in terms of mechanical time. For example, New Keynesians are associated with a normative concern for the consequences of disturbances in the short run, although there is agreement on the nature of the long-run equilibrium position. But then, what does the mechanical short run mean in terms of historical time? Rational expectations theorists who define all positions in historical time as equilibrium positions are ambiguous on the connection between the unit of mechanical time in which individuals acquire information and act on it, and the corresponding unit of historical time; one of the major critiques of rational expectations theory is the implication that information is acquired and assimilated quickly in historical time (Laidler, 1981; Hahn, 1983). We now consider particular areas of policy as illustrations of the impact of theoretical framework on the formulation and treatment of policy questions.

Inflation and unemployment policy

The key policy issues within the broad mainstream school of thought have been whether or not there is a trade-off between inflation and unemployment, and the capacity for either fiscal or monetary policy to have a real impact on the economy. Given a conclusion as to the preferred policy stance, the important question then is whether government policy should be governed by rules, or be discretionary.

The conventional stance of the neo-classical synthesis in the 1950s and 1960s had been based on the empirical regularity of the Phillips curve, which implied a trade-off between inflation and unemployment. It was open to government then to choose a preferred combination of the two, and to use discretion in fine-tuning fiscal and monetary policy to generate that combination, on the basis of an IS-LM analysis of the goods and money markets. The challenge to this consensus came first from the monetarists, then from the rational expectations theorists. The challenge gained credibility from the simultaneous rise in both inflation and unemployment in the 1970s, which seemed to negate the presumption of a trade-off, and thus the rationale for stabilization policy. The events of the 1970s were portrayed as demonstrating the failure of conventional policy (Lucas, 1981). On a factual basis this judgement was rather unfair, given the policy successes of the previous two decades, and given the fact that the 1970s, when the problems began to emerge, also saw an increasing application of monetarist policies notably at the instigation of the International Monetary Fund (see Dow and Earl, 1982, Chapter 16).

Nevertheless, the argument which proved to be persuasive was that the previous consensus had been based on apparent empirical regularities rather than on an axiomatic model. The development of the alternative, expectations-augmented, Phillips curve was explicitly grounded in rational individual behaviour. (The analysis developed from Friedman, 1968b, and Phelps, 1968.) This analysis portrayed the trade-off between inflation and unemployment as a short-run phenomenon, resulting from the lag with which expectations adjust to rising inflation. The coincidence of inflation and unemployment in the 1970s could thus be explained by a continuing upward shift in the short-run Phillips curve, as expectations adjusted ever more rapidly to ever-increasing inflation. As a corollary, if governments chose a low unemployment/high-inflation trade-off, expectations would adjust to the increasing inflation, negating attempts to reduce unemployment.

The argument was conducted in terms of expansionary monetary policy (Friedman, 1975). A key element in the argument, then, was the long-run neutrality of money; expansionary monetary policy could induce an increase in output and employment in the short run, but in the long run they would return to their equilibrium values. The rational expectations development of the argument suggested that, if the government announced its expansionary monetary policy, then expectations would adjust very rapidly, allowing little scope even for short-run non-neutrality. Friedman (1969) advocated rules for monetary policy, given that the beneficial effects of discretionary policy were short-lived, and overtaken by the lasting effects on the rate of inflation. Monetary growth should be kept in line with real growth, to keep inflation at zero. The rational expectations argument was stronger: *any* rule would be incorporated in individuals' expectations, neutralizing its effect on real variables. The only scope for a non-neutral monetary policy would be given by a random (and thus unpredictable) monetary policy, which of course would be unlikely to serve any government goal (Sargent and Wallace, 1976).

At the same time as the Phillips curve analysis was being brought into the fold of the general equilibrium deductive system, fiscal policy was likewise being investigated for its interdependencies with the rest of the system. In particular, the financial aspects of fiscal policy were being integrated into monetary policy analysis in what came to be known as the 'crowding out' literature (see Blinder and Solow, 1973; Dow and Earl, 1982, Chapter 10). It was pointed out that money-financed government expenditure added to the stock of money and bond-financed expenditure added to the stock of bonds, each of which would have further repercussions as portfolios were adjusted to achieve an equilibrium configuration. At the same time, the resulting additions to wealth would have repercussions for private-sector expenditure plans. These considerations added further dimensions to the arguments about the relative effectiveness of fiscal and monetary policy in determining the level of aggregate demand.

'Crowding out' refers to the specific consequences of bond-financed government expenditure, which puts pressure on bond markets, thus discouraging private-sector expenditure. If the demand for real money balances is insensitive to the rate of interest, then the interest rate rise required to encourage the sale of new government bonds will be so high as to discourage as much private-sector expenditure as the increase in public-sector expenditure. Since the long-run neutrality of money result rests on the interest inelasticity of the demand for money in the long run, the implication is that crowing out is complete in the long run. The degree of crowding out in the short-run depends on how interest elastic the demand for money is in the short-run. Thus, fiscal policy is also powerless in the long run, just as the expectations augmented Phillips curve analysis showed monetary policy to be powerless in the long-run.

The connection between the crowding out analysis and the Phillips curve analysis can be provided by additional considerations as to the supply-side consequences of increased government expenditure and taxation. The argument (as expressed more in Britain) rests on the presumption that non-market expenditure cannot in general be as efficient as market expenditure (Bacon and Eltis, 1976), and (as expressed more in the United States) that taxation distorts market behaviour from its optimal configuration (Gilder, 1981). Increased government expenditure and taxation thus both ensure a higher natural rate of unemployment than would otherwise be the case. Thus, the natural rate of unemployment, which is the long-run equilibrium rate, will be higher, the greater the proportion of expenditure in the public sector and the greater the extent of taxation. Thus, in the long-run, expansionary fiscal policy only shifts out the long-run Phillips curve, increasing unemployment.

Some supply-siders, such as Gilder, also maintain that inflation (movement up the Phillips curve) is the result of excessive taxation rather than excessive monetary growth. And indeed attempts to cure inflation by curbing monetary growth may jeopardize attempts to reduce unemployment (and possibly inflation) by reducing taxation if much of the monetary excess has arisen in the first place from financing the government's budget deficit. The two sets of policies can only be compatible if expenditure is controlled even more stringently than taxation, allowing a reduction in the budget deficit, or if the deficit is financed by bond issues rather than of taxation, the fiscal policy emphasis has been on reducing expenditure, an approach which is designed to be compatible with controlling monetary growth. In the United States, where the supply-side emphasis has been more on reducing taxation, restrictive monetary policy has been maintained by increased bond-financing of the budgetary deficit, with the consequence of rising interest rates.

The supply-side concern with freeing market processes has also been expressed by New Keynesians, whose primary concern is with market rigidities. Some New Keynesians see a role for stabilization policy to offset the fluctuations caused by these rigidities amplifying the effects of exogenous shocks. But generally there is a concern that there might be a similar amplified reaction to government-induced shocks. The focus then is on removing rigidities, e.g. in the labour market (Snowdon *et al.*, 1994, Chapter 7). This reinforces the withdrawal of interest in stabilization policy in mainstream macroeconomics, a trend to which the real business cycle theory and the shift in attention to growth theory have both added a significant impetus.

The conduct of monetary policy

The technique of monetary control as a means of combatting inflation provides a good example of the significance of analysis being conducted in terms of mechanical time. Reducing the rate of growth of the money supply has been the predominant policy prescription within this school of thought for reducing the rate of inflation. This prescription follows naturally from the theoretical conclusion that money is neutral in the long run, implying a causal relationship between the money supply and the general price level. Two important features of the underlying theoretical framework are the assumed exogeneity of the money supply, and the fixed behavioural and institutional structure of the economy; both of these features are necessary to allow the theoretical connection between money and prices to carry forward into an active policy context. The application of theory to policy is seriously undermined if the policy act itself changes features of the actual economic structure for which the theory is an analogue.

For monetary policy in general, either the money supply or interest rates can be the policy target. The monetary authorities can aim for a target interest rate, and accept the money supply that is required to maintain it, or vice versa. The move towards monetary control with a view to controlling inflation in the 1970s encouraged a move in favour of a money supply target, rather than an interest rate target. This rendered the money supply more explicitly exogenous, the variable which was to be controlled. Nevertheless, interest rates remained an important instrument for achieving the money supply target. Thus, open-market operations would be used to establish an interest rate at which the demand for money was compatible with the target rate of monetary growth. Such a policy requires that the demand for money is a stable function of the interest rate. If, however, demand continues to rise in spite of rising interest rates, then the target is not reached. As long as the monetary authorities perform the function of lender of last resort, excess demand for money can be satisfied. If credit needs increase (either for distress borrowing in a recession or to financial speculative ventures in a boom), the banks can back their new lending by new reserves acquired from the monetary authorities. The supply of money is then not exogenous.

Suppose, however, that the monetary authorities act to raise interest rates until they are penal, i.e. to succeed in discouraging borrowing and to maintain their control over the money supply. It is unlikely then that the structure of the financial system would remain unchanged. In a recession, rapidly rising interest rates force bankruptcies and defaults among borrowers, causing difficulties for the lending institutions, among whom there may also be failures. In an extreme case there is danger of collapse of the entire financial system. In a boom, when there is optimism about speculative gains on assets, there will be a strong incentive for the private sector to devise new ways of conserving liquid resources, and of generating new credit. These structural changes themselves alter the demand for money by any one definition, requiring adjustment to the target specified in terms of that particular aggregate (see Goldfeld, 1976, Paulus and Axilrod, 1976; Porter *et al.*, 1979). The effects of attempts at monetary control on the range of assets which actually perform money functions is evident in the repeated redefinitions of the official money supply variable to include ever more assets (see Berkman, 1980; Johannes and Rasche, 1981; Davis, 1979–80 on the United States changes; Coleby, 1983; Gowland, 1982; Artis and Lewis, 1981, on Britain). Of particular theoretical importance is the fact that the changes in financial structure which occur in response to policy initiatives are both discrete and irreversible. At some critical interest rate there is an incentive to introduce a new financial instrument; once it has been introduced it is extremely rare for it then to be removed once financial conditions become easier. There is thus a ratchet effect in the process of financial innovation which is incompatible with the reversibility of mechanical time.

Because of the difficulties experienced in reaching a money supply target with the interest rate as the instrument, both the United States and United Kingdom moved at the end of the 1970s towards a more direct system of monetary control, expressed specifically in terms of the monetary base. The monetary base consists primarily of the reserves of the banking system, the basis for credit creation. The argument rested on the presumption that there was a stable relationship between the monetary base and the broader monetary aggregates which had previously been the basis for targets. Monetary base control had long been advocated by monetarists (see Anderson and Jordan, 1968, for example). In 1979 the United States monetary authorities announced a greater focus on the monetary base (together with a move towards deregulation of the financial system), while in Britain, a similar move was made in 1981 following the public debate on the issue initiated by the 1980 Green Paper (UK, 1980). But the attempt has been hampered, particularly in Britain, by the continued availability of the lender-of-last-resort facility, and by the practice of bank lending by overdraft; since borrowing on overdraft is unpredictable in terms of both amount and timing, the banks are unable to plan their reserve requirements. Monetary growth in both countries did eventually contract, but it is impossible to identify the contraction as the result of control of supply, or contraction of demand for other reasons: curtailed willingness of banks to lend to firms in a recession combined with an unwillingness on the part of borrowers to increase their indebtedness. In other words, evidence of contracting growth of monetary aggregates does not necessarily support the theoretical assumption of money supply exogeneity.

It is paradoxical that the theoretical structure which most clearly suggests control of monetary growth as the means of controlling inflation should be the least equipped to handle the consequences of such a policy. The monetary authorities have not been able to control the money supply in the way they have intended, indicating that the money supply is not exogenous in the sense of being under the control of the monetary authorities. Further, the consequences of attempts to control monetary growth have consistently been structural change within the financial system of a discrete and irreversible kind which modellers have been incapable of predicting at all accurately. The comparative static method has proved particularly unsuited for estimating the effects of monetary control.

International policy

Just as domestic policy discussions were influenced by the theoretical developments designed to bring policy variables explicitly within a unified theoretical framework, so international macroeconomics developed along lines which brought the international economy also into the system. Indeed, the global economy could be analysed in exactly the same way as a domestic economy within a theoretical framework which is designed to be universally applicable. The main distinguishing feature of the global economy is that there are institutional impediments to relative price flexibility between the component countries. If exchange rates are variable, then domestic prices change *en bloc* relative to foreign prices when the exchange rate changes. Further, there may be impediments to the free flow of goods and factors which allow more scope for relative prices to differ from their optimal values than would be the case domestically. (Indeed, within the domestic model, scope is rarely given for imperfect goods and factor mobility between regions or sectors, so that prices of goods and factors are assumed to be uniform throughout the domestic economy.)

The general tenor of policy discussions from a global perspective is in favour of removing impediments to trade and factor flows, since this would promote speedier adjustment of relative prices to their Pareto efficient levels. Nevertheless, there has been more attention paid in the international literature to reasons for modifying that position than in the domestic macro literature, although the arguments do have general applicability; this may reflect an awareness of national, as opposed to global, interest. First, the Second-Best Theorem was initially expressed in terms of the free trade argument; it was shown that, if the starting point is a general system of tariffs, then it is not necessarily Pareto efficient for any one country to remove its tariffs (Lipsey and Lancaster, 1956–57). Second, Mundell (1976) and Hahn (1983) have pointed out the significance of the marked differences in size between countries. If producers in some countries are price-makers and in others price-takers in international markets, and if their competitive position differs markedly between the international and domestic markets, then the conventional general equilibrium results need not apply. Third, although the predominant emphasis is on the stability of foreign exchange markets, there has been more exploration of the possibility of destabilizing speculation than in analysis of any other market (see, for example, Frenkel and Johnson, 1978).

The area of policy debate which has had most impact on macroeconomics has, however, surrounded the effect of international economic relations on the domestic money supply, and the significance of the exchange rate regime adopted for the success of monetary control. Indeed global monetarism emerged at a time when there was little theory extant on the monetary implications of the balance of payments; its results thus found a ready niche in the neo-classical synthesis (Frenkel and Johnson, 1976). The approach stresses the transitional nature of a balance-of-payments imbalance, which involves a changing stock of domestic financial assets (a continuing fall in the base of a deficit, and rise in the case of a surplus). Attention is thus focused instead on the equilibrium position at which stocks are at the desired levels. Thus the full stock equilibrium theory of the domestic economy is simply extended to the international economy, with its broader selection of goods and assets.

If relative prices internationally depart from those consistent with full stock equilibrium (and thus payments imbalance arises), adjustment is effected either by the resulting changes in the money stock if the exchange rates are fixed, or by exchange rate changes if they are flexible. Here the preferences between the two regimes are coloured by whether the process of transition is regarded as a disequilibrium process, and how seriously the short-run consequences of any disequilibrium are regarded (Laidler, 1981; Friedman, 1971). Otherwise, the preference is determined by a judgement as to whether governments should reap the results of their own actions. If exchange rates are fixed, a government can increase the money supply, and adjustment is effected by the resulting balance-of-payments deficit which distributes the additional money internationally, adding to the world money stock and thus the world price level. However, if exchange rates are flexible, then the additional money is retained in the domestic economy, increasing the domestic price level; the international price level is protected by the resulting depreciation in the first country's exchange rate.

In general, just as in domestic macroeconomics, government is singled out as a major source of exogenous shocks which disturb private-sector equilibrium, alongside real shocks, such as changing technology. It is government actions on which international analysis hangs; without the existence of separate currencies whose supply is controlled by national governments, without tariffs and other trade barriers, and without institutional impediments to capital and labour flows, the presumption is that the private sector at the global level would generate a Pareto efficient outcome.

9.4   Post Keynesian Policy

Relation between theory and policy

For most macroeconomists, a major purpose of theory is policy prescription. This is as true within the mainstream school of thought (see, for example, Samuelson, 1948; Weintraub, 1979; Hahn, 1973a; Lucas, 1980) as it is within Post Keynesian thought (see, for example, Robinson, 1977; Davidson and Weintraub, 1978; Eichner, 1979; Eatwell and Milgate, 1983). There is, however, an important difference between choosing the policy questions according to what constitutes good theory, and choosing theory according to what constitute important policy questions. The two approaches can overlap; because of this, there is much in common between the policy discussions of some neo-classical economists (such as Tobin, 1981, for example) and those of some Post Keynesians (although important differences remain at the theoretical level).

But it is a pertinent generalization that Post Keynesian theory starts, in the Classical tradition, with policy questions and selects a theoretical approach accordingly. This contrasts with the mainstream school of thought, where it is always a more powerful argument that a particular theory is consistent with the overall axiomatic system, than that it directly addresses a particular policy question. Thus, for example, the fact that Keynesian uncertainty cannot be modelled deterministically is not regarded as adequate justification for excluding it from Post Keynesian theory, since uncertainty is regarded as playing such an important part in investment behaviour. More generally, critical realism, which many Post Keynesians now explicitly espouse, is explicitly directed at understanding deep structures in order to change them (Lawson, 1995a).

Post Keynesian theory is expressed in historical time which, although less tractable theoretically than mechanical time, allows a more direct application to policy issues. Further, the practice of employing partial equilibrium analysis allows for some variables to be treated as 'givens', which, in another piece of analysis might be treated as dependent. The overall methodological approach is thus geared to application to particular historical contexts, choosing givens to suit the particular situation. The use of this method within a historical time framework also allows for explicit treatment of institutional change.

It is not being implied that other theorists do not adjust their policy statements for application to particular situations. Rather, it is being suggested that Post Keynesian theory is distinctive in being designed for that purpose. It is also distinctive in that the resulting method appears rather *ad hoc*, thereby attracting the disapproval of those who regard an axiomatic system as the only basis for scientific theory (see for example Cross, 1982, on Post Keynesian theory and Lucas, 1980, on Keynes). However it is interesting to note that when Klamer asks New Classical economists about Post Keynesian and Marxian economics, the answers are non-commital on the grounds of lack of knowledge. The attack on non-axiomatic method is reserved rather for neo-classical economists (Klamer, 1984; see also Dow and Earl, 1984).

Any theory, however geared to dealing with policy issues, is still an abstraction from reality. The scope within Post Keynesian economics for empirical testing of the connection between theory and reality is viewed as being limited by the recognition that structural change is the norm (particularly as a response to deliberate acts of government policy), as well as the importance of unquantifiable variables (like the state of long-run expectations). Nevertheless, with these qualifications in mind, empirical work is undertaken to add an important dimension to the understanding of actual economic developments. It is regarded as being of particular importance in discerning long-term trends in output, employment and distribution, to provide a basis for governments to plan intervention of a structural (rather than stabilizing) nature.

The world view brought to policy issues, and thus determining to a certain extent their selection, is that economies are potentially unstable. (This contrasts with the world view of neo-Austrian theory which presumes stability.) Instability is seen as arising predominantly from a conflict between individual actions and the social outcome. It is thus open to a government, which represents the social interest (or at least some part of it), to act in such a way that conflict between the individual and social levels is reduced. The presumption is therefore that there is a potential role for government in implementing macroeconomic policy. Since much of individual action is in any case regarded as socially determined, by conventions and group expectations as much as by formal institutions, there would appear to be scope for action at the macro level to promote social and individual goals together. In addition, since ability to pursue individual goals within a market economy is largely determined by income and wealth, the government is seen as having as additional role in promoting a more equal distribution of market power.

Because the approach to policy is so broad, encompassing influence on conventions and institutions as much as more conventional policy instruments, the theory of policy-making is much less cut and dried than the targets-and-instruments framework of mainstream policy theory. Not only is the uncertainty of the environment within which policy is implemented not regarded as the sort which can be converted into 'certainty equivalents', but also there is an emphasis on the structural changes which can occur as a direct result of policy action.

Finally, there are differences within Post Keynesian thought as to the extent of government intervention required to stabilize economies and promote growth, depending on the view taken as to the effectiveness under normal conditions of the price mechanism. The following is an analogy, to consider along with that quoted in the previous section. It represents a view more consistent with inherent stability than many, but nevertheless illustrates well the Post Keynesian view of the rôle of stabilization policy.

> Imagine yourself in a Buck Rogers interplanetary adventure, looking at a highway in a City of Tomorrow. The highway is wide and straight, and its edges are turned up so that it is almost impossible for a car to run off the road. What appears to be a runaway car is speeding along the road and veering off to one side. As it approaches the rising edge of the highway, its front wheels are turned so that it gets back on to the road and goes off at an angle, making for the other side, where the wheels are turned again. This happens many times, the car zigzagging but keeping on the highway until it is out of sight. You are wondering how long it will take for it to crash when another car appears which behaves in the same fashion. When it comes near you it stops with a jerk. A door is opened, and an occupant asks whether you would like a lift. You look into the car, and before you can control yourself, you cry out, 'Why there's no steering wheel ...' (Lerner, 1951, p.3)

Note that the disturbances depicted in the analogy are partly systematic, although always involving an element of uncertainty. Such disturbances pose different policy problems from the random disturbances of the Parkin and Bade analogy. A complete Post Keynesian analogy would in addition have the position of the road, and the strength of its upturned edges, influenced by the path taken by car travelling on it (see Leijonhufvud's, 1981, Chapter 6, corridor analogy).

Inflation and unemployment policy

The traditional Keynesian explanation for involuntary unemployment as the norm is effective demand failure, given the inability of the market sector to co-ordinate activity in such a way as to ensure full employment. Since neither the supply of labour nor the demand for it is determined by the real wage, a reduction in the real wage could not reduce unemployment even if it could be brought about by the parties concerned. Keynes's policy solution is for government spending (particularly capital spending) to increase effective demand to the point of full employment. In the long run, an increased government presence in investment spending reduces the scope for unpredictable fluctuations in private-sector investment to occur. In addition, it allows for more planning of the industrial structure of the economy, given that private investment (the major driving force of the economy) is undertaken with a view to accumulation, rather than the fulfilment of any particular need of society.

The crowding-out argument against increased government expenditure is accepted, in the sense that, to the extent that interest rates rise as a result, some private-sector expenditure may be discouraged, *other things being equal*. But the circumstances in which fiscal expansion is seen as most necessary are those in which the demand for money is highly interest elastic: indeed government intervention in a recession *could* have a sufficiently buoyant effect on financial markets that interest rates would be under little pressure. But in any case, the accelerator effect of increased government investment combined with beneficial effects on long-term expectations can be expected to increase private-sector investment at any interest rate. Thus the focus is on the effect of government spending on expectations in financial markets and among investors, rather than on given behavioural relations as assumed in the IS-LM context of the general equilibrium exposition of the crowding out issue. The results do, however, rest on a theory of expectations which assumes that the correctness of the policy is perceived; otherwise, if all individuals concerned happen to hold that there is a hundred per cent crowding out of government expenditure, then the expectations effect will be perverse (McCallum, 1983). Ultimately, it is argued by some, following Keynes (1936, Chapter 24) that private sector volatility can only be avoided by a continued presence of the government in investment, rather than simply periodic pump-priming.

Investment planning is also an integral part of anti-inflationary policy. In the 1930s, Keynes advocated that such government intervention be accompanied by gradually rising prices, to encourage further private-sector investment to take over from the government's pump-priming action. In the 1980s, however, it is conventional among neoclassical 'Keynesians' to argue against attempts to expand the economy on the grounds that inflation would be further fuelled. It is argued that the stagflation inherited from the 1970s presents quite different problems from the deflationary recession of the 1930s. Let us consider, then, the Post Keynesian explanation for inflation accompanying the stagnation of output.

While mainstream theorists are compelled by their methodology to search for explanations of inflation in isolated exogenous variables, Post Keynesian methodology allows for several factors to interact within the overall structural development of an economy to generate inflation. In other words, rather than isolating universal exogenous variables, this approach attempts to identify the main features of a *process* which, in particular circumstances, are associated with inflation. The conventional contrast between the mainstream explanation of inflation and the Post Keynesian is often perceived as between demand-pull inflation, depending on money supply increases, on the one hand, and cost-push inflation, depending on wage increases, on the other. Such a contrast is in fact an expression of orthodox methodology, whereby Post Keynesians are also perceived as searching for the causal exogenous variable (in this case, money wages). While the setting of money wages plays an important part in the Post Keynesian theory of inflation, and policy proposals for its control, it is only part of a broader analysis (Eichner, 1979; Applebaum, 1982; Weintraub, 1978).

The major element of realism retained in the abstractions of Post Keynesian labour-market theory is the absence of perfect competition in most of the labour market, and indeed in most product markets, preventing the specification of labour supply and demand schedules. Determination of the level of employment and of real wages are thus viewed as occurring independently of each other, the former influenced primarily by the level of effective demand, and the latter by the relative capacities of unions and firms to influence money wages and product prices, respectively. To the extent that money wage increases are required to attract additional labour into employment once full employment is reached, the resulting inflation is as much due to the initial anticipation of rising product demand as to the resulting increase in money wages. In general, there is no complete theory of money wages (Weintraub, 1978–79), only pointers as to the most likely influences in particular circumstances (Applebaum, 1979; Tylecote, 1981; Keynes, 1936, Chapter 19).

To the extent that union power, fuelled often by real wage uncertainty once inflation has already started to accelerate, achieves money wage increases which further fuel inflation, incomes policies are proposed as a preventative policy measure. A variety of schemes has been explored which would penalize excessive money wage increases, or reward their absence. (See Colander, 1979, for a review, and Wallich and Weintraub, 1971, for the most widely discussed scheme). As a permanent institution, incomes policies would remove the uncertainty about gross divergence in relative money wage trends, and thus much of the impetus for leap-frogging behaviour among unions. Preventing significant relative wage movement would, according to general equilibrium theory, prevent the efficient allocation of resources. While this is recognized as a drawback to a certain extent, the assumptions of the Post Keynesian model are that an unfettered wage-bargaining process bears little relation to the efficient market process assumed by general equilibrium theory; wage inflation itself arguably interferes with the allocative function of the market in any case. (However, see Tylecote, 1981, for a critical appraisal of incomes policies from an institutional perspective.)

The importance of nominal wage levels for inflation stems from the close relationship between wage settlements and product prices. Keynes viewed this relationship in terms of competitive product markets, whereby changes in wage income translated generally into changes in the same direction of effective demand and thus of prices. The Kalecki tradition rests rather on the lack of competitiveness of markets in manufactured products, which allows a mark-up system of pricing, i.e. a direct mechanism whereby prices move in tandem with wages. As a corollary, any change in the competitive structure of industry alters the degree to which wage increases ensure that higher prices can in fact be sustained. (See Domberger, 1979, on the British evidence for increased inflationary pressure with greater concentration of industry.) In turn, the impetus for wage increases and the degree to which they can be passed on determine the distribution of income between profit earners and wage earners. (See Sylos-Labini, 1979, which also includes empirical analysis of the cost-price relationship.)

A crucial factor in firms' pricing policy is the provision of internal finance for investment; the mechanism depends on the competitive structure of industry (Seccareccia, 1984). According to Keynes's competitive framework, expenditure in the capital goods sector, in expectation of favourable returns from investment, puts upward pressure on capital goods prices, and attracts resources more readily to the capital goods sector than to the consumption goods sector. Increased employment earnings in the capital goods sector, however, increases demand for consumption goods, raising their prices and reducing the real value of labour income. As was postulated by the neo-Austrians, the resulting forced savings ultimately provide the finance for new investment (which had been financed in the first instance by bank credit). The Kaleckian oligopolistic framework, on the other hand, envisages a simultaneous rather than sequential rise in the prices of capital and consumption goods. Consumption goods producers finance their demands on the capital goods sector directly by means of raising the mark-up on product prices. The theory was developed by Steindl (1945, 1952) and Eichner (1973) (see also Harcourt and Kenyon, 1976; Shapiro, 1977) that producers' risk aversion with respect to external finance encourages price increases in anticipation of investment returns. Seccareccia (1984) found evidence supporting both the Keynesian sequential pricing pattern and the Kalecki simultaneous pattern from Canadian data, concluding that this could be interpreted as reflecting the competitive/oligopolistic mix of the Canadian industrial structure.

The policy significance of the view of the impetus behind price changes is that incomes policy by itself is insufficient to control inflation. Inflationary pressure comes not only from attempts to preserve profits' share, but also starts with investment plans, the willingness of the banking sector to finance the resulting pressure on the capital goods sector and the market power of firms attempting to general investment finance directly through rising product prices. The more investment decisions are conducted within, or influenced by, the public sector, the greater scope there is for guiding the pattern of expansion and reducing the incidence of bottlenecks in both capital goods and consumption good production. But as long as market power is allowed to become more concentrated (as happens particularly during a recession), the more scope there is for firms to act independently of external sources of finance by self-financing through prices increases.

The overall Post Keynesian policy package for dealing with unemployment and inflation, then, is fiscal expansion to increase effective demand and generate more private-sector optimism, incomes policy to defuse the anxieties attached to wage bargaining, intervention in investment planning to direct activity in such a way that consumption output groups concomitantly with investment output, so as not to give rise to inflationary pressures, and competition policy to limit the market power which allows anticipatory self-finance by increased mark-up on product prices.

It is important to note that each component of the package refers to, and depends on, an institutional structure and set of conventions which will vary markedly in character from economy to economy, and period to period. None of the components is without difficulties in application which will take on a different character in different contexts. The policy measures are expressed in a very general form, because the particular elements of realism retained in the theoretical structure are those which prevent the construction of a formal model with universal application. There is no scope for abstract policy rules. But as a result, there is less difficulty in shifting from the theory of policy to policy itself than is apparent in the case of mainstream theory.

The conduct of monetary policy

Mainstream theorists may acknowledge that all the inflationary pressures outlined above are important, but that they are only effective in so far as money supply increases validate them; money supply control, according to this view, can deal with whatever inflationary pressures are present. This view requires that money supply increases are a necessary condition for inflation, and that decreases are thus sufficient to reverse the process.

Post Keynesian monetary theory is inconsistent with this view of money (see section 8.4). Their alternative view of money includes a view of the nature of money and of the process by which it enters the economic system which has direct implications for the technique, as well as the direction, of monetary policy (Davidson and Weintraub, 1973). Money is seen as any asset which possesses certain attributes; these attributes are part institutional and part judgemental. If monetary control encourages innovation which generates new assets which have the attributes of money, then what performs the money functions has now changed and the object of monetary control needs to be redefined. Second, the *process* of money creation is endogenous in the sense that credit creation must start with the demand for credit. Nevertheless there is a necessary exogenous element in the financial system in the sense that assets only perform money functions if they inspire confidence. Aside from commodity money, that confidence is derived from confidence in the issuer of assets which back the money asset and the authority which regulates the issuers of money assets (primarily the banks); conventionally the issuer of the reserve asset is the government, whose taxing power ensures its solvency. What does and does not inspire confidence, however, is a matter of judgement – at the market rather than the individual level. The technique of monetary control itself can alter that confidence – if, for example, the monetary authorities withdraw the lender-of-last-resort facility, thus generating lack of confidence in the banks.

Indeed the mainstream preference for monetary base control is institutionally alien to the historical development of banking systems, since it requires ultimately a removal of the lender-of-last-resort facility and, in Britain, the overdraft facility. Similarly, a return to interest rate volatility is alien to the way in which banking systems themselves have developed to promote financial stability. The financial system in general contributes most effectively to the day-to-day operations of an economy, as well as its long-term development, if there is considerable confidence in expectations as to the values of financial assets, and this confidence is well-founded. On the one hand, this confidence requires that there be confidence in the institutions to which recourse for credit is made in the event of disappointment of expectations: the central monetary authority in the case of banks, banks in the case of producers and consumers. The lender-of-last-resort facility and a flexible credit response by banks allow individual investors to behave as if disappointments are not going to occur. On the other hand, confidence in asset prices requires an absence of volatility in interest rates and credit conditions in general. The euphoric, unrealistic over-extension of credit in an unfettered speculative boom, as well as the frenzied rush for liquidity once the euphoria collapses (which are the focus of Minsky's, 1975, 1982, work), do not contribute to the maintenance of a high and stable level of employment. Rather, they divert financial market activity in the first case into speculative assets and in the second case to idleness.

The power of financial markets to influence the pace of capital accumulation is regarded as rendering them a dangerous arena for anti-inflationary policy. The primary role for monetary policy suggested by Post Keynesian theory, therefore, is to promote financial market stability. Public sector regulatory control over financial institutions can thus be exercised to limit the scope for overextension of credit or borrowing by individual institutions and the danger that poses for ripple effects through the system. In addition, this power can be exercised to attempt to co-ordinate the allocation of credit with investment planning (whether through market incentives, directives, or public ownership) (see further, Minsky, 1982, Introduction and Chapters 7, 8 and 13; Dow and Earl, 1982, Chapters 11, 12, and 17, 1984).

These policy conclusions arise directly from a focus on money as an institution, which is not immutable when the monetary authorities change their relationship with the private sector in order to control monetary aggregates. In addition they arise from the focus on the possibility of financial instability and its consequences. The foundation of the financial system on confidence is regarded as obviating its analysis in terms of deterministic behaviour within a given structure.

International policy

Within the sphere of international policy also the emphasis is on the scope for instability. Not only may effective demand failure in one economy spread to others through falling export demand, but there is scope also for polarization at a global level between high-growth and low-growth economies. Since these trends (particularly the latter) evolve over long periods, in an irreversible manner, and are influenced by the institutional arrangements governing trade and payments, the method of analysis emphasizes historical developments and institutional arrangements rather than marginal responses within a given historical structure. (See Singh, 1977, for an example of this approach applied to the issue of Britain's de-industrialization in a world setting; see also Gray, 1976.)

Without impediments to trade, market forces operating internationally are seen as potentially exacerbating pre-existing differences in productivity, income and wealth. Kaldor (1970) in particular has stressed the importance of exports as the component of demand which acts most directly on investment plans, and income growth in general. Further, he argues that productivity growth is cumulative, so that the disparity between economies with strong export growth and those with weak export growth tends to widen. This tendency is exacerbated if the latter are primary product producers, selling in competitive markets while the former are manufacturers, selling in oligopolistic markets, with the resulting capacity to general self-finance for investment via price increases (Myrdal, 1964; Burbridge, 1979). The means proposed for offsetting these tendencies includes the imposition of import controls, to generate growth of domestic demand, and thus domestic productivity growth.

The potentiality (though not inevitability) of increasing international disparities is also evident in the behaviour of international capital markets. Large multinational corporations can operate independently of capital markets to the extent that self-finance is available through product price increase: transfer pricing facilitates the international movement of these internal savings beyond the reach of national taxing authorities. But, in addition, the criteria for international capital market lending favour liquid rather than illiquid economies, i.e. those which have less need but more credit worthiness. Illiquidity ultimately enforces balance-of-payments adjustment, in the form of demand deflation and/or exchange depreciation. The first exacerbates income disparities, while the second adds to domestic inflation, as import price rises feed into domestic prices and wages. This adjustment can be enforced by the activity of short-term capital flows away from currencies expected to depreciate, thus making the illiquidity position more immediate. Exchange controls can be employed to attempt to limit the volatility of short-term capital flows.

Keynes recognized the consequences for international economic relationships of the asymmetrical distribution of the burden of adjustment. His plan for an International Clearing Union (Great Britain, 1943) involved an attempt at symmetrical intervention by the Union in the economic policies of those countries in balance of payments surplus and those in deficit. In addition, he advocated controls on short-term capital flows in an attempt to limit the scope for disruptive speculative capital movements (de Cecco, 1979). In a more recent expression of Post Keynesian international economic policy, Davidson (1982) also emphasizes the importance of international co-operation to provide a stable environment for world economic activity. One aspect of that environment would be fixed exchange rates. Another which he sees as necessary if international struggles for shares of world income are not to be inflationary is an international incomes policy; that such a policy seems impossible to implement is an indication of the inevitability of inflation due to international forces.

For a complete parallel with the domestic-policy package, the policy is also advocated of influencing, at the international level, the pricing and investment activity of multinational corporations. This, together with the more indirect influence on economic activity exerted by the International Monetary Fund (preferably modified to apply symmetrically to countries in deficit and surplus, as advocated by Keynes), would defuse the inflationary component of investment finance, as well as promote goals with respect to international income distribution.

Finally, international co-operation is necessary given the advocacy of impediments to international flows of goods and factors as a means of isolating individual economies from forces for divergence. These impediments can discourage beneficial as well as harmful flows, so that judgement is required in their use. What would be particularly damaging would be the widespread, rather than selective, use of such impediments, which would damage world trade and finance (Burbridge, 1979). If import and exchange controls are to be used only selectively, without retaliation, supervision by an international body is required.

The general tenor of Post Keynesian policy can thus be seen to stem from the initial assumption (backed by historical analysis) of the potential for international instability, with the consequences analysed in terms of market processes and the alternative institutional arrangements which could be introduced by policy-makers.

9.5   Marxian Policy

Marxian theory does not lend itself to a discussion of policy issues in the sense in which the other schools of thought have done in the last three sections. Even neo-Austrian theory which severely circumscribes the scope for government macroeconomic policy still expresses a view as to the relevance of theory for policy. Nor are Marxian theorists reticent because of the type of difficulties of relating theory to policy which are experienced particularly by mainstream theorists. Marxian theory is presented as being grounded in objective reality, identifying the actual material forces at work, in contrast to the misleading appearances of reality on which bourgeois theory dwells. While Marx employed abstraction for analytical purposes, this was merely a means toward the end of identifying the nature and consequences of actual material forces. There is, therefore, no room for doubt about the direct application of the analysis to actual experience.

The avoidance of policy prescription is the result, rather, of the content of the theory of reality. Events are viewed as being the inevitable outcome of historical forces. Inevitability does not mean predictability in particular contexts, necessarily. But, in retrospect, it is possible to interpret events in terms of the theory and indeed future developments can be predicted in broad terms, like the eventuality of crises, and the falling rate of profit. Government policy is simply regarded as part of this historical process. Thus Marxian discussions of contemporary policy to deal with inflation and unemployment, for example, analyse government policy in terms of class struggle, and criticize it as ineffectual in its attempts to modify the capitalist process (see, for example Mandel, 1980; Magdoff and Sweezy, 1981; Rowthorn, 1977; Gonick, 1975). Gonick devotes significant attention to the question, 'what can be done?' (Gonick, 1975, Chapter 8), but the solution lies with labour action, not with government policy. Mandel (1980, Chapter 5) also discusses strategy for the transition from capitalism to socialism in terms of workers' action, although state expropriation of private capital is seen as part of the process, resulting from political pressure from the working class. The only effective solution to inflation and unemployment is the fundamental redistribution of the ownership of the means of production which would spell the end of capitalism. Since inflation and unemployment are seen as the direct consequence of the capitalist process, it is natural that their cure should be identified with an ending of that process.

Chernomas (1983) provides an interesting account from a Marxian perspective of the differences in macroeconomic policy stance represented by different schools of bourgeois thought. The stagflation of the 1970s he identifies as the outcome of traditional post-war Keynesian fiscal and monetary policy, which was designed to limit the scope for economic downturns. This required subsidizing, through fiscal means or public ownership, firms which would otherwise have been taken over at reduced value, or gone bankrupt. Monetary policy designed to keep interest rates low, in addition, encouraged firms to survive and expand which would not otherwise have done so. Such policies were adopted for legitimation purposes, because of the large working-class support on which these governments depended. But employment could only be maintained at high levels by these means at the cost of inflation, as capitalists struggled to maintain their share of total income. Such policy measures are doomed to failure because they prevent the cleansing crisis necessary to restore the profit rate, for a time, to its earlier level. In contrast, monetarist policy helps the underlying forces along by acceding to, and even contributing to, the emergence of the crisis. The mandate of the New Right is to restore the rate of profit by encouraging the weeding out of weaker firms, and creating unemployment to discipline the labour force. Such policy cannot succeed in the long term, because each succeeding crisis carries the seeds of further falls in the rate of profit. But in the short term, it is perfectly consistent with the interests of the capitalist class.

Chernomas differentiates Post Keynesian policy from traditional 'Keynesian' policy, emphasizing the role of state-directed investment and incomes policies. From the standpoint of Marxian theory, he correctly points out that even these policies do not fully address the problems associated with the continuation of a capitalist class, whose aim is accumulation rather than meeting the needs of the working class. Mandel (1980, Chapter 5) argues that increasing state ownership requires not only the political acquiescence of the capitalist class, but also an increased tax burden, which is only tolerated by capitalists if net profits can be maintained through rising prices. At the same time, he argues that incomes policies tackle only a proportion of unit costs, the major element of costs being determined by production conditions (state of technology, etc.) and credit conditions; incomes policies can thus be interpreted as a means of limiting the share of labour in national income.

Incomes policies are often put forward as a means of promoting international competitiveness, which militates against the interests of the working class on a global scale. Export-led growth is not possible simultaneously for all countries. And indeed, the view of international development is one of growing disparities. Even if low-wage countries attract foreign investment by multinational corporations, these corporations then extract the surplus, leaving problems of deteriorating terms of trade and foreign indebtedness. The pattern of international trade, argues Shaikh (1980), is governed by absolute advantage rather than comparative advantage, so that internationally as well as domestically there are forces towards growing disparities in terms of income and wealth. Again, the only solution lies in political action by workers, this time at a global level. As Shaikh concludes, with respect to the widening gap between rich and poor countries under capitalism: 'This gap and its attendant consequences are symptoms, not causes: the cure must address itself to the disease' (Shaikh, 1980, p.232).

The radical Marxist rejection of any type of reformist policy is typified by Mandel's (1980, p.202) statement: 'The mixed economy is a myth', meaning that *any* private ownership of capital constrains the role of government to further the ends of private capital. But the problems of transition for individual economies do require a policy stance for a mixed economy. Such a stance is set out by Thomas (1974), based on the experience of Tanzania. The strategy he proposes includes state ownership of key sectors, and a direction of activity toward the satisfaction of local needs rather than export, as a means both of direction production for use value rather than exchange value and also of reducing the scope for capitalist forces to influence the domestic economy through trade and financial relationships. Such transitional policies bear a strong family resemblance to Post Keynesian policies for mixed economies. Although incomes policies are viewed by Marxians as a means of exploiting the working class, they can only work if they are widely agreed upon as a more acceptable means of distributing income than free competitive forces. Implicit in Marxian analysis of the transition to socialism is a broad consensus among the working population on relative wages being determined largely within the state sector.

There are sufficient similarities between the Marxian and Post Keynesian analysis of the divergence-promoting nature, and potential instability of, market behaviour governed by the accumulation motive that it is not surprising that in practice there should be some common ground on policy issues. The major divergence occurs in terms of the inevitability or otherwise of periodic crises culminating in the end of capitalism. Post Keynesian policy is, in contrast to Marxian views, reformist with an optimistic view of the capacity for co-operation between classes and countries. Marxians deny that capacity for such co-operation to have any long-lasting effect on the underlying forces of capitalism.

9.6   Conclusion

Each school of thought, it transpires, not only differs over specific policy measures, but also differs as to the proper rôle of government policy.

Neo-Austrians deny the capacity for government (or indeed, by implication, any economist) to have knowledge of particular situations superior to that of the individuals involved. Given their faith in the capacity of market forces to generate the best attainable outcome, individuals' interests are best served by the least possible interference from outside bodies. Macroeconomic policy thus consists of a strategy for the transition to an absence of macroeconomic policy; ideally, the money supply should even be produced privately to remove any vestige of the macroeconomic presence of government.

Nevertheless, neo-Austrians are caught in a conundrum. One of the features of market behaviour which sustains their faith is its capacity to generate institutions (for gathering information for example) where these are necessary for promoting individuals' interests. There is no apparent logical reason for regarding government and its agencies any differently. There is no logical basis for an economist to advocate a change in government macroeconomic policy in either direction; activist macroeconomic policy may be a public good. Indeed, neo-Austrian *theory* does not provide a logical basis for an economist to advocate anything. It is only the quite separate confidence in market forces which justified their policy statements.

The mainstream position on policy is more directly related to their method, although often influenced by an independent confidence in market forces. First, the axiomatic method, which generated equilibrium solutions in mechanical time, does not yield results directly applicable to situations in historical time. Only the instrumentalist approach, which itself translates mechanical time theory into predictions based on historical data, provides a basis for policy statements. But both approaches are also hamstrung by two further methodological features of the theory: the structure of preferences, production and institutions are assumed constant regardless of changes in policy variables, and there is a strict dual between exogenous variables (which include policy variables) and endogenous variables. The first presumes that observing a correlation between variables in the past is a sufficient basis for identifying causality, and that a policy-induced change in the causal variable will have the same (lack of) effect on structure as non-policy-induced changes in the past. The second practice (of defining policy variables as exogenous) ensures that any changes, past or future, are defined as policy-induced; the most important exogenous variable is the money supply. However, not only are financial institutions notorious (or famous) for their capacity to adapt in the face of monetary controls, changing the structure of the environment being modelled, but one consequence is that the money supply (in the sense of that which is closely related to expenditure, not necessarily any one aggregate like M_0) is endogenous. In the face of such difficulties, policy proposals have been extended to try to mould the economic environment to resemble more closely its analogue model.

Post Keynesians' interpretation of history rules out confidence in the capacity of markets to promote social welfare, and provides the case for some form of government intervention. At the same time, the method of analysis includes study of institutional and structural change in response to events, including changing policy stance. Indeed the method is designed for generating policy proposals and predicting the institutional response as well as the direction of change of strictly economic variables. As a result, the policy statements arising from general theory are necessarily incomplete: specific statements must themselves be context specific. General statements about the causes and possible cures of the current inflation and unemployment and implications for monetary and international policy, however, provide pointers for particular cases.

On the one hand, inflation and unemployment are analysed as the natural outcome of the cyclical path of capitalist economies, where there is not automatic mechanism ensuring full employment and where unemployment is in fact a potential mechanism for limiting workers' power to protect or increase their share of national income. Inflation in turn is the outcome of the struggle for income shares between capital and labour, with price increases used as a primary mechanism for financing accumulation. The acceleration of these trends can, however, be halted by reintroducing rigidities, or 'normalcies' into the economic system: in wage bargaining, in financial markets, and in international economic relations. In contrast to mainstream policy conclusions, then, Post Keynesian policies take the causes of inflation and unemployment as being endogenous to the capitalist economic system, and the cures in a combination of increased government intervention in investment spending and of reintroducing the type of conventional rigidities which mainstream theorists see as having caused problems in the first place. The viability of Post Keynesian policies depends on the co-operative group behaviour which is inherent of Post Keynesian theory, rather than the atomistic behaviour of mainstream theory.

The purpose of Marxian theory is to identify the objective material forces underlying history; the history of capitalism includes government policy as well as the behaviour of capitalists and workers. Unlike other schools of thought, then, the government sector is regarded as completely endogenous to the capitalist process. Macroeconomic problems as we know them are identified as problems of capitalism. The policy content of Marxian analysis is thus restricted to advice on the political activities of workers and on the transition from capitalism to socialism.

The policy for economies in the period of transition to socialism (which by definition are still mixed economies) has elements in common with Post Keynesian policy. (Post Keynesian policy is wrongly identified by some as promoting workers' exploitation through incomes policies; this misconception arises from the application of orthodox methodology to Post Keynesian policy analysis, involving a search for exogenous causes of problems and thus unidirectional cures.) The underlying difference between the two schools of thought is that, while Post Keynesians envisage co-operation between groups within a mixed economy, Marxians only envisage the democratization of policy with a full commitment to the eradication of capitalism.

10 Conclusion

It has been the aim of the previous chapters to demonstrate the range of views held across the various schools of thought in macroeconomics, and how this range can be traced through the different levels of analysis: mode of thought, methodology, theory and policy. What appear on the face of it to be incomprehensible differences of opinion over policy issues, for example, make sense when considered in terms of the structure of thought and theory underlying each position. The type of approach adopted here is designed to promote greater understanding of debates which do not explicitly recognize the methodological content of arguments.

The methodological approach in addition allows us to go further in taking a more constructive approach to differences of opinion within macroeconomics. It allows a categorization of theories and arguments according to how far they are founded on a common methodological framework. More effective communication is possible among those who share a particular use of the equilibrium concept, for example, than among those who do not. Attempts to express in terms of a common framework theories which have been devised on the basis of different frameworks can be expected to lead to a frustrating lack of communication. Conducting the monetarist-Keynesian debate in terms of IS-LM analysis is a case in point. While the conclusion drawn on the basis of irreconcilable methodological differences might be that attempts at communication are unlikely to be fruitful, this conclusion can be constructive in channelling energies in more productive directions.

Some readers may be unpersuaded by the particular categorization used here. There will inevitably be differences of opinion as to what are fundamental methodological differences. The important point is that it is the methodological level at which the discussion should take place. The force of the argument presented here is that the debate over whether or not the mainstream school of thought, for example, should be categorized as such should refer not to positions on policy questions, but to use of methodological concepts and indeed to criteria for recognizing arguments as acceptably 'scientific' in the first place. Within any school of thought there will be differences on theory and policy questions. But if there is a shared methodological position, there is scope for effective discussion of those differences. The tendency to play down methodological differences has been most noticeable among non-Marxian economists. Traditional methodology has infused the profession to the extent that there has been an (often implicit) acceptance of the notion that there is a unique set of criteria for scientific endeavour. The result has been not only confusion in debates where different criteria have been (often implicitly) employed, but also a divergence between professed methodology and practice. More seriously, the dualistic reaction against methodological principles altogether, which is much more widespread than among those who profess postmodernism, has encouraged a lack of concern with theoretical and methodological fragmentation. Yet the methodological principles of closed, axiomatic systems still exert power in the discipline which goes unaddressed. Non-mainstream schools of thought address these issues, but find it difficult to communicate in the current environment.

Marxian economists have in the past been so aware of differences in mode of thought and methodology that an intellectual barrier has been erected between Marxian and non-Marxian economics. However, reflecting a recent trend among non-orthodox Marxians, the discussion here has highlighted some points held in common by Marxian and non-Marxian economists, which would allow constructive exchanges of ideas. In this case, greater methodological awareness all round would point to avenues of fruitful discussion.

In tune with the methodological stance adopted in this analysis, categorization by school of thought does not have dualistic, 'either/or', implications. It is not intended that the conclusion be drawn that theory can be parcelled up irrevocably into mutually-exclusive groups within which communication is possible, but between which communication is impossible. Rather, the appropriate conclusion concerns the type of communication which can reasonably be expected to be fruitful, and in what sense it would be fruitful. In general terms, discussion is likely to enhance mutual understanding, the greater the awareness of methodological differences. In that sense, greater tolerance of differences may ensue, enhancing the freedom with which economists in different schools of thought may fully develop their ideas. But in addition, cross-paradigm discussion can act as a catalyst for new ideas, as has so often been the case in the past. Given that no one school of thought has a monopoly of approximation to truth, cross-fertilization of ideas may be an important factor in the development of the discipline.

Many of the benefits of methodological awareness outlined above stem from the particular methodological position adopted here. But one aspect of that position is that there are no ultimate criteria for appraising methodologies, any more than for appraising theories. Indeed, those who still adhere to traditional methodological principles will arrive at different conclusions as to the relevance of methodological differences between schools of thought; the norm in the past has been to select one school of thought, in effect, as most scientific, and to reject the rest. Nevertheless, if the dialogue between those adopting this traditional position and others could be conducted at the methodological level, where it belongs, significant progress would have been made. Far too often, the dialogue is conducted at different levels, without reference to methodology, resulting in a frustrating lack of communication.

While, at the methodological level or at the level of theory, the position adopted here has eschewed universal criteria, it has also eschewed dualism; there is no necessity for the alternative to be methodological or theoretical nihilism. The reason for the absence of universal criteria is that each individual or group approaching a body of theory cannot but do so in terms of their own mode of thought and view of the world. There is no basis on which any individual or group can specify criteria for other individuals or groups. But this by no means precludes the capacity of each to make the case for their preferred methodology or theory, in terms of their own mode of thought and view of the world.

More generally, any economist, if consistent, must employ a body of theory when addressing particular theoretical or policy questions. (This body of theory may or may not fit into one of the categories chosen for discussion here.) That economist can then employ the reasons for that choice of body of theory to persuade others of the merits of her choice. Dramatic conversions from one school of thought to another are unusual. More common are marginal shifts in position as the result of persuasion by other economists. It is these shifts which, cumulatively, can generate paradigm shifts. At the level of theory rather than of the individuals involved, these shifts can be very dramatic.

While some economists specialize in methodology, most are engaged in practice. However, methodological awareness among all economists not only provides a guide for that practice, but also allows most effective use of the diversity of methodological stances. At the individual level we each have opinions as to which is the best methodological stance and body of theory, by our own criteria. But, given the range of experience with which any social science must deal, it is surely to be welcomed that, at the level of society, there is some diversity of ideas. It has been the limited aim of this study to demonstrate the existence of this diversity within macroeconomics, by employing a methodological framework, and thereby to persuade readers of the benefits to be derived from a focus on methodology.

Bibliography

When more than one date is given, as in Smith (1776; 1976), reference is being made to succeeding editions; page numbering in references refers to the latest edition.

Addison, J.L., Burton, J. and Torrance, T.S. (1980), 'On the Causes of Inflation', *The Manchester School*, 48 (June)

Ahmad, S. (1970), 'Is Money Net Wealth?', *Oxford Economic Papers*, 22 NS (November)

Alchian, A. and Allen, W.R. (1974), *University Economics*, London: Prentice-Hall International

Althusser, L. (1968; 1977), *Lenin and Philosophy and Other Essays*, translated by B. Brewster, London: New Left Books

Amariglio, J.L. (1988), 'The Body, Economic Discourse and Power: An Economist's Introduction to Foucault', *History of Political Economy*, 29(4)

Amariglio, J.L. and Ruccio, D. (1995), 'Keynes, Postmodernism and Uncertainty', in S.C. Dow and J. Hillard eds, Chapter 19

Anderson, L.C. and Jordan, J.L. (1968), 'The Monetary Base - Explanation and Analytical Use', *Federal Reserve Bank of St. Louis Review* (August)

Applebaum, E. (1979), 'The Labour Market', in A.S. Eichner (ed.), *A Guide to Post-Keynesian Economics*, London: Macmillan

Applebaum, E. (1982), 'The Incomplete Incomes Policy Vision', *Journal of Post Keynesian Economics*, 4 (Summer)

Archibald, G.C. and Lispey, R.C. (1958), 'Monetary and Value Theory: A Critique of Lange and Patinkin', *Review of Economic Studies*, 25 (69)

Arestis, P. (1992), *The Post-Keynesian Approach to Economics: An Alternative Analysis of Economic Theory and Policy*, Aldershot: Elgar

Arrow, K.J. (1959), 'Towards a Theory of Price Adjustment', in M. Bramovitz (ed.), *The Allocation of Economic Resources*, Stanford: Stanford University Press

Arrow, K.J. and Debreu, G. (1954), 'Existence of an Equilibrium for a Competitive Economy', *Econometrica*, 22 (July)

Arrow, K.J. and Hahn, F.H. (1971), *General Competitive Analysis*, Edinburgh: Oliver and Boyd

Artis, M.J. and Lewis, M.K. (1981), *Monetary Control in the United Kingdom*, Oxford: Philip Allen

Asimakopulos, A. (1980-81), 'Themes in a Post Keynesian Theory of Income Distribution', *Journal of Post Keynesian Economics*, 3 (Winter)

Azariadis, C. (1975), 'Implicit Contracts and Underemployment Equilibria', *Journal of Political Economy*, 83 (December)

Backhouse, R.E. (1992), 'The Constructivist Critique of Methodology', *Methodus*, 4(1)

Backhouse, R.E. (ed.) (1994), *New Directions in Economic Methodology*, London: Routledge

Bacon, R. and Eltis, W. (1976), *Britain's Economic Problems: Too Few Producers*, London: Macmillan

Baily, M.N. (1974), 'Wages and Employment Under Uncertain Demand', *Review of Economic Studies*, 41 (January)

Ball, R.J. (1964), *Inflation and the Theory of Money*, London: Allen and Unwin

Baran, P.A. and Sweezy, P.M. (1966), *Monopoly Capital: An Essay on the American Economic and Social Order*, New York: Monthly Review Press

Barens, I. (1983), Review of *Keynes's Economics and the Theory of Value and Distribution, Contributions to Political Economy*, 2 (March)

Barro, R.J. (1976), 'Rational Expectations and the Rôle of Monetary Policy, *Journal of Monetary Economics*, 2 (January)

Barro, R.J. (1979), 'Second Thoughts on Keynesian Economics', *American Economic Review, Papers and Proceedings*, 69 (May)

Barro, R.J. and Grossman, H.I. (1971), 'A General Disequilibrium Model of Income and Employment', *American Economic Review*, 61 (March)

Barry, N.P. (1979), *Hayek's Social and Economic Philosophy*, London: Macmillan

Bateman, B.W. and Davis, J.B. (eds) (1991), *Keynes and Philosophy: Essays on the Origin of Keynes's Thought*, Aldershot: Elgar

Baumol, W.J. (1952), 'The Transactions Demand for Cash: An Inventory Theoretic Approach', *Quarterly Journal of Economics*, 66 (November)

Bausor, R. (1982-83), 'Time and the Structure of Economic Analysis', *Journal of Post Keynesian Economics*, 5 (Winter)

Becker, G. (1962), 'Material Behaviour and Economic Theory', *Journal of Political Economy*, 70 (February)

Becker, G. (1976), *The Economic Approach to Human Behaviour*, Chicago: Chicago University Press

Begg, D.K.H. (1982), 'Rational Expectations, Wage Rigidity and Involuntary Unemployment', *Oxford Economic Papers*, 34 (March)

Berkman, N.G. (1980), 'Some Comments on the New Monetary Aggregates', *New England Economic Review*, (March/April)

Bhaskar, R. (1978), *A Realist Theory of Science*, Brighton: Harvester

Blaug, M. (1976), 'Kuhn versus Lakatos on Paradigms versus Research Programmes in the History of Economics', in S.J. Latsis (ed.), *Method and Appraisal in Economics*, Cambridge: Cambridge University Press

Blaug, M. (1980; 1992), *The Methodology of Economics; Or How Economists Explain*, Cambridge: Cambridge University Press

Bleaney, M. (1991), 'An Overview of Emerging Theory', in D. Greenaway *et al.*, (eds), *Companion to Contemporary Economic Thought*, London: Routledge

Blinder, A. and Solow, R.M. (1973), 'Does Fiscal Policy Matter?', *Journal of Public Economics*, 2 (November)

Böhm-Bawerk, E.V. (1889; 1959), *Capital and Interest: A Critical History of Economic Theory*, translated by G.D. Huncke, South Holland, Ill.: Libertarian Press

Boland, L.A. (1982), *The Foundations of Economic Method*, London: George Allen and Unwin

Boland, L.A. (1991), 'The Theory and Practice of Economic Methodology', *Methodus*, 3(2)

Bonadei, R. (1994), 'John Maynard Keynes: Contexts and Methods', in A. Marzola and F. Silva (eds), *John Maynard Keynes: Language and Method*, Aldershot: Elgar, Chapter 2

Brainard, W. (1967), 'Uncertainty and the Effectiveness of Policy', *American Economic Review, Papers and Proceedings*, 57 (May)

Bronfenbrenner, M. (1971), 'The "Structure of Revolutions" in Economic Thought', *History of Political Economy*, 3 (Spring)

Brunner, K. and Meltzer, A.H. (1963), 'The Place of Financial Intermediaries in the Transmission of Monetary Policy', *American Economic Review*, 53 (May)

Buchanan, J.M. (1991), 'Economics in the Post-Socialist Century', *Economic Journal*, 101(404)

Buchanan, J.M. and Thirlby, G.F. (eds.) (1973) *L.S.E. Essays on Cost*, London: Weidenfeld and Nicolson, for London School of Economics and Political Science

Burbridge, J.B. (1979), 'The International Dimension', in A.S. Eichner (ed.), *A Guide to Post Keynesian Economics*, London: Macmillan

Cagan, P. (1956), 'The Monetary Dynamics of Hyperinflation', in M. Friedman (ed.), *Studies in the Quantity Theory of Money*, Chicago: University of Chicago Press

Caldwell, B.J. (1982), *Beyond Positivism: Economic Methodology in the Twentieth Century*, London: Allen and Unwin

Caldwell, B.J. (1988), 'Hayek's Transformation', *History of Political Economy*, 20(4)

Caldwell, B.J. (1989), 'Post-Keynesian Methodology: An Assessment', *Review of Political Economy*, 1(1)

Cameron, R. (1967), *Banking in the Early Stages of Industrialisation: A Study in Comparative Economic History*, Oxford: Oxford University Press

Canterbery, E.R. (1976), *The Making of Economics*, Belmont, California: Wadsworth

Capra, F. (1975), The Tao of Physics: *An Exploration of the Parallels Between Modern Physics and Eastern Mysticism*, London: Wildwood

Carabelli, A. (1985), 'Keynes' Idea of the Possible: His Concepts of Cause', in T. Lawson and M.H. Pesaran (eds), *Keynes' Economics: Methodological Issues*, London: Croom Helm

Carabelli, A. (1988), *On Keynes's Method*, London: Macmillan

Carabelli, A. (1994), 'The Methodology of the Critique of Classical Theory: Keynes on Organic Interdependence', in A. Marzola and F. Silva (eds), *John Maynard Keynes: Language and Method*, Aldershot: Elgar

Carabelli, A. (1995), 'Uncertainty and Measurement in Keynes: Probability and Organicness', in S.C. Dow and J. Hillard (eds), Chapter 8

Carvalho, F. (1983-84), 'On the Concept of Time in Shacklean and Sraffian Economics', *Journal of Post Keynesian Economics*, 6 (Winter)

Casson, M. (1981), *Unemployment: A Disequilibrium Approach*, Oxford: Martin Robertson

Casson, M. (1982), *The Entrepreneur*, Oxford: Martin Robertson

Chernomas, B. (1983), 'Keynesian, Monetarist and Post-Keynesian Policy: A Marxist Analysis', *Studies in Political Economy*, 10 (Winter)

Chick, V. (1983), *Macroeconomics After Keynes: A Reconsideration of the General Theory*, Oxford: Philip Allan

Chick, V (1995), '"Order Out of Chaos" in Economics', in S.C. Dow and J. Hillard (eds), Chapter 2

Clower, R.W. (1965), 'The Keynesian Counterrevolution: A Theoretical Appraisal', in F.H. Hahn and F.P.R. Brechling (eds), *The Theory of Interest Rates*, London: Macmillan

Coats, A.W. (1969), 'Is There A "Structure of Scientific Revolutions" in Economics?', *Kyklos*, 22

Coddington, A. (1975), 'The Rationale of General Equilibrium Theory', *Economic Inquiry*, 13 (December)

Coddington, A. (1976), 'Keynesian Economies: The Search for First Principles', *Journal of Economic Literature*, 14 (December)

Coddington, A. (1982), 'Deficient Foresight: A Troublesome Theme in Keynesian Economics', *American Economic Review*, 72 (June)

Colander, D. (1979), 'Incomes Policies: MIP, WIPP, and TIP', *Journal of Post Keynesian Economics*, 1 (Spring)

Coleby, A.L. (1983), 'The Bank's Operational Procedures for Meeting Monetary Objectives', *Bank of England Quarterly Bulletin*, (June)

Cottrell, A. (1994), 'Post-Keynesian Monetary Economics', *Cambridge Journal of Economics*, 18(6)

Cowen, T. and Kroszner, R. (1994), *Explorations in the New Monetary Economics*, Oxford: Blackwell

Cross, R. (1982), *Economic Theory and Policy in the UK*, Oxford: Martin Robertson

Cross, R. (ed.) (1988), *Unemployment, Hysteresis and the Natural Rate Hypothesis*, Oxford: Martin Robertson

Crotty, J.R. (1980), 'Post-Keynesian Economic Theory: An Overview and Evaluation', *American Economic Review, Papers and Proceedings*, 70 (May)

Cuthbertson, K. (1979), *Macroeconomic Policy*, London: Macmillan

Davidson, P. (1972; 1978), *Money and the Real World*, London: Macmillan

Davidson, P. (1977), 'Money and General Equilibrium', *Economie Appliquée*, 30 (4)

Davidson, P. (1981), 'Post-Keynesian Economics', in D. Bell and I. Kristol (eds), *The Crisis in Economic Theory*, New York: Basic Books

Davidson, P. (1982), *International Money and the Real World*, London: Macmillan

Davidson, P. (1983a), 'The Dubious Labor Market Analysis in Meltzer's Restatement', *Journal of Economic Literature*, 21 (March)

Davidson, P. (1983b), 'The Marginal Product Curve is not the Demand Curve for Labor and Lucas's Labor Supply Function is not the Supply Curve for Labor in the Real World', *Journal of Post-Keynesian Economics*, 6 (Fall)

Davidson, P. (1994), *Post-Keynesian Macroeconomic Theory: A Foundation for Successful Economic Policies for the Twenty-First Century*, Aldershot: Elgar

Davidson, P. and Weintraub, S. (1973), 'Money as Cause and Effect', *Economic Journal*, 83 (December)

Davidson, P. and Weintraub, S. (1978), 'A Statement of Purposes', *Journal of Post Keynesian Economics*, 1 (Fall)

Davis, R.G. (1979-80), 'The Monetary Base as an Intermediate Target for Monetary Policy', *Federal Reserve Bank of New York Quarterly Review*, 4 (Winter)

de Brunhoff, S. (1973; 1976), *Marx on Money*, translated by M.J. Goldbloom, New York: Urizon

de Cecco, M. (1979), 'Origins of the Post-War Payments System', *Cambridge Journal of Economics*, 3 (March)

de Marchi, N. (1991), 'Introduction', in M. Blaug and N. de Marchi (eds), *Appraising Economic Theories: Studies in the Methodology of Research Programme*, Aldershot: Elgar

de Vroey, M. (1980), 'The Transition from Classical to Neoclassical Economics: A Scientific Revolution', in W.J. Samuels (ed.), *The Methodology of Economic Thought*, London: Transactions

Deane, P. (1978), *The Evolution of Economic Ideas*, Cambridge: Cambridge University Press

Deane, P. (1983), 'The Scope and Method of Economic Science', *Economic Journal*, 93 (March)

Debreu, G. (1959), *Theory of Value*, New York: Wiley

Desai, M. (1981), *Testing Monetarism*, London: Pinter

Dixon, H. and Rankin, N (1994), 'Imperfect Compeition and Macroeconomics: A Survey', *Oxford Economic Papers*, April

Dobb, M. (1973), *Theories of Value and Distribution Since Adam Smith: Ideology and Economic Theory*, Cambridge: Cambridge University Press

Dolan, E.G. (ed.) (1976), *The Foundations of Modern Austrian Economics*, Kansas City: Sheed and Ward

Domberger, S. (1979), 'Price Adjustment and Market Structure', *Economic Journal*, 89 (March)

Dow, A.C. and Dow, S.C. (1985), 'Animal Spirits and Rationality', in T. Lawson and M.H. Pesaran (eds), *Keynes' Economics: Methodological Issues*, London: Croom Helm

Dow, A.C. and Dow, S.C. (1989), 'Endogenous Money Creation and Idle Balances', in J. Pheby (ed.), *New Directions in Post Keynesian Economics*, Aldershot: Elgar

Dow, S.C. (1986-87), 'A Post Keynesian Theory of Money in an Open Economy', *Journal of Post Keynesian Economics*, 9(2)

Dow, S.C. (1988), 'What Happened to Keynes's Economics?', in O. Hamouda and J. Smithin (eds.), *Keynes and Public Policy After Fifty Years*, I

Dow, S.C. (1990a), 'Beyond Dualism', *Cambridge Journal of Economics*, 14(2)

Dow, S.C. (1990b), 'Post Keynesianism as Political Economy: A Methodological Discussion', *Review of Political Economy*, 2(3)

Dow, S.C. (1991), 'Are There Signs of Postmodernism in Economics?', *Methodus*, 3

Dow, S.C. (1995), 'Uncertainty About Uncertainty', in S.C. Dow and J. Hillard (eds), Chapter 7

Dow, S.C. (forthcoming, a), 'Why the Financial System Should be Regulated', *Economic Journal*

Dow, S.C. (forthcoming, b), 'The Appeal of Neoclassical Economics: Some Lessons from Keynes's Epistemology', *Cambridge Journal of Economics*

Dow, S.C. (forthcoming, c), 'Endogenous Money', in G.C. Harcourt and P. Riach (eds), *The Second Edition of the General Theory,* London: Routledge

Dow, S.C. (forthcoming, d), 'Whither Mainstream Economics?', *Cambridge Journal of Economics*

Dow, S.C. (forthcoming, e), 'Post Keynesian Methodology', in J.B. Davis *et al.* (eds), *The Handbook on Methodology*, Aldershot: Elgar

Dow, S.C. and Earl, P.E. (1982), *Money Matters: A Keynesian Approach to Monetary Economics*, Oxford: Martin Robertson

Dow, S.C. and Earl, P.E. (1984), 'Methodology and Orthodox Monetary Policy, *Economie Appliquée*, 37(1)

Dow, S.C. and Hillard, J. (eds) (1995), *Kenes, Knowledge and Uncertainty*, Aldershot: Elgar

Dow, S.C. and Smithin, J. (1995), 'Change in Financial Markets and the First Principles of Monetary Economics', Universities of Stirling and York, mimeo

Dowd, K. (1993), *Laissez-Faire Banking*, London: Routledge

Drakopoulos, S. (1991), *Values and Economic Theory*, Aldershot: Gower

Dubois, D. and Prade, H. (1980), *Fuzzy Sets and Systems: Theory and Applications*, London: Academic Press

Duhem, P. (1906; 1954), *The Aim and Structure of Physical Theory*, translated by P.P. Wiener, Princeton: Princeton University Press

Dutt, A.K. and Amadeo, E.J. (1990), *Keynes's Third Alternative? The Neo-Ricardian Keynesians and the Post Keynesians*, Aldershot: Elgar

Earl, P.E. (1983), *The Economic Imagination: Towards a Behavioural Theory of Choice*, Brighton: Wheatsheaf

Earl, P.E. (1984), *The Corporate Imagination: How Big Companies Make Mistakes*, Brighton: Wheatsheaf

Earl, P.E. (1995a), *Microeconomics for Business and Marketing*, Aldershot: Elgar

Earl, P.E. (1995b), 'Liquidity-Preference, Marketability and Pricing', in S.C. Dow and J. Hillard (eds), Chapter 15

Eatwell, J. (1979), 'Theories of Value, Output and Employment', *Thames Papers in Political Economy* (Summer)

Eatwell, J. and Milgate, M. (eds) (1983), 'Introduction', in *Keynes's Economics and the Theory of Value and Distribution*, London: Duckworth

Edgeworth, F.Y. (1881), *Mathematical Psychics*, London: Routledge

Eichner, A.S. (1973), 'A Theory of the Determination of the Mark-up Under Oligopoly', *Economic Journal*, 83 (December)

Eichner, A.S. (1976), *The Megacorp and Oligopoly: Microfoundations of Macro Dynamics*, Cambridge: Cambridge University Press

Eichner, A.S. (1979), 'Introduction', in A.S. Eichner (ed.), *A Guide to Post-Keynesian Economics*, White Plains: M.E. Sharpe

Ekelund, R.B. and Hebert, R.F. (1975), *A History of Economic Theory and Method*, London: McGraw-Hill

Evans, G. (1984) 'The Stability of Rational Expectations in Macroeconomic Models', in R. Frydman and E. Phelps (eds), *Individual Forecasting and Aggregate Outcomes: Rational Expectations Examined*, Cambridge, Cambridge University Press, Chapter 4

Feyerabend, P.K. (1970), 'Consolations for the Specialist', in I. Lakatos and A. Musgrave, (eds), *Criticism and the Growth of Knowledge*, Cambridge: Cambridge University Press

Feyerabend, P. (1978), *Science in a Free Society*, London: New Left Books

Feyerabend, P.K. (1981), 'How to Defend Society Against Science', in I. Hacking (ed.), *Scientific Revolutions*, Oxford: Oxford University Press

Feynman, R.P. (1965), The Character of Physical Law, Cambridge, MA: MIT Press

Fishburn, P.C. (1991), 'Decision Theory: The Next 100 Years', *Economic Journal*, 101(404)

Fisher, D. (1978), *Monetary Theory and the Demand for Money*, Oxford: Martin Robertson

Fisher, I. (1911; 1963), *The Purchasing Power of Money*, New York: Augustus Kelley

Fisher, I. (1930; 1965), *The Theory of Interest as Determined by Impatience to Spend Income and Opportunity to Invest It*, New York: Augustus Kelley

Fitzgibbons, A. (1988), *Keynes's Vision: A New Political Economy*, Oxford: Clarendon

Frank, A.G. (1967), *Capitalism and Underdevelopment in Latin America*, New York: Monthly Review Press

Frenkel, J.A. and Johnson, H.G. (1976; 1977), *The Monetary Approach to the Balance of Payments*, Toronto: University of Toronto Press

Frenkel, J.A. and Johnson, H.G. (1978), *The Economics of Exchange Rates*, Reading, MA: Addison-Wesley

Friedman, M. (1953), 'The Methodology of Positive Economics', in *Essays in Positive Economics*, Chicago: University of Chicago Press

Friedman, M. (1956), 'The Quantity Theory of Money: A Restatement', in M. Friedman, *Studies in the Quantity Theory of Money*, Chicago: Chicago University Press

Friedman, M. (1957), *A Theory of the Consumption Function*, Princeton: Princeton University Press

Friedman, M. (1968a), *Dollars and Deficits: Living with America's Economic Problems*, Englewood Cliffs: Prentice-Hall

Friedman, M. (1968b), 'The Rôle of Monetary Policy', *American Economic Review*, 58 (March)

Friedman, M. (1969), *The Optimum Quantity of Money*, Chicago: Aldine

Friedman, M. (1971), 'A Monetary Theory of Nominal Income, *Journal of Political Economy*, 79 (March/April)

Friedman, M. (1975), 'Unemployment Versus Inflation? An Evaluation of the Phillips Curve', *IEA Lecture*, 2, London: IEA

Friedman, M. and Schwartz, A. (1963a), *A Monetary History of the United States: 1867-1960*, Princeton: Princeton University Press for NBER

Friedman, M. and Schwartz, A. (1963b), 'Money and Business Cycles', *Review of Economics and Statistics*, 45 (Supplement)

Friedman, M. and Schwartz, A. (1982), *Monetary Trends in the United States and the United Kingdon: Their Relationship to Income, Prices, and Interest Rates, 1867-1975*, Chicago: University of Chicago Press for NBER

Frydman, R. and Phelps, E. (eds.) (1984), *Individual Forecasting and Aggregate Outcomes: Rational Expectations Examined*, Cambridge: Cambridge University Press

Gale, D. (1982), *Money: In Equilibrium*, Welwyn: Nisbet; Cambridge: Cambridge University Press

Gale, D. (1983), *Money: In Disequilibrium*, Welwyn: Nisbet; Cambridge: Cambridge University Press

Garegnani, P. (1978), 'Notes on Consumption, Investment and Effective Demand: I, *Cambridge Journal of Economics*, 2 (December)

Garegnani, P. (1979), 'Notes on Consumption, Investment and Effective Demand, II', *Cambridge Journal of Economics*, 3 (March)

Garrison, R.W. (1984), 'Time and Money: The Universals of Macroeconomic Theorizing', *Journal of Macroeconomics*, Spring

Garrison, R.W. (1989), 'The Austrian Theory of the Business Cycle in the Light of Modern Macroeconomics', *Review of Austrian Economics*

Georgescu-Roegen, N. (1971), *The Entropy Law and the Economic Process*, Cambridge, Mass: Harvard University Press

Gerrard, B. (1989), *Theory of the Capitalist Economy: Towards a Post-Classical Synthesis*, Oxford: Blackwell

Gerrard, B. (1990), 'On Matters Methodological in Economics', *Journal of Economic Surveys*, 4(2)

Gerrard, B. (1992), 'Human Logic in Keynes's Thought: Escape from the Cartesian Vice', in P. Arestis and V. Chick (eds), *Recent Developments in Post-Keynesian Economics*, Aldershot: Elgar

Gerrard, B. (ed.) (1993), *The Economics of Rationality*, London: Routledge

Gerrard, B. (1995), 'The Scientific Basis of Economics: A Review of the Methodological Debates in Economics and Econometrics', *Scottish Journal of Political Economy*, 42(2)

Gerrard, B. and Hillard, J. (eds.) (1992), *The Philosophy and Economics of J.M. Keynes*, Aldershot: Elgar

Gilder, G. (1981), *Wealth and Poverty*, New York: Basic Books

Glass, J.C. and Johnson, W. (1989), *Economics: Progression, Stagnation or Degeneration?*, Brighton: Harvester Wheatsheaf

Goldfeld, S.M. (1976), 'The Case of the Missing Money', *Brookings Papers on Economic Activity*, 3

Gonick, C. (1975), *Inflation or Depression: The Continuing Crisis of the Canadian Economy*, Toronto: Lorimer

Goodhart, C.A.E. (1994), 'What Should Central Banks Do? What Should Be Their Macroeconomic Objectives and Operations?', *Economic Journal*, 104(427)

Gordon, D.F. (1974), 'A Neo-Classical Theory of Keynesian Unemployment', *Economic Inquiry*, 12 (December)

Gordon, R.J. (1978), *Macroeconomics*, Boston: Little, Brown & Co

Gordon, R.J. (1990), 'What is New-Keynesian Economics?', *Journal of Economic Literature*, 27 (September)

Gordon, S. (1991), *The History and Philosophy of Social Sciences*, London: Routledge

Gowland, D. (1982), *Controlling the Money Supply*, London: Croom Helm

Gram, H. and Walsh, V. (1983), 'Joan Robinson's Economics in Retrospect', *Journal of Economic Literature*, 21 (June)

Grandmont, J.M. and Laroque, G. (1977), 'On Temporary Keynesian Equilibrium', in G.C. Harcourt, *The Microeconomic Foundations of Macroeconomics*, London: Macmillan

Gray, H.P. (1976), *A Generalized Theory of International Trade*, London: Macmillan

Great Britain (1943), *International Clearing Union*, text of a paper containing proposals by British experts for an International Clearing Union, New York: British Information Services

Green, H.A.J. (1977), 'Aggregation Problems of Macroeconomics', in G.C. Harcourt (ed.), *The Microeconomic Foundations of Macroeconomics*, London: Macmillan

Greenwald, B. and Stiglitz, J. (1993), 'New and Old Keynesians', *Journal of Economic Perspectives*, 7

Grossman, S.J. and Stiglitz, J.E. (1980), 'On the Impossibility of Informationally Efficient Markets', *American Economic Review*, 70 (June)

Gutting, G. (ed.) (1980), *Paradigms and Revolutions: Applications and Appraisals of Thomas Kuhn's Philosophy of Science*, Notre Dame, Ind: University of Notre Dame Press

Hacking, I. (ed.) (1981), *Scientific Revolutions*, Oxford: Oxford University Press

Hahn, F.H. (1952), 'Expectations and Equilibrium', *Economic Journal*, 72 (December)

Hahn, F.H. (1973a) 'The Winter of our Discontent', *Economica*, 40 (August)

Hahn, F.H. (1973b), *On the Notion of Equilibrium in Economics*, Cambridge: Cambridge University Press

Hahn, F.H. (1977), 'Keynesian Economics and General Equilibrium Theory: Reflections on Some Current Debates', in G.C. Harcourt (ed.), *The Microeconomic Foundations of Macroeconomics*, London: Macmillan

Hahn, F.H. (1980), 'Monetarism and Economic Theory', *Economica*, 47 (February)

Hahn, F.H. (1981), 'General Equilibrium Theory', in D. Bell and I. Kristol (eds), *The Crisis in Economic Theory*, New York: Basic Books

Hahn, F.H. (1983), *Money and Inflation*, Cambridge, MA: MIT Press

Hahn, F.H. (1991), 'The Next Hundred Years', *Economic Journal*, 101(404)

Hall, R.E. (1980), 'Employment Functions and Wage Rigidity', *Brookings Papers in Economic Activity*, 1

Hanson, N.R. (1965), *Patterns of Discovery: An Inquiry into the Conceptual Foundations of Science*, Cambridge: Cambridge University Press

Harcourt, G.C. (1972), *Some Cambridge Controversies in the Theory of Capital*, Cambridge: Cambridge University Press

Harcourt, G.C. (ed.) (1977), *The Microeconomic Foundations of Macroeconomics*, London: Macmillan

Harcourt, G.C. (1982), 'Post-Keynesianism: Quite Wrong And/Or Nothing New?' *Thames Papers in Political Economy*, (Summer)

Harcourt, G.C. (1987), 'The Legacy of Keynes: Theoretical Methods and Unfinished Business', in D. Reese (ed) *The Legacy of Keynes: Nobel Conference XXII*, San Francisco: Harper and Row, Chapter 1

Harcourt, G.C. and Kenyon, P. (1976), 'Pricing and the Investment Decision', *Kyklos*, 29

Harcourt, G.C. and O'Shaughnessy, T.J. (1983), 'Keynes's Unemployment Equilibrium: Some Insights from Joan Robinson, Piero Sraffa and Richard Kahn', *University of Cambridge Faculty of Economics and Politics Research Paper Series*, No. 3 (November)

Harding, S.G. (ed.) (1976), *Can Theories be Refuted? Essays on the Duhem-Quine Thesis*, Boston: Reider

Harris, D.J. (1975), 'The Theory of Economic Growth: A Critique and Reformulation', *American Economic Review, Papers and Proceedings*, 65 (May)

Harrod, R.F. (1939), 'An Essay in Dynamic Theory', *Economic Journal*, 49 (March)

Harvey, D. (1982), *The Limits to Capital*, Chicago: University of Chicago Press

Hausman, D.M. (1989), 'Economic Methodology in a Nutshell', *Journal of Economic Perspectives*, 3(2)

Hausman, D. (1992), *The Inexact and Separate Science of Economics*, Cambridge: Cambridge University Press

Hawtrey, R.G. (1919), *Currency and Credit*, London: Longman

Hayek, F.A. (1931a; 1935), *Prices and Production*, London: Routledge and Kegan Paul

Hayek, F.A. (1931b, 1932), 'Reflections on the Pure Theory of Money of Mr J.M. Keynes', *Economica*, 11 (August), 12 (February)

Hayek, F.A. (1931c), 'The Pure Theory of Money: A Rejoinder to Mr Keynes', *Economica*, 11 (November)

Hayek, F.A. (1933), *Monetary Theory and the Trade Cycle*, London: Jonathan Cape

Hayek, F.A. (1937), 'Economics and Knowledge', *Economica*, NS 4

Hayek, F.A. (1941), *The Pure Theory of Capital*, London: Routledge and Kegan Paul

Hayek, F.A. (1948), 'Economics and Knowledge', in F.A. Hayek, *Individualism and Economic Order*, London: Routledge and Kegan Paul, Chapter 2

Hayek, F.S. (1949), 'Socialist Calculation. I The Nature and History of the Problem', in F.A. Hayek, *Individualism and Economic Order*, London: Routledge and Kegan Paul

Hayek, F. A. (1960), *The Constitution of Liberty*, London: Routledge and Kegan Paul

Hayek, F.A. (1967), *Studies in Philosophy, Politics and Economics*, London: Routledge and Kegan Paul

Hayek, F.A. (1972), *A Tiger by the Tail: The Keynesian Legacy of Inflation*, London: Institute of Economic Affairs

Hayek, F.A. (1975), 'Full Employment at Any Price', *Hobert Paper*, 45, London: IEA

Hayek, F.A. (1978), 'Denationalisation of Money: The Argument Refined', *Hobert Paper*, 70, London: IEA

Heiner, R.A. (1983), 'The Origin of Predictable Behaviour', *American Economic Review*, 73 (September)

Heinsohn, G. and Steiger, O. (1984), 'Marx and Keynes - Private Property and Money', *Economies et Societes, X, Monnaie et Production*, 1

Hendry, D.F. (1993), *Econometrics: Alchemy or Science?*, Oxford: Blackwell

Hendry, D.F. and Ericsson, N.R. (1983), 'Assertion Without Empirical Basis: An Econometric Appraisal of Friedman and Schwartz' Monetary Trends in the United Kingdom', in Bank of England Panel of Academic Consultants, *Panel Paper*, No. 22 (October)

Hey, J.D. (1981), *Economics in Disequilibrium*, Oxford: Martin Robertson

Heyting, A. (1971), *Intuitionism: An Introduction*, Amsterdam: North-Holland

Hicks, J.R. (1937), 'Mr Keynes and the Classics: A Suggested Interpretation', *Econometrica*, 5 (April)

Hicks, J.R. (1939), *Value and Capital*, Oxford: Clarendon Press

Hicks, J.R. (1974), *The Crisis in Keynesian Economics*, Oxford: Basil Blackwell

Hicks, J.R. (1976), 'Some Questions of Time in Economics', in A.M. Tang, F.M. Westfield and J.S. Worley (eds), *Evolution, Welfare and Time in Economics: Essays in Honor of Nicholas Georgescu-Roegen*, Lexington, Mass: Lexington Books

Hicks, J.R. (1979a), *Causality in Economics*, Oxford: Basil Blackwell

Hicks, J.R. (1979b), Review of *Microfoundations: The Compatibility of Microeconomics and Macroeconomics, Journal of Economic Literature*, 17 (December)

Hicks, J.R. (1980-81), 'IS-LM: An Explanation', *Journal of Post Keynesian Economics*, 3 (Winter)

Hicks, J.R. (1981), 'LSE and the Robbins Circle', in J.R. Hicks, *Collected Essays on Economic Theory, I: Wealth and Welfare*, Oxford: Martin Robertson

Hilferding, R. (1910; 1981) *Finance Capital: A Study of the Latest Phase of Capitalist Development*, edited by T. Bottomore, translated by M. Watnick and S. Gordon, London: Routledge and Kegan Paul

Hodgson, G.M., Samuels, W.J. and Tool, M.R. (eds) (1994), *The Elgar Companion to Institutional and Evolutionary Economics*, Aldershot: Elgar

Hollander, S. (1979) *The Economics of David Ricardo*, Toronto: University of Toronto Press

Hollis, M. and Nell, E.J. (1975), *Rational Economic Man: A Philosophical Critique of Neo-Classical Economics*, Cambridge: Cambridge University Press

Hume, D. (1752; 1955), 'Of Money', in E. Rotwein (ed.), *D. Hume: Writings on Economics*, Edinburgh: Nelson

Hunt, E.K. (1979), *History of Economic Thought: A Critical Perspective*, Belmont, Ca: Wadsworth

Hutchison, T.W. (1981), *The Politics and Philosophy of Economics: Marxians, Keynesians and Austrians*, Oxford: Basil Blackwell

Jenssen, M.C.W. (1993), *Microfoundations: A Critical Inquiry*, London: Routledge

Johannes, J.M. and Rasche, R.H. (1981), 'Can the Reserves Approach to Monetary Control Really Work?', *Journal of Money, Credit and Banking*, 13 (August)

Johnson, H.G. (1971), 'The Keynesian Revolution and the Monetarist Counter-Revolution, *American Economic Review*, 61 (May)

Johnson, L.E. (1983), 'Economic Paradigms: A Missing Dimension', *Journal of Economic Issues*, 17 (December)

Johnston, J. (1991), 'Econometrics: Retrospect and Prospect', *Economic Journal*, 101 (404)

Jorgenson, D.W. (1963), 'Capital Theory and Investment Behaviour', *American Economic Review*, 53 (May)

Kaldor, N. (1960), 'Keynes' Theory of the Own Rates of Interest', in N. Kaldor, *Essays on Economic Stability and Growth*, London: Duckworth

Kaldor, N. (1970), 'The Case for Regional Policies', *Scottish Journal of Political Economy*, 17 (November)

Kaldor, N. (1972), 'The Irrelevance of Equilibrium Economics', *Economic Journal*, 82 (December)

Kaldor, N. (1982), *The Scourge of Monetarism*, Oxford: Oxford University Press

Kaldor, N. (1983), 'Keynesian Economics After Fifty Years', in D. Worswick and J. Trevithick (eds), *Keynes and the Modern World*, Cambridge: Cambridge University Press

Kalecki, M. (1937; 1954), *The Theory of Economic Dynamics*, New York: Rinehart

Kalecki, M. (1971), 'Entrepreneurial Capital and Investment', in M. Kalecki, *Selected Essays on the Dynamics of the Capitalist Economy, 1933-1970*, Cambridge: Cambridge University Press

Kantor, B. (1979), 'Rational Expectations and Economic Thought', *Journal of Economic Literature*, 17 (December)

Kay, N. (1982), *The Evolving Firm: Strategy and Structure in Industrial Organisation*, London: Macmillan

Keller, R.R. and Carson, J.L. (1982), 'A neglected chapter in *The General Theory*', *Journal of Post Keynesian Economics*, 4 (Spring)

Kelly, G.A. (1963), *A Theory of Personality: The Psychology of Personal Constructs*, New York: Norton

Keynes, J.M. (1925), 'Freudian Psycho-analysis', letter to the editor of *The Nation and Atheneum*, 29 (August)

Keynes, J.M. (1926), *The End of Laissez-Faire*, London: Hogarth

Keynes, J.M. (1936), *The General Theory of Employment, Interest and Money*, London: Macmillan

Keynes, J.M. (1937), 'The General Theory of Employment', *Quarterly Journal of Economics*, 51

Keynes, J.M. (1971), *A Treatise on Money, II: The Applied Theory of Money, Collected Writings, VI*, London: Macmillan, for the Royal Economic Society

Keynes, J.M. (1972a), *Essays in Persuasion, Collected Writings, IX*, London: Macmillan, for the Royal Economic Society

Keynes, J.M. (1972b), 'My Early Beliefs', in *Essays in Biography, Collected Writings, X*, London: Macmillan, for the Royal Economic Society

Keynes, J.M. (1972c), 'Newton the Man', in *Essays in Biography, Collected Writing, X*, London: Macmillan, for the Royal Economic Society

Keynes, J.M. (1973a), *A Treatise on Probability, Collected Writings, VIII*, London: Macmillan, for the Royal Economic Society

Keynes, J.M. (1973b), *The General Theory and After Part I: Preparation, Collected Writings, XIII*, London: Macmillan, for the Royal Economic Society

Keynes, J.M. (1973c), *The General Theory and After Part II: Defence and Development, Collected Writings, XIV*, London: Macmillan, for the Royal Economic Society

Keynes, J.M. (1982), *Social, Political and Literary Writings, Collected Writings, XXVIII*, London: Macmillan, for the Royal Economic Society

Keynes, J.N. (1891; 1904) *The Scope and Method of Political Economy*, London: Macmillan

Kirzner, I.M. (1973), *Competition and Entrepreneurship*, Chicago: Chicago University Press

Kirzner, I.M. (1976), 'On the Method of Austrian Economics', in E.G. Dolan (ed.), *The Foundations of Modern Austrian Economics*, Kansas City: Sheed and Ward

Klamer, A. (1984), *Conversations with Economists: New Classical Economists and Opponents Speak Out on the Current Controversy in Macroeconomics*, Totawa, NJ: Rowman and Allenheld; Brighton: Wheatsheaf

Klamer, A. (1995), 'The Conception of Modernism in Economics: Samuelson, Keynes and Harrod', in S.C. Dow and J. Hillard (eds), Chapter 18

Koopmans, T. (1957), *Three Essays on the State of Economic Science*, London: McGraw-Hill

Kregel, J.A. (1976), 'Economic Methodology in the Face of Uncertainty', *Economic Journal*, 86 (June)

Kregel, J.A. (1980a), 'Economic Dynamics and the Theory of Steady Growth: An Historical Essay on Harrod's "Knife-Edge"', *History of Political Economy*, 12 (Spring)

Kregel, J.A. (1980b), 'Markets and Institutions as Features of a Capitalist Production System', *Journal of Post Keynesian Economics*, 3 (Fall)

Kregel, J.A. (1983), 'The Microfoundations of the "Generalisation of *The General Theory*" and "Bastard Keynesianism": Keynes's Theory of Employment in the Long and the Short Period', *Cambridge Journal of Economics*, 7 (September/December)

Kuhn, T.S. (1962; 1970), *The Structure of Scientific Revolutions*, Chicago: Chicago University Press

Kuhn, T.S. (1970), 'Reflections on my Critics', in I. Lakatos and A. Musgrave (eds), *Criticism and the Growth of Knowledge*, Cambridge: Cambridge University Press

Kuhn, T.S. (1974), 'Second Thoughts on Paradigms', in F. Suppe (ed.), *The Structure of Scientific Theories*, Urbana: University of Illinois Press

Kuhn, T.S. (1977), *The Essential Tension*, Chicago: Chicago University Press

Kunin, L. and Weaver, F. (1971), 'On the Structure of Scientific Revolutions in Economics', *History of Political Economy*, 3 (Fall)

Kydland, F.E. and Prescott, E.C. (1982), 'Time to Build on Aggregate Fluctuations', *Econometrica*, 50

Lachmann, L.M. (1943), 'The Role of Expectations in Economics as a Social Science', *Economica*, 10 (February)

Lachmann, L.M. (1956), *Capital and its Structure*, London: London School of Economics and Political Science

Lachmann, L. (1973), 'Macroeconomic Thinking and the Market Economy', *Hobart Paper*, 56, London: IEA

Lachmann, L. (1976a), 'On Austrian Capital Theory', in E.G. Dolan (ed.), *The Foundations of Modern Austrian Economics*

Lachmann, L.M. (1976b), 'Towards a Critique of Macroeconomics', in E.G. Dolan (ed.), *The Foundations of Modern Austrian Economics*

Lachmann, L.M. (1976c), 'From Mises to Shackle: An Essay on Austrian Economics and the Kaleidic Society', *Journal of Economic Literature*, 14 (March)

Lachmann, L.M. (1977), *Capital, Expectations, and the Market Process: Essays on the Theory of the Market Economy*, Kansas City: Sheed Andrews and McMeel

Lachmann, L.M. (1986), *The Market as an Economic Process*, Oxford: Blackwell

Laidler, D.E.W. (1981), 'Monetarism: An Interpretation and an Assessment', *Economic Journal*, 91 (March)

Laidler, D. (1983), 'The Buffer Stock Notion in Monetary Economics', *Economic Journal*, 93 (Supplement)

Lakatos, I. (1970) 'Falsification and the Methodology of Scientific Research Programmes', in I. Lakatos and A. Musgrave (eds.), *Criticism and the Growth of Knowledge*, Cambridge: Cambridge University Press

Lakatos, I. (1981) 'History of Science and its Rational Reconstructions', in I. Hacking (ed.), *Scientific Revolutions*, Oxford: Oxford University Press

Lakatos, I. and Musgrave, A. (eds) (1970), *Criticism and the Growth of Knowledge*, Cambridge: Cambridge University Press

Lange, O. and Taylor, F.M. (1964), *On the Economic Theory of Socialism*, London: McGraw-Hill

Lapavitsas, C. (1994), 'The Banking School and Karl Marx's Monetary Thought', *Cambridge Journal of Economics*, 18(5)

Latsis, S.J. (ed.) (1976), *Method and Appraisal in Economics*, Cambridge: Cambridge University Press

Laudan, L. (1977), *Progress and its Problems: Towards a Theory of Scientific Growth*, London: Routledge and Kegan Paul

Lavoie, D. (1983), 'Some Strengths in Marx's Disequilibrium Theory of Money', *Cambridge Journal of Economics*, 7 (March)

Lavoie, M. (1992), *Foundations of Post-Keynesian Economic Analysis*, Aldershot: Elgar

Lawson, T. (1983) 'Different Approaches to Economic Modelling', *Cambridge Journal of Economics*, 7 (March)

Lawson, T. (1985a), 'Keynes, Predictions and Econometrics', in T. Lawson and M.H. Pesaran (eds), *Keynes' Economics: Methodological Issues*, London: Croom Helm

Lawson, T. (1985b), 'Uncertainty and Economic Analysis', *Economic Journal*, 95(380)

Lawson, T. (1989), 'Abstraction, Tendencies and Stylised Facts: A Realist Approach to Economic Analysis', *Cambridge Journal of Economics*, 13(1)

Lawson, T. (1994), 'A Realist Theory for Economics', in R.E. Backhouse (ed)

Lawson, T. (1995a), 'Economics and Expectations', in S.C. Dow and J. Hillard (eds), Chapter 5

Lawson, T. (1995b), 'The "Lucas Critique": A Generalisation', *Cambridge Journal of Economics*, 19(2)

Lawson, T. and Pesaran, M.H. (eds) (1985), *Keynes's Economics: Methodological Issues*, London: Croom Helm

Lazonick, W. (1979), 'Industrial Relations and Technical Change: The Case of the Self-Acting Mule', *Cambridge Journal of Economics*, 3 (September)

Leijonhufvud, A. (1967), 'Keynes and the Keynesians: A Suggested Interpretation', *American Economic Review*, 57 (May)

Leijonhufvud, A. (1968), *On Keynesian Economics and the Economics of Keynes*, Oxford: Oxford University Press

Leijonhufvud, A. (1974), 'Keynes's Employment Function', *History of Political Economy*, 6 (Summer)

Leijonhufvud, A. (1981), *Information and Coordination: Essays in Macroeconomic Theory*, Oxford: Oxford University Press

Lenin, V. (1916; 1939), *Imperialism, the Highest Stage of Capitalism*, London: Lawrence and Wishart

Lerner, A.P. (1951), *Economics of Employment*, New York: McGraw-Hill

Levhari, D. and Patinkin, D. (1968), 'The Rôle of Money in a Simple Growth Model', *American Economic Review*, 58 (September)

Lipsey, R.G. and Lancaster, K. (1956-57), 'The General Theory of Second Best', *Review of Economic Studies*, 24

Littlechild, S.C. (1978), *The Fallacy of the Mixed Economy: An 'Austrian' Critique of Economic Thinking and Policy*, London: Institute for Economic Affairs

Littlechild, S.C. (1981), 'Misleading Calculations of the Social Costs of Monopoly Power', *Economic Journal*, 91 (June)

Loasby, B.J. (1976), *Choice, Complexity and Ignorance*, Cambridge: Cambridge University Press

Loasby, B.J. (1983), 'Economics of Dispersed and Incomplete Knowledge', in I.M. Kirzner (ed.), *Method, Process and Austrian Economics: Essays in Honor of Ludwig von Mises*, Lexington, Mass: Lexington Books

Loasby, B.J. (1991), 'The Austrian School', in Mair and Miller (eds), chapter 3

Losee, J. (1972; 1980), *A Historical Introduction to the Philosophy of Science*, Oxford: Oxford University Press

Lucas, R.E., Jr. (1972), 'Expectations and the Neutrality of Money', *Journal of Economic Theory*, 4 (April)

Lucas, R.E., Jr. (1976), 'Econometric Policy Evaluation: A Critique', in K. Brunner and A.H. Meltzer (eds), *The Phillips Curve and Labour Markets*, Amsterdam: North-Holland

Lucas, R.E., Jr. (1977), 'Understanding Business Cycles', in K. Brunner and A.H. Meltzer (eds), *Stabilisation of the Domestic and International Economy, Journal of Monetary Economics*, 5 (Supplement)

Lucas, R.E., Jr. (1980), 'Methods and Problems in Business Cycle Theory', *Journal of Money Credit and Banking*, 12 (November)

Lucas, R.E., Jr. (1981), 'Tobin and Monetarism: A Review Article', *Journal of Economic Literature*, 19 (June)

Lucas, R.E., Jr. (1988), 'On the Mechanics of Economics Development', *Journal of Monetary Economics*, July

Lucas, R.E., Jr. and Sargent, T.J. (1981), 'After Keynesian Macroeconomics', in R.E. Lucas, Jr. and T.J. Sargent (eds), *Rational Expectations and Econometric Practice*, London: George Allen and Unwin

McCallum, J. (1983), 'Policy "Credibility" and Economic Behaviour', *Journal of Post Keynesian Economics*, 6 (Fall)

McCloskey, D.N. (1983), 'The Rhetoric of Economics', *Journal of Economic Literature*, 21 (June)

McCloskey, D.N. (1986), *The Rhetoric of Economics*, Brighton: Wheatsheaf

McCloskey, D.N. (1994), *Knowledge and Persuasion in Economics*, Cambridge: Cambridge University Press

Macfie, A.L. (1955), 'The Scottish Tradition in Economic Thought', *Scottish Journal of Political Economy*, 2 (June)

Machlup, F. (1967), 'Theories of the Firm: Marginalist, Behavioral, Managerial', *American Economic Review*, 57 (March)

Machlup, F. (1974), 'Friedrich von Hayek's Contributions to Economics', *Swedish Journal of Economics*, 76

Magdoff, D. and Sweezy, P.M. (1981), *The Deepening Crisis of US Capitalism*, New York: Monthly Review Press

Magnani, M. (1983), 'Keynesian Foundamentalism': A Critique', in J. Eatwell and M. Milgate (eds), *Keynes's Economics and the Theory of Value and Distribution*, London: Duckworth

Mair, D. and Miller, A.G. (eds) (1991), *A Modern Guide to Economic Thought: An Introduction to Comparative Schools of Thought in Economics*, Aldershot: Elgar

Maki, U. (1989), 'On the Problem of Realism in Economics', *Ricerche Economiche*, 43(1-2)

Malinvaud, E. (1977), *The Theory of Unemployment Reconsidered*, Oxford: Basil Blackwell

Malinvaud, E. and Younes, Y. (1977), 'Some New Concepts for the Microeconomic Foundations of Macroeconomics', in G.C. Harcourt (ed.), *The Microeconomic Foundations of Macroeconomics*, London: Macmillan

Malthus, T. (1824), 'Political Economy', *Quarterly Review* (January)

Mandel, E. (1968), *Marxist Economic Theory*, translated by B. Pearce, London: Merlin

Mandel, E. (1980), *The Second Slump: A Marxist Analysis of Recession in the Seventies*, London: Verso

Mankiw, N.G. and Romer, D. (eds) (1991), *New Keynesian Economics*, Cambridge, MA: MIT Press

Marshall, A. (1890), *Principles of Economics*, London: Macmillan

Marshall, A. (1923), *Money, Credit and Commerce*, London: Macmillan

Marx, K. (1857-58; 1973), *Grundrisse der Kritik der Politischen Okonomie*, translated by M. Nicolaus, Harmondsworth: Penguin

Marx, K. (1867; 1976), *Capital: A Critique of Political Economy*, Vol. I, translated by B. Fowkes, Harmondsworth: Penguin, with *New Left Review*

Marx, K. (1894; 1909), *Capital: A Critique of Political Economy*, Vol. III, translated by E. Untermann, Chicago: Charles H. Kerr

Marx, K. (1975), *Texts on Method*, edited and translated by T. Carver, Oxford: Basil Blackwell

Mayer, T. (1993), *Truth Versus Precision in Economics*, Aldershot: Elgar

Menger, C. (1871; 1981), *Principles of Economics,* ed. by J. Dingwall and B.F. Hoselitz, New York: New York University Press

Menger, C. (1883; 1963), *Problems of Economics and Sociology*, edited by L. Schneider, translated by F.J. Nock, Urbana: University of Illinois Press

Metzler, L. (1951), 'Wealth, Saving and the Rate of Interest', *Journal of Political Economy*, 59 (April)

Milgate, M. (1983), *Capital and Employment: A Study of Keynes's Economics*, London: Academic Press

Mill, J.S. (1836; 1967), 'On the Definition of Political Economy', in J.M. Robson (ed.), *Collected Works: Essays on Economy and Society*, Vol. 4, Toronto: University of Toronto Press

Mill, J.S. (1848; 1965), *Principles of Political Economy: With Some of Their Applications to Social Philosophy*, edited by W.J. Ashley, New York: A.M. Kelly

Minsky, H. (1975; 1976), *John Maynard Keynes*, London: Macmillan

Minsky, H.P. (1980), 'Money, Financial Markets and the Coherence of a Market Economy', *Journal of Post Keynesian Economics*, 3 (Fall)

Minsky, H.P. (1982), *Inflation, Recession and Economic Policy*, Brighton: Wheatsheaf

Mises, L. (1912; 1953), *The Theory of Money and Credit*, translated by H.E. Batson, New Haven: Yale University Press

Mises, L. (1949), *Human Action*, New Haven: Yale University Press

Modigliani, F. (1944), 'Liquidity Preference and the Theory of Interest and Money', *Econometrica*, 12 (January)

Moore, B. (1988), *Horizontalists and Verticalists: The Macroeconomics of Credit Money*, Cambridge: Cambridge University Press

Muellbauer, J. and Portes, R. (1978), 'Macroeconomic Models with Quantity Rationing', *Economic Journal*, 88 (December)

Mundell, R.A. (1976), 'The International Distribution of Money in a Growing World Economy', in J.A. Frenkel and H.G. Johnson (eds), *The Monetary Approach to the Balance of Payments*

Muth, J.F. (1961), 'Rational Expectations and the Theory of Price Movements', *Econometrica*, 29 (July)

Myrdal, G. (1953), *The Political Element in the Development of Economic Theory*, London: Routledge and Kegan Paul

Myrdal, G. (1964), *Economic Theory and Underdeveloped Regions*, London: Methuen

Neill, T.P. (1949), 'The Physiocrats' Concept of Economics', *Quarterly Journal of Economics*, 63 (November)

Nell, E.J. (1983), Review of *Capital and Employment: A Study of Keynes's Economics, Contributions to Political Economy*, 2 (Spring)

Newton-Smith, W.H. (1981), *The Rationality of Science*, London: Routledge and Kegan Paul

Norton, B. (1992), 'Radical Theories of Accumulation and Crisis: Developments and Directions', in Roberts and Feiner (eds.), Chapter 5

O'Donnell, R.M. (1989), *Keynes's Philosophy, Economics and Politics: The Philosophical Foundations of Keynes's Thought and Their Influence on his Economics and Politics*, London, Macmillan

O'Donnell, R.M. (ed.) (1991), *Keynes as Philosopher-Economist*, London: Macmillan

O'Driscoll, G.P. Jr. (1977), *Economics as a Coordination Problem*, Kansas City: Sheed, Andrews and McMeel

O'Driscoll, G.P., Jr. and Rizzo, M.J. (1985), *The Economics of Time and Ignorance*, Oxford: Blackwell

Panico, C. (1980), 'Marx's Analysis of the Relationship Betwen the Rate of Interest and the Rate of Profits', *Cambridge Journal of Economics*, 4 (December)

Panico, C. (1983), 'Interest and Profit: A Study in Marx's Writings', *University of Cambridge Faculty of Economics and Politics Research Paper Series*, 26-8 (March)

Parkin, M. and Bade, R. (1982), *Modern Macroeconomics*, Oxford: Philip Allen

Patinkin, D. (1956; 1965), *Money, Interest and Prices*, New York: Harper and Row

Paulus, J. and Axilrod, S.H. (1976), *Recent Regulatory Changes and Financial Innovations Affecting the Growth of the Monetary Aggregates*, Washington, DC: Federal Reserve Board

Pencavel, J. (1991), 'Prospects for Economics', *Economic Journal*, 101 (404)

Perry, G.L. (1984), 'Reflections on Macroeconomics', *American Economic Review, Papers and Proceedings*, 74 (May)

Pesaran, M.H. (1982), 'A Critique of the Proposed Tests of the Natural Rate - Rational Expectations Hypothesis', *Economic Journal*, 92 (September)

Pesaran, M.H. and Smith, R. (1985), 'Keynes on Econometries', in T. Lawson and M.H. Pesaran (eds), *Keynes' Economics: Methodological Issues*, London: Croom Helm

Pesek, B. and Saving, T. (1967), *Money, Wealth and Economic Theory*, New York: Macmillan

Pheby, J. (1988), *Methodology and Economics: A Critical Introduction*, London: Macmillan

Phelps, E.S. (1968), 'Money Wage Dynamics and Labor Market Equilibrium, *Journal of Political Economy*, 76 (July/August)

Phelps, E.S. (ed.) (1970), *Microeconomic Foundations of Employment and Inflation Theory*, New York: Norton

Phelps, E.S. (1972), *Inflation Policy and Unemployment Theory: The Cost-Benefit Approach to Monetary Planning*, New York: W.W. Norton

Phelps, E.S. (1990), *Seven Schools of Thought in Macroeconomics*, Oxford: Oxford University Press

Pigou, A.C. (1941), *Employment and Equilibrium*, London: Macmillan

Piore, M.J. (1979), *Unemployment and Inflation: Institutional and Structural Views*, Whilte Plains, Ill: M.E. Sharpe

Pirsig, R.M. (1974; 1976), *Zen and the Art of Motor Cycle Maintenance*, London: Corgi

Poole, W. (1970), 'Optimal Choice of Monetary Policy Instruments in a Simple Stochastic Macro Model', *Quarterly Journal of Economics*, 84 (May)

Popper, K.R. (1934; 1972), *The Logic of Scientific Discovery*, London: Hutchinson

Popper, K. R. (1944; 1957), *The Poverty of Historicism*, Boston: Beacon Press

Popper, K.R. (1945; 1963), *The Open Society and Its Enemies*, Princeton, Princeton University Press

Popper, K.R. (1963; 1969), *Conjectures and Refutations: The Growth of Scientific Knowledge*, London: Routledge and Kegan Paul

Popper, K.R. (1970), 'Normal Science and Its Dangers', in I. Lakatos and A. Musgrave (eds), *Criticism and the Growth of Knowledge* , Cambridge: Cambridge University Press,

Porter, R.D., Simpson, T.D. and Mauskopf, E. (1979), 'Financial Innovation and Monetary aggregates', *Brookings Papers on Economic Activity*, 1,

Prigogine, I and Stengers, I. (1984), *Order out of Chaos: Man's New Dialogue with Nature,* London, Heineman

Quine, V. van O. (1953), *From a Logical Point of View*, Cambridge, Mass: Harvard University Press.

Radcliffe, Lord (1959), *The Committee on the Working of the Monetary System: Report*, Cmnd 827. London: HMSO.

Redman, D.A. (1991), *Economics and the Philosophy of Science*, Oxford: Oxford University Press

Resnick, S. and Wolff, R. (1992), 'Radical Economics: A Tradition of Theoretical Differences', in Roberts and Feiner (eds), Chapter 1

Reynolds, P.J. (1987), *Political Economy: A Synthesis of Kaleckian and Post Keynesian Economics,* Brighton: Wheatsheaf

Ricardo, D. (1809-23; 1951-5), *The Works and Correspondence of David Ricardo,* Edited by P. Sraffa. Cambridge: Cambridge University Press.

Ricardo, D. (1817; 1971), *On the Principles of Political Economy, and Taxation,* edited by R.M Hartwell, Harmondsworth: Penguin.

Richardson, G.B. (1960), *Information and Investment,* Oxford: Oxford University Press

Rizzo, M.J. (1979), 'Disequilibrium and All That: An Introductory Essay', in M.J. Rizzo (ed.), *Time, Uncertainty and Disequilibrium,* Lexington: Lexington Books

Robbins, L. (1932; 1935), *An Essay on the Nature and Significance of Economic Science,* London: Macmillan

Roberts, B. and Feiner, S. (eds) (1992), *Radical Economics,* Boston: Kluwer.

Robertson, D.E.H. (1928), *Money,* London: Nisbet

Robertson, D.E.H. (1940), *Essays in Monetary Theory,* London: King

Robinson, J. (1965), '*The General Theory* after Twenty-Five Years', in *Collected Economic Papers, III.* Oxford: Basil Blackwell

Robinson, J. (1977), 'What are the Questions?', *Journal of Economic Literature,* 15

Robinson, J. (1978), 'History versus Equilibrium', in J. Robinson, *Contributions to Modern Economics,* Oxford: Basil Blackwell

Robinson, J. (1979), 'Garegnani on Effective Demand', *Cambridge Journal of Economics,* 3 (September)

Roemer, J. (1981), *Analytical Foundations of Marxian Economic Theory,* Cambridge: Cambridge University Press

Romer, D. (1993), 'The New Keynesian Synthesis', *Journal of Economic Perspectives,* 7

Roncaglia, A. (1982), 'Hollander's Ricardo', *Journal of Post Keynesian Economics,* 4 (Spring)

Rothbard, M.N. (1976a), 'Praxeology: The Methodology of Austrian Economics', in E.G. Dolan (ed.), *The Foundations of Modern Austrian Economics,* Kansas City: Steed and Ward

Rothbard, M.N. (1976b), 'The Austrian Theory of Money', in E.G. Dolan (ed.), *The Foundations of Modern Austrian Economics,* Kansas City: Steed and Ward

Rotheim, R.J. (1981), 'Keynes' Monetary Theory of Value' (1933), *Journal of Post Keynesian Economics,* 3 (Summer)

Rotwein, E. (1973), 'David Hume as an Economist', in H.C. Recktenwald (ed.), *Political Economy: A Historical Perspective,* London: Collier-Macmillan

Rowthorn, R.E. (1977), 'Conflict, Inflation and Money', *Cambridge Journal of Economics,* 1 (September)

Runde, J. (1990), 'Keynesian Uncertainty and the Weight of Arguments', *Economics and Philosophy,* 6

Runde, J. (1991), 'Keynesian Philosophy and the Instability of Beliefs', *Review of Political Economy,* 3(2)

Runde, J. (1994), 'Keynesian Uncertainty and Liquidity Preference', *Cambridge Journal of Economics,* 18 (2)

Russell, B. (1946; 1961), *History of Western Philosophy and its Connection with Political and Social Circumstances from the Earliest Times to the Present Day,* London: George

Allen and Unwin

Samuels, W.J. (1995), 'The Present State of Institutionalist Economics', *Cambridge Journal of Economics*, 19 (4)

Samuelson, P. (1938), 'A Note on the Pure Theory of Consumer Behaviour', *Economica*, 5 (17)

Samuelson, P. (1947), *Foundations of Economic Analysis*, New York: Atheneum

Samuelson, P.A. (1948; 1976), *Economics*, London: McGraw-Hill

Samuelson, P. (1963), 'Problems of Methodology – Discussion', *American Economic Review, Papers and Proceedings*, 53 (May)

Sardoni, C. (1987), *Marx and Keynes on Economic Recession: The Theory of Unemployment and Effective Demand*, Brighton: Wheatsheaf

Sargent, T.J. (1973), 'Rational Expectations, the Real Rate of Interest, and the Natural Rate of Unemployment', *Brookings Papers on Economic Activity*, 2

Sargent, T.J. (1984), 'Autoregressions, Expectations and Advice', *American Economic Review,* 74 (2)

Sargent, T.J. and Wallace, N. (1975), 'Rational Expectations, the Optimal Monetary Instrument and the Optimal Money Supply Rate', *Journal of Political Economy*, 83 (April)

Sargent, T.J. and Wallace, N. (1976), ' Rational Expectations and the Theory of Economic Policy', *Journal of Monetary Economics*, 2 (April)

Sawyer, M.C. (1982), 'Towards a Post-Kaleckian Macroeconomics', *Thames Paper in Political Economy* (Autumn)

Say, J.B. (1803; 1834), *A Treatise on Political Economy*, translated by C.C. Biddle, Philadelphia: Grigg and Elliot

Sayer, D. (1979; 1983), *Marx's Method: Ideology, Science and Critique in Capital*, Brighton: Harvester

Schmalansee, R. (1991), 'Continuity and Change in Economic Inquiry', *Economic Journal*, 101 (404)

Schumpeter, J. (1934), *The Theory of Economic Development*, Cambridge, MA: Harvard University Press

Schumpeter, J. (1954), *History of Economic Analysis*, London: George Allen and Unwin

Scott, A.G. (1991), 'Marxian and Radical Economics', in Mair and Miller (eds), Chapter 9

Seccareccia, M.S. (1984), 'The Fundamental Macroeconomic Link Between Investment Activity, the Structure of Employment and Price Changes: A Theoretical and Empirical Analysis', *Economies et Societes, X: Monnaie et Production*, 1

Shackle, G.L.S. (1955), *Uncertainty and Economics*, Cambridge: Cambridge University Press

Shackle, G.L.S. (1966), *The Nature of Economic Thought: Selected Papers 1955-1964*, Cambridge: Cambridge University Press

Shackle, G.L.S. (1967), *The Years of High Theory*, Cambridge: Cambridge University Press

Shackle, G.L.S. (1968), *A Scheme of Economic Theory*, Cambridge: Cambridge University Press

Shackle, G.L.S. (1972), *Epistemics and Economics*, Cambridge: Cambridge University Press

Shackle G.L.S. (1979), *Imagination and the Nature of Choice*, Edinburgh: Edinburgh University Press

Shaikh, A. (1980), 'The Laws of International Exchange', in E.J. Nell (ed.), *Growth, Profits and Property: Essays in the Revival of Political Economy*, Cambridge: Cambridge University Press

Shaikh, A. (1992), 'Values and Value Transfers: A Comment on Itoh', in Roberts and Feiner (eds), Chapter 2

Shapiro, N. (1977), 'The Revolutionary Character of Post-Keynesian Economics, *Journal of Economic Issues*, 11 (September)

Shapiro, N. (1978), 'Keynes and Equilibrium Economics', *Australian Economic Papers*, 17 (December)

Sherman, H.J. (1992), 'Rhetoric and Radical Economics: A Comment on Resnick and Wolff', in Roberts and Feiner (eds), chapter 1

Simon, H. (1955), 'A Behavioural Theory of Rational Choice', *Quarterly Journal of Economics*, 69 (February)

Simon, H. (1976), 'From Substantive to Procedural Rationality', in S.J. Latsis (ed.), *Method and Appraisal in Economics*, Cambridge: Cambridge University Press

Singh, A. (1977), 'U.K. Industry and the World Economy: a Case of De-industrialisation?' *Cambridge Journal of Economics*, 1 (June)

Sismondi, J.C.L. (1819), *Nouveaux Principes d'Economie Politique*, Vols I and II, Paris: Delaunay

Skidelsky, R. (1983), *John Maynard Keynes, Vol. 1. Hopes Betrayed 1883-1920*, London: Macmillan

Skinner, A.S. (1979), 'Adam Smith: An Aspect of Modern Economics?' *Scottish Journal of Political Economy*, 26 (June)

Smith, A. (1759; 1976), *The Theory of Moral Sentiments*, edited by D.D. Raphael and A.L. Macfie (Glasgow edition), Oxford: Clarendon

Smith, A. (1795; 1980), 'History of Astronomy', in W.P.D. Wightman (ed.), *Essays on Philosophical Subjects* (Glasgow edition), Oxford: Clarendon

Snowdon, B., Vane, H. and Wynarczyk, P. (1994), *A Modern Guide to Macroeconomics*, Aldershot: Elgar

Solow, R.M. and Stiglitz, J. (1968), 'Output, Employment and Wages in the Short Run', *Quarterly Journal of Economics*, 82 (November)

Sowell, T. (1974), *Classical Economics Reconsidered*, Princeton: Princeton University Press

Sraffa, P. (1960), *Production of Commodities by Means of Commodities*, Cambridge: Cambridge University Press

Steindl, J. (1945), 'Capitalist Enterprise and Risk', *Oxford Economic Papers*, 7 (March)

Steindl, J. (1952), *Maturity and Stagnation in American Capitalism*, Oxford: Basil Blackwell

Stiglitz, J. and Weiss, A. (1981), 'Credit Rationing in Markets with Imperfect Information', *American Economic Review*, 71 (3)

Stohs, M. (1983), "Uncertainty" in Keynes *General Theory*: A Rejoinder', *History of Political Economy*, 15 (Spring)

Sweezy, P.M. (1942), *The Theory of Capitalist Development*, New York: Monthly Review Press

Sylos-Labini, P. (1979), 'Prices and Income Distribution in Manufacturing Industry', *Journal of Post Keynesian Economics*, 2 (Fall)

Tavlas, G.S. (1977), 'Chicago Schools Old and New on the Efficacy of Monetary Policy', *Banca Nazionale del Lavoro Quarterly Review*, 120 (March)

Termini, V. (1981), 'Logical, Mechanical and Historical Time in Economics', *Economic Notes* by Monte dei Paschi di Siena, 10 (3)

Theil, H. (1961), *Economic Forecasts and Policy*, Amsterdam: North-Holland

Thomas, C.Y. (1974), *Dependence and Transformation: The Economics of the Transition to Socialism*, New York: Monthly Review Press

Tinbergen, J. (1952), *On the Theory of Economic Policy*, Amsterdam: North-Holland

Tinbergen, J. (1965), *Central Planning*, New Haven: Yale University Press

Tobin, J. (1958), 'Liquidity Preference as Behaviour Towards Risk', *Review of Economic Studies*, 25 (February)

Tobin, J. (1963), 'Commercial Banks as Creators of "Money"', in D. Carson (ed.), *Banking and Monetary Studies*, Homewood, Ill.: Irwin,

Tobin, J. (1980b), *Asset Accumulation and Economic Activity: Reflections on Contemporary Macroeconomic Theory*, Oxford: Basil Blackwell

Tobin, J. (1981), 'The Monetarist Counter-Revolution Today – An Appraisal', *Economic Journal*, 91 (March)

Tobin, J. and Brainard, W.C. (1963), 'Financial Intermediaries and the Effectiveness of Monetary Controls', *American Economic Review*, 53 (May)

Townshend, H. (1937), 'Liquidity Premium and the Theory of Value', *Economic Journal*, 47 (March)

Tylecote, A. (1981), *The Causes of the Present Inflation*, London: Macmillan

UK (1980), *Monetary Control* (Green Paper), Cmd 7858 (March), London: HMSO

Veblen, T.B. (1898; 1900a), 'Why Economics is not an Evolutionary Science', *Quarterly Journal of Economics*, 12 (February)

Veblen, T.B. (1899a; 1899b; 1900b), 'The Preconceptions of Economic Science', *Quarterly Journal of Economics*, 13 (January), 13 (July), 14 (February)

Veblen, T.B. (1899c; 1934), *The Theory of the Leisure Class*, New York: Modern Library

Wallich, H.C. and Weintraub, S. (1971), 'A Tax-based Incomes Policy', *Journal of Economic Issues*, 5 (June)

Walsh, V. and Gram, H. (1979), *Classical and Neoclassical Theories of General Equilibrium: Historical origins and Mathematical Structure*, Oxford: Oxford University Press

Weintraub, E.R. (1979), *Microfoundations: The Compatibility of Microeconomics and Macroeconomics*, Cambridge: Cambridge University Press

Weintraub, E.R. (1985), *General Equilibrium Analysis*, Cambridge: Cambridge University Press

Weintraub, E.R. (1989), 'Methodology Doesn't Matter. But the History of Economic Thought Might', *Scandinavian Journal of Economics*, 91

Weintraub, S. (1956), 'A Microeconomic Approach to the Theory of Wages', *American Economic Review*, 46 (December)

Weintraub, S. (1978), *Capitalism's Inflation and Unemployment Crisis*, Reading, Mass: Addison-Wesley

Weintraub, S. (1978-79), 'The Missing Theory of Money Wages', *Journal of Post Keynesian Economics*, 1 (Winter)

Wells, P. (1983), 'A Post Keynesian View of Liquidity Preference and the Demand for Money', *Journal of Post Keynesian Economics*, 5 (Summer)

Whitehead, A.N. (1938), *Modes of Thought*, Cambridge: Cambridge University Press

Wicksell, K. (1934-35), *Lectures on Political Economy*, edited by L. Robbins, translated by E. Classen, London: Routledge and Kegan Paul

Wicksell, K. (1936; 1965), *Interest and Prices*, translated by R.F. Kahn, New York: Augustus M. Kelly

Wiles, P. (1979-80), 'Ideology, Methodology and Neoclassical Economics', *Journal of Post Keynesian Economics*, 2 (Winter)

Williamson, O.E. (1985), *The Economic Institutions of Capitalism*, New York: Free Press

Wimsatt, W.C. (1981), 'Robustness, Reliability and Overdetermination', in M.B. Brewer and B.E. Collins (eds), *Scientific Inquiry and the Social Sciences*, San Francisco: Jossey Bass

Winslow, T. (1986), 'Keynes and Freud: Psychoanalysis and Keynes's Account of the "Animal Spirits" of Capitalism', *Social Research,* 53 (Winter)

Winslow, T. (1995), 'Uncertainty and Liquidity Preference', in S.C. Dow and J. Hillard (eds), Chapter 13

Wong, S. (1973), 'The 'F-twist' and the Methodology of Paul Samuelson', *American Economic Review*, 63 (June)

Wong, S. (1978), *The Foundations of Paul Samuelson's Revealed Reference Theory*, London: Routledge and Kegan Paul

Wood, A. (1975), *A Theory of Profits*, Cambridge: Cambridge University Press

Wray, L.R. (1990), *Money and Credit in Capitalist Economies*, Aldershot: Elgar

Ziman, J. (1979), *Reliable Knowledge: An Exploration of the Grounds for Belief in Science*, Cambridge: Cambridge University Press

Author Index

Subject Index